Electrical Systems
including Tapes and Radios

By David Rowlands
and the Autobooks team of Technical Writers

Autobooks

Autobooks Ltd. Golden Lane Brighton BN1 2QJ England

Acknowledgements

The Publishers wish to thank the following firms for their assistance in the preparation of this book:

Smiths Electrics Limited

Joseph Lucas Limited

Lumenition Limited

Mobelec Limited

Mullard Limited

Cover Photography: Walter Gardiner

First Published 1975

ISBN 0 85147 576 0

651

Printed and bound in Brighton England for Autobooks Ltd by G. Beard & Son Ltd

CHAPTER 1

Introduction to electricity and electrical systems

1 :1 Electrical theory

Electricity is a form of energy that is very easily controlled and directed to the points where it is used, the consumer units. In a car these units can use the electricity to produce heat and light, like lamps, motion, like solenoids and motors, or sparks to fire the engine, like the ignition circuit. However, a full understanding of the working of the car's electrical system needs a grasp of some basic principles of electricity and, going further back into the theory, a look at the nature of materials.

All materials – solids, liquids and gases – are composed of atoms which are themselves made up of even smaller particles, electrons, protons and neutrons. The atom is not a very stable unit – the protons and neutrons are tightly bound into the nucleus of the atom but the electrons are in constant motion, orbiting the nucleus like Planets around the Sun (see **FIG 1 :1**).

In a perfect atom there are as many electrons as there are protons. The protons have a positive electrical charge and have an attraction for the negatively charged electrons which keeps them in their orbits around the nucleus. But there are many ways in which this fragile bond can be broken to split electrons from their proton partners.

When an electron is pried free from its atom it may very quickly be attracted to orbit the nucleus of an adjacent atom which has a vacant orbital space. In relation to its size the electron can also travel an enormous distance through a material until it is once again captured by an atom. This ability of the electron to hop around from atom to atom within a material takes place in random order and direction. But there are ways in which the movement of electrons can be ordered into an overall flow of electrons from one end of the material to the other.

Although there are many significant applications of the flow of electrons in liquids and gases to be found in cars it is sufficient at this stage in the theory to concentrate on the flow through solid materials.

To envisage electron flow through a solid material, a good model is to liken the material to a drainpipe packed with ping-pong balls. If a few more ping-pong balls are stuffed into one end of the pipe the same number of balls will pop out of the other end – they aren't the same ones that were packed in but the net effect is that there has been a flow of ping-pong balls through the drainpipe (see **FIG 1 :2**).

Electrons behave in a similar way to these ping-pong balls. Push some electrons into one end of a piece of material and some electrons will be emitted at the other end. Electricity is this flow of electrons within a material.

But to start the flow a source of electrons is required. The simplest source is the battery which is a chemical generator of electrons with one terminal – the negative terminal – rich in electrons ready to flow, and another terminal – the positive terminal – full of atoms which haven't got enough electrons.

Another source of electricity is an electromagnetic generator – the dynamo or alternator on a car. This machine works like a pump. Magnetic forces excite electrons within the generator's wire windings into movement and, like a pump acting on a liquid, the direction of the forces is such that the electrons are made to flow in one direction. One terminal of the generator – the negative terminal – has a pressure of electrons trying to escape, while the positive terminal has atoms from which the electrons have fled.

So connecting the electron-rich negative terminal of a source of electrons like a battery or generator to one end of a piece of material, say copper, and connecting the other end of the copper to the electron-depleted positive

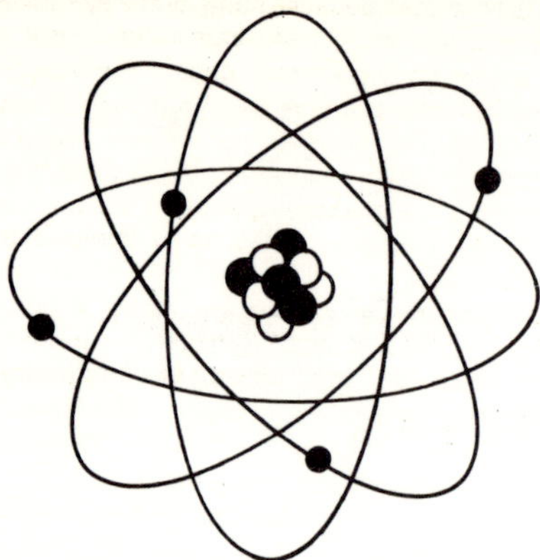

FIG 1:1 The structure of the atom

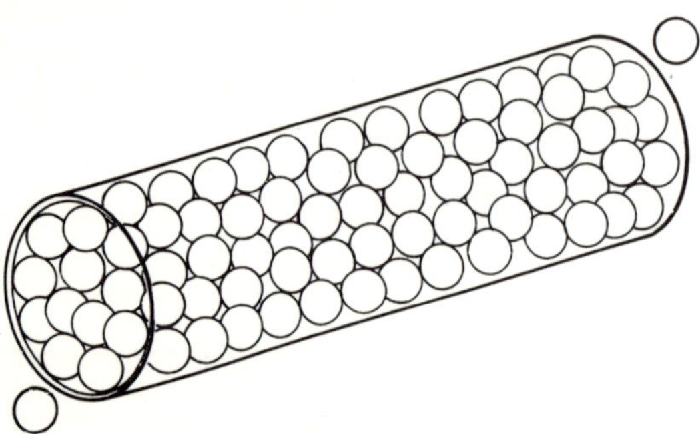

FIG 1:2 Electron flow model

terminal enables the electrons to flow from one end of the copper to another.

Note that theoretically electricity is the flow of electrons from negative terminal to positive terminal. Unfortunately this theory was elucidated long after electricity had been put to use and this long period of ignorance allowed a convention to arise that is still in use today.

For practical purposes the convention is that electrical current flows from the positive terminal of a battery or generator, through a circuit to the negative terminal.

1:2 Conductors and insulators

Some electron movement will take place in all materials in response to a pressure of electrons trying to pass through the material. But there are many materials in which electrons are much freer to jump from atom to atom than others.

Materials in which an almost unrestricted flow of electrons can be induced are called conductors. The best conductors are to be found among the metals; copper, silver, aluminium, platinum and mercury are all excellent conductors. Steel, nickel, lead and gold are not quite so good but are used as conductors in specific applications.

Conductivity is not confined exclusively to metals. One very important non-metallic conductor is carbon.

Many materials possess chemical and physical properties which restrict electron movement and thus little or no electricity can flow through them. These materials, when they are used to actively prevent the flow of electricity from one conductor to another, are called insulators. Examples of insulators commonly found in cars are polyvinylchloride (pvc) and other plastics, glass and porcelain ceramics, and even air.

1:3 The concept of an electrical circuit

It has already been stated that for electricity to flow a conductor must be connected between a source of electrons (for example, the negative terminal of a battery) and an electron-depleted area (the battery's positive terminal). This arrangement is the simplest, but most impractical, circuit. In fact it is so damaging to the source of electrons (the battery or generator) that it has earned its own name, the short circuit. In a short circuit; **1** electrons flow back to the electron-depleted atoms quickly and wastefully thus neutralizing the battery's ability to supply more electrons and **2** the uncontrolled flow of electrons in the conductor causes a rapid heat rise which can actually burn or melt the conductor.

To harness the energy available in the electron flow a properly controlled electrical circuit must be constructed. Such a circuit consists of a wire conductor from one of the electron source's terminals to a switch, which is simply a mechanical way of breaking the conductive path. From the other side of the switch the conductor is led to an electrical load or consumer unit, such as a light bulb. From the load's second terminal a wire is led back to the electron source's other terminal thus completing the circuit (see **FIG 1:3**).

There are various ways an electrical circuit can be completed:

Parallel circuit. A circuit in which each of two or more electrical loads or consumer units are connected separately across the two supply terminals (see **FIG 1:4**).

Series circuit. A circuit in which two or more electrical loads or consumer units are connected end to end between the two supply terminals (see **FIG 1:5**).

Series-parallel circuit. A circuit in which both types of connection are used (see **FIG 1:6**).

1:4 The concept of resistance

However good a conductor may be at allowing electrons to flow along it there are obstacles within the material that resist the electrons' movement. Electrons are slowed by collisions with each other, with the atoms of the material and by hitting the occasional atom of an impurity which doesn't behave in the same way as the atoms of the conductor.

Resistance to electron flow is a very useful property of materials, because it is one way of making the flow of electrons give up its electrical energy. Conductors that are specially resistant to heat can be made to glow in a controlled way–this is a simple electric heater. If the conductor can glow white hot it will give out usable light and this is the principle of the light bulb filament.

All consumer units present a resistance to electrical flow although not all of them utilise this property of releasing energy in the form of heat.

No conductor is really perfect so, unfortunately, heat is a by-product of any flow of electrons through a material

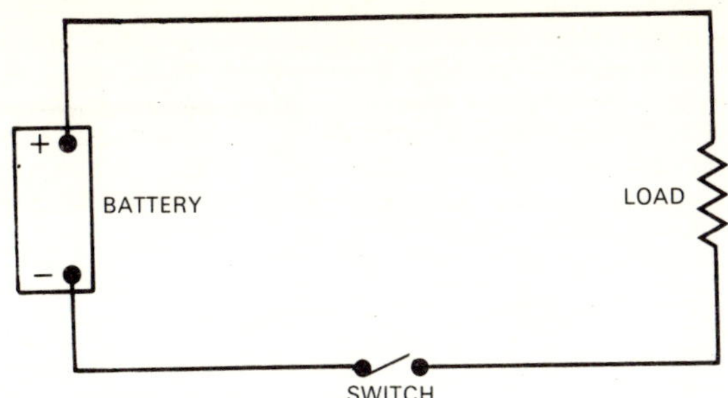

FIG 1:3 Simple circuit

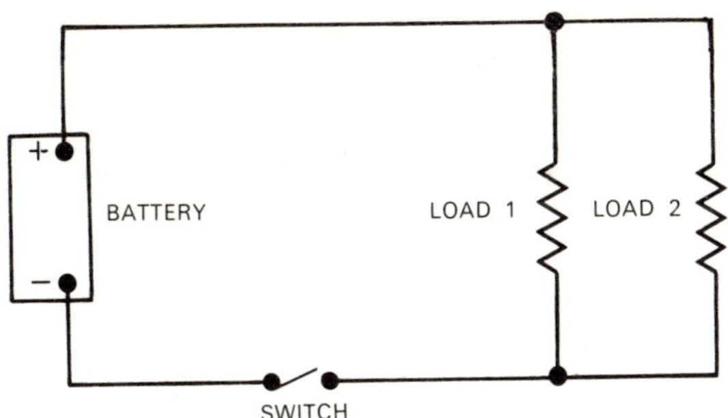

FIG 1:4 Parallel circuit

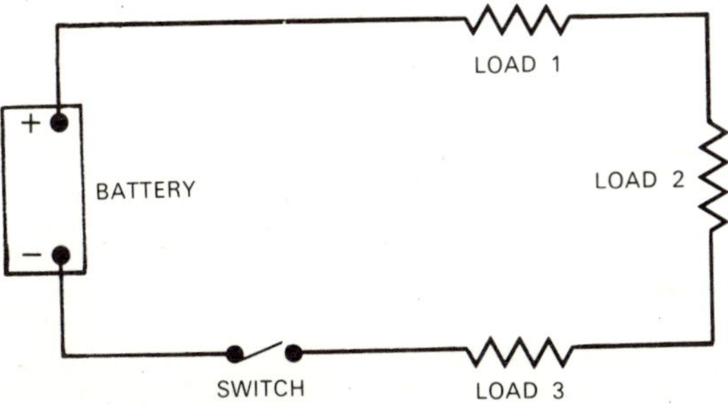

FIG 1:5 Series circuit

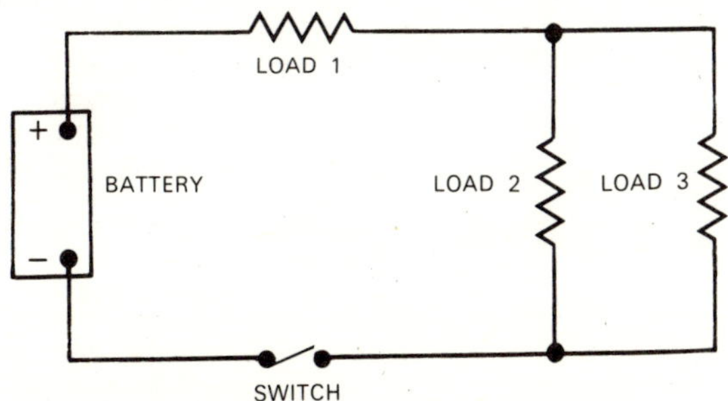

FIG 1:6 Series-parallel circuit

and the amount of heat obtained is proportional to the number of electrons flowing. So great care has to be taken to ensure that the wires in a circuit do not heat up to the point at which they are damaged, or to a temperature at which other materials nearby are damaged.

Heat is produced because some of the electrons' energy is dissipated and this means that there is less available energy at the consumer unit end of the wire than was originally put into the wire by the battery. Thus circuits not only must be designed to reduce the amount of unwanted heat produced but also to provide the amount of usable electrical energy required by the consumer unit. So the circuit's resistance has to be lowered to within acceptable levels.

Resistance can be lowered in many ways. First the conducting materials must be made as pure as possible. Then the cross-sectional area of the conductor can be increased – the thicker the conductor the more electrical energy it will carry without producing an unacceptable heat rise or an appreciable loss of electrical energy.

It is at this point that important factors like the cost of materials intrude. Cars, like all consumer goods, are built down to a price and for this reason it is generally true that car electrical circuits are made from the thinnest conducting materials consistent with the amount of electrical energy, usually small, that they have to carry.

But the design of electrical circuits is not a matter of trial and error – all the parameters of electrical energy and flow can be measured or calculated very accurately and quite simply.

1:5 Measuring and calculating electrical energy

Having established that the flow of electrons through conductors represents energy flow it is easier to consider this movement as an **electric current**. The current can be measured using an instrument called the **ammeter** (see **Chapter 8**) and the unit of measurement is the **ampere**. One ampere is defined as the current that flows when a certain number (6.28×10^{18}) of electrons pass a given point in a circuit in one second.

The amount of current that flows depends on two factors. First there is the pressure that makes the electrons flow. This pressure, sometimes known as the **electromotive force (emf)** or **potential difference (pd)**, is measured in **volts** with a **voltmeter** (see **Chapter 8**). Current and electromotive force are simply related. The higher the electromotive force, or voltage, the more electrons flow and so the higher the current is.

The third important parameter is resistance, explained earlier. Resistance can be measured too and the unit used is the **ohm**, named after George Simon Ohm. His major contribution to the understanding of electricity was Ohm's Law which stated the precise relationship between current, electromotive force, and resistance:

$$\mathbf{E} = \mathbf{I} \times \mathbf{R},$$

where **I** = the current in amps, **E** = the electromotive force in volts, **R** = the resistance in ohms. Ohm's Law is a very useful equation because if two of the quantities are known or can be measured, the third factor can be calculated. If $\mathbf{E} = \mathbf{I} \times \mathbf{R}$, $\mathbf{I} = \mathbf{E} \div \mathbf{R}$ and $\mathbf{R} = \mathbf{E} \div \mathbf{I}$.

When electricity is used to make a piece of apparatus work its energy is dissipated. The rate at which the energy is dissipated or used is termed the electrical **power** of the load. The unit to measure power is the **watt.**

Power is directly related to the current and electromotive force in another important equation:

Power (**watts**) = Current (**amps**) × Electromotive force (**volts**).

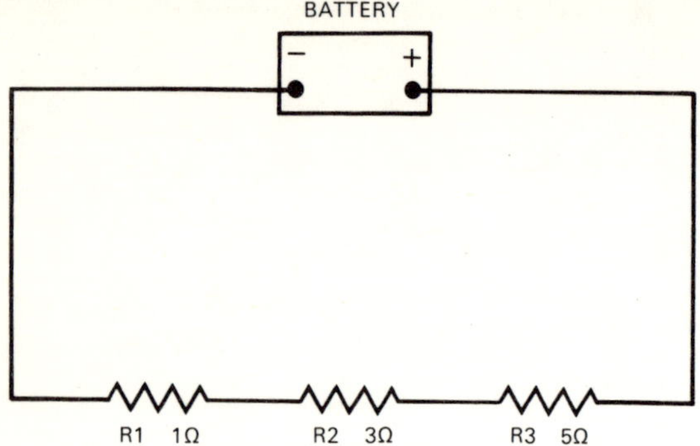

FIG 1:7 Resistances in series

In common usage electrical units are abbreviated as follows: amperes = amps = A (or mA = milliamps = thousandths of an amp); volts = V (or kV = kilovolts = thousands of volts); watts = W (or kW = kilowatts = thousands of watts); ohms = Ω.

Calculating electrical values:

The following are some simple calculations of electrical values designed to show how various parameters of electrical circuits can be worked out.

Resistances in series:

The total value of several resistances in series is given by adding their individual values together. So the total resistance **R** in the circuit shown in **FIG 1:7** is found like this:

$\mathbf{R} = \mathbf{R1} + \mathbf{R2} + \mathbf{R3}$.

In the example shown, $\mathbf{R} = 1\Omega + 3\Omega + 5\Omega = 9\Omega$

Resistances in parallel:

The total resistance **R** in the circuit in **FIG 1:8** can be calculated from

$$\frac{1}{\mathbf{R}} = \frac{1}{\mathbf{R1}} + \frac{1}{\mathbf{R2}} + \frac{1}{\mathbf{R3}}.$$

So in **FIG 1:8**,

$$\frac{1}{\mathbf{R}} = \frac{1}{2} + \frac{1}{4} + \frac{1}{16} = \frac{13}{16} \quad \therefore \mathbf{R} = \frac{16}{13}\Omega = 1.23\Omega.$$

As a general rule, the total resistance of resistances in parallel is always less than the value of the lowest resistance in the circuit.

Resistances in a series-parallel circuit:

First find the combined value **RX** of the resistances in parallel by the method already described. In the circuit shown in **FIG 1:9** the value **RX** of **R1** and **R2** = 1.33Ω.

Then the total resistance **R** is added up as for resistances in series:

$\mathbf{R} = \mathbf{RX} + \mathbf{R3} + \mathbf{R4}$.

In **FIG 1:9**,

$\mathbf{R} = 1.33\Omega + 17\Omega + 200\Omega = 218.33\Omega$.

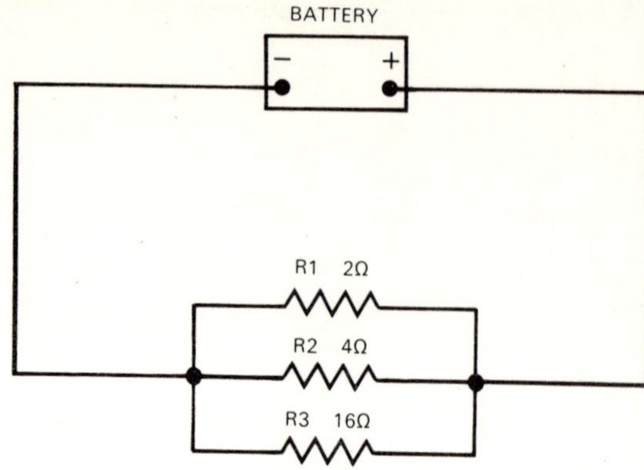

FIG 1:8 Resistances in parallel

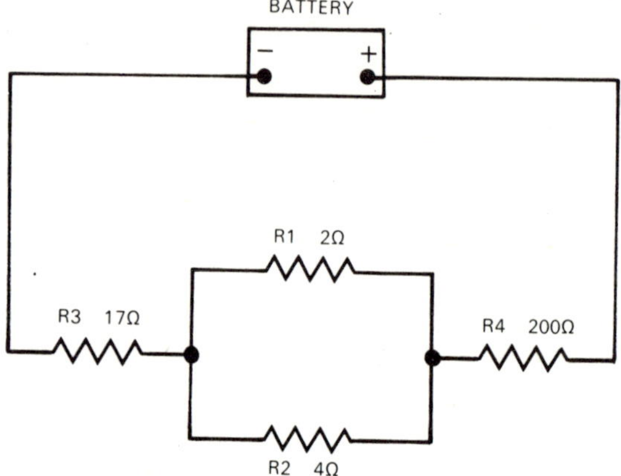

FIG 1:9 Resistances in series and in parallel

Power of an electrical load:

The power of the light bulb, **X**, in **FIG 1:10** is calculated from the current flowing in the circuit and the battery voltage:

$\mathbf{X} = 5A \times 12V = 60$ watts.

Current flowing in a circuit:

Using the power equation it is also possible to calculate the current flowing in a circuit if the power of the consumer unit and the circuit voltage are known. If W = A × V, then A = W ÷ V.

In **FIG 1:11**,

$A = \frac{25}{12}$ amps = 2.08 amps.

Voltage drop:

Having explained the simple theory of electric current flow and resistance, and seen how some of these parameters can be calculated, the concept of the drop in voltage that occurs over a resistance may be more easily understood.

In the circuit in **FIG 1:12** a battery of 12 volts is connected across a load of 12 ohms. Therefore by

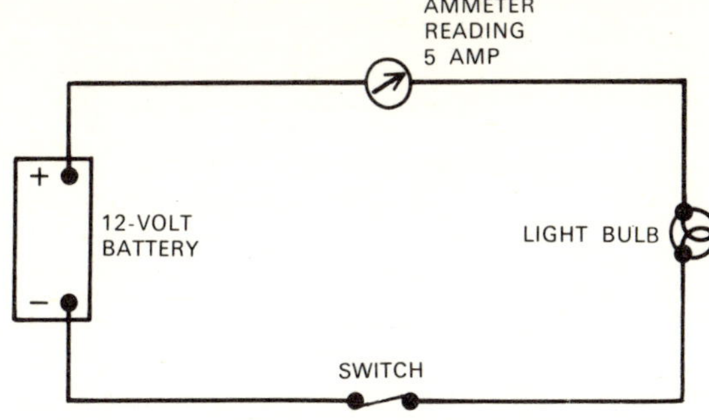

FIG 1:10 Calculating the power of an electrical load

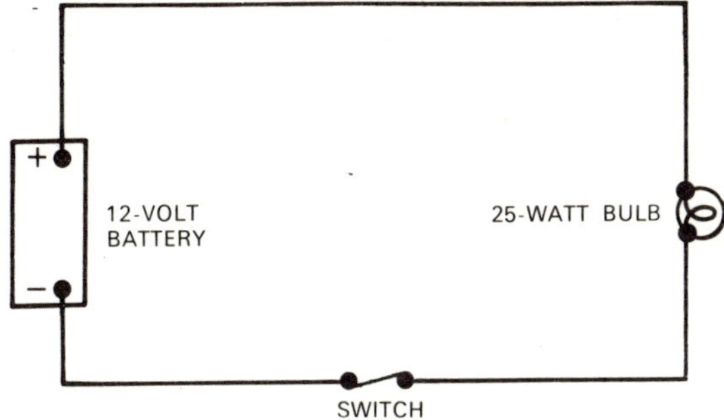

FIG 1:11 Calculating the current flowing in a circuit

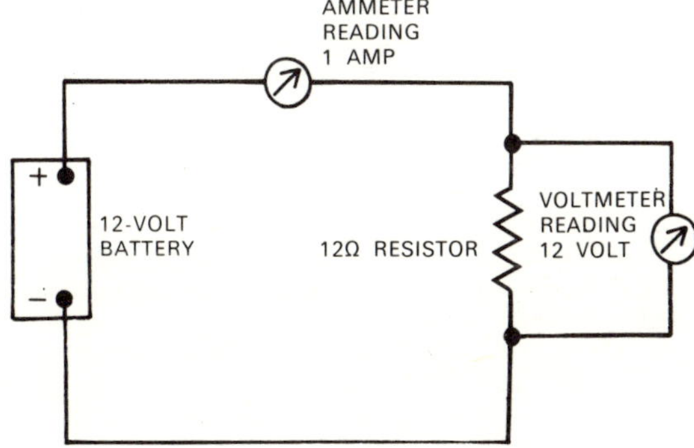

FIG 1:12 Calculating the voltage across a load

applying Ohm's Law the current flowing in the circuit is 1 amp.

But suppose that load of 12 ohms were composed of two resistances of 6 ohms each, connected in series as in the circuit in **FIG 1:13**.

As the total load has remained the same and the battery voltage is the same the current flowing in the circuit (and thus constant at all points in the circuit) is again 1 amp. However, what has happened to the voltage in the wire connecting the two halves of the load? Ohm's law comes to the rescue again. The current is 1 amp, the load is 6 ohms, therefore the voltage is 6 volts.

The resistance has thus reduced the voltage by 6 volts. This voltage reducing effect is true of all resistances and it has many applications in car circuitry. One use of the voltage drop across a resistance, the ballast resistor in the

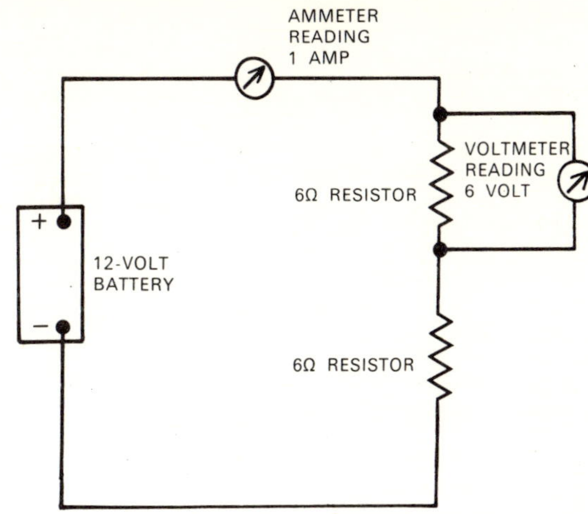

FIG 1:13 Calculating the voltage across loads in series

ignition circuit, is explained in **Chapter 5**. However, the most important effect of this relationship between voltage and the total circuit resistance is in the restriction of the electrical energy available to the consumer unit by unplanned resistances in the circuit.

These resistances can arise at any electrical connection point in the circuit if perfect metal to metal contact is not achieved. In the worst case it can even be the resistance of the electrical wiring itself that restricts the electrical energy available because too thin a wire has been used for a particular application. With all these resistances in series in the circuit, what may have started off as a voltage of 12V at the battery terminals has been reduced to say, 10V by the time it reaches the headlamp. In **Chapter 2** it is explained how the voltage drop betrays circuit faults and how it can be used to track down the resistant connection.

1:6 Earth and polarity in car circuits

There is one important difference between the simple circuits described above and those found in a car. It is that the car's steel body, a large and efficient conductor, is used as a common lead to complete the majority of the circuits from battery to consumer unit and back to the battery. Using the body, known as the **earth** of the system, halves the amount of wiring required for each circuit, thus it is cheaper, reduces the clutter of wiring and makes fault finding much easier.

A typical car circuit will consist of a supply lead from one battery terminal fed, through a switch, to the consumer unit. The other terminal of the consumer unit is fixed to the car's body. The body, or earth, is firmly connected to the other terminal of the battery by a stout metal **earthing strap**.

For many years Japanese, American and European car manufacturers have connected the battery's negative terminal to the car body – the vehicle is then said to have **negative earth**. In Britain, until very recently, car manufacturers connected the positive terminal of the battery to the car's body. The **positive earth** system was known to have an advantage in preventing corrosion of some electrical components. However, the use of better materials and the need to standardize some items of equipment have dictated a change by British manufacturers to the negative earth system.

The type of earth system a car uses is sometimes referred to as its **polarity**; a positive earth car has positive polarity.

Although the term is old-fashioned, a car's polarity has growing importance because more and more modern electrical devices contain components that are **polarity conscious**. This means that they will not operate correctly or they may be irreparably damaged by connection to a system of the wrong polarity. Examples of polarity conscious devices include radios and tape-players – these contain transistors which will be damaged by connection to cars of the wrong earth system – and some motors which will operate in the reverse direction if connected into circuits the wrong way.

The advantage to the motorist having a negative earth car is that many modern accessories, like high performance ignition systems, and some radios and tape-players, are produced exclusively for negative polarity vehicles. For the motorist with a positive polarity car, the choice of some accessories is limited and the possibilities of exchanging some of the car's electrical units for those of a more recent model is reduced. Changing a car's polarity can sometimes be carried out relatively simply and the technique is explained in **Chapter 3**.

1:7 Protection against overloads

Earlier it was explained how a short circuit can allow a damaging amount of current to flow, creating enough heat to burn up the circuit wires. Short circuits can occur frequently during electrical work unless proper precautions are taken to prevent them. In addition a short circuit can happen as the result of chafed or worn wire insulation allowing a feed wire to connect with the bare metal of the car body. Sometimes this accidental contact between a supply wire and the earth can occur inside an electrical unit, perhaps as a result of overheating or plain old age.

Clearly it is prudent to guard against the possibility of a short circuit setting the wiring alight and perhaps igniting other materials, resulting in the car's destruction.

Quite apart from the risk of fire an excessive current flow may damage sensitive units like the car's current and voltage regulator box or leave the car immobile with a flat battery.

Car manufacturers do build in some circuit protection by arranging that most of the car's circuits are supplied with electricity via **fuses**. At its simplest, a fuse is a short length of wire with a resistance such that any current flow greater than its working value (measured in amps) will cause it to heat up, melt and thus break the circuit.

In cars the most common type of fuse is a small glass or ceramic cartridge enclosing the fuse wire which is connected internally to the metal caps at each end of the capsule. The fuse cartridge is designed to fit into clips in the car's fuse box, which may contain a number of fuses. Another type of fuse consists of a thin strip of metal mounted on a short ceramic rod which again clips into a fuse carrier or box. This type of fuse is used mainly by European car manufacturers.

Many older cars only have two fuses. One protects circuits supplied direct from the battery, the other protects those circuits which are supplied via the ignition switch. But nowadays more delicate equipment is used in cars and more comprehensive protection against current overload is required. So most modern cars have, in addition to main circuit fuses (for example, in the lighting circuit), some fuses which protect circuits to individual electrical units. Sometimes it is convenient to connect the fuse cartridge into a supply lead rather than a central fuse box and this type of fuse mounted in a special plastics carrier, is called a **line fuse**.

Fuses can be designed to carry different amounts of current – the value of a fuse is usually marked on it in terms of its current carrying capacity in amps. But beware! The current rating of some fuses is set according to a confusing convention. Some fuses will only carry their marked current value for approximately ten seconds. In continuous operation these fuses will only carry half their marked value.

For example, a 25 amp fuse will carry a current of only 12.5 amps continuously. It will accept momentary current surges (for example, immediately after switching on a heavily loaded circuit) up to and slightly over 25 amps. But currents of several hundred amps flowing as a result of a short circuit will blow the fuse almost instantaneously.

Other fuses are marked with their continuous current rating – in other words, a 25 amp continuous rated fuse will carry a 25 amp current and will accept surges of up to or slightly over 50 amps.

It is important to check which type of fuse marking is used on a vehicle before replacing a fuse cartridge.

Electrical equipment manufacturers are aware of the confusion that exists about fuse ratings and some have begun to mark their fuses with both current values – for example, '30 amps (15 amps CR).'

The use of fuses and how to calculate the required value of a fuse is described in **Chapter 9**.

There is another type of circuit protection used on some cars when it is considered necessary to protect a circuit from overloading without breaking the circuit completely and depriving the motorist of the use of a piece of electrical equipment. This type of protection is provided by a thermostatic interrupter.

A thermostatic interrupter is a device consisting of a specially designed metal strip that bends when it is heated by a current flow in excess of its rated working value. The metal strip is firmly mounted to one contact of the interrupter and touches the other contact to complete the circuit. When it overheats it bends away from the contact and breaks the circuit. This action allows the strip to cool down and once again it makes contact and completes the circuit. This oscillation of the metal strip allows the circuit to function with a limited current flow until such time as a repair can be made. It is a type of protection sometimes found in a lighting circuit, for example, on Vauxhalls. Operation of the thermostatic interrupter causes the lights to flicker on and off but allows the motorist to continue driving in relative safety. Nevertheless the fault which is causing the interruption must be cured as soon as possible.

An interrupter is sometimes used to protect the electrical circuit of motors which may be subject to accidental overloads. An example is the electric window winding motors found on some expensive cars – a thermostatic interrupter prevents damage to the motor if a window becomes jammed in its runners.

1:8 Magnetism and electricity

It has been mentioned already that electricity can be made to work by producing light or heat. The third application of electricity is in the creation of magnetism.

When an electric current passes through a wire a magnetic field is generated around the wire. Current flowing in a straight wire produces a very weak magnetic field but this effect can be multiplied by forming the wire into a coil. The strength of the magnetic field produced will be increased by the number of turns or windings in the coil and by increasing the current flowing through it.

Just as electricity can only be conducted by certain materials the lines of magnetic force which comprise a magnetic field will only be sustained in magnetic materials like iron and steel. Inserting a soft iron core into a coil concentrates the magnetic field produced by the current flowing in the coil. This is the principle of a simple electromagnet.

Soft iron has no ability to retain a magnetic field. Once the current in the coil is switched off the magnetic field collapses. If the coil is then reconnected so the current flows in the opposite direction through its windings the magnetic field in the iron core will be recreated. However, it will differ in a fundamental sense to the previous field because magnetism exhibits a curious property called polarity.

There are two magnetic poles, north and south, named according to the Earth's natural magnetism. If an electromagnet consisting of a coil wrapped round a soft iron rod were freely suspended by its connections (say, they were very thin wires) and balanced so it was horizontal the rod might swing a little but it would eventually come to rest, like a compass needle, pointing in a north-south direction.

A peculiar property of magnetic poles is that unlike poles are attracted to each other and like poles are repelled. The suspended electromagnet has obeyed this rule – its north pole is attracted to the Earth's south pole and equally its south pole is attracted to the Earth's north pole.

But if the direction of the current flow through the coil is reversed the polarity of an electromagnet will also be reversed; what was its north pole will become its south pole and vice versa. Under these conditions the suspended electromagnet would swing through 180 degrees to realign itself with the Earth's poles.

The compass needle isn't an electromagnet – the needle is made from a material that retains magnetism, thus it is a permanent magnet. Steel is a material that retains magnetism and special grades of steel can be made that can be used to produce extremely strong permanent magnets.

If an ordinary piece of steel, like the blade of a screwdriver, is inserted into the middle of a current carrying coil it becomes magnetised just like a piece of soft iron. But in the case of steel, switching off the current does not destroy the magnetic field; the screwdriver blade becomes permanently magnetised.

Both electromagnets and permanent magnets are at the heart of numerous electrical units used in cars.

1:9 Motors

The magnetic property of attraction between unlike poles and repulsion of like poles is turned to advantage in the electric motor. The simplest electric motor consists of a permanent magnet with its north and south poles arranged on each side of a current carrying coil which is free to rotate. An additional stipulation is that the rotation causes the current flow to be switched in alternate directions with each half turn of the coil. Thus the magnetic poles are alternately switching from end to end of the coil and being alternately attracted and repelled by the poles of the permanent magnet (see **FIG 1:14**).

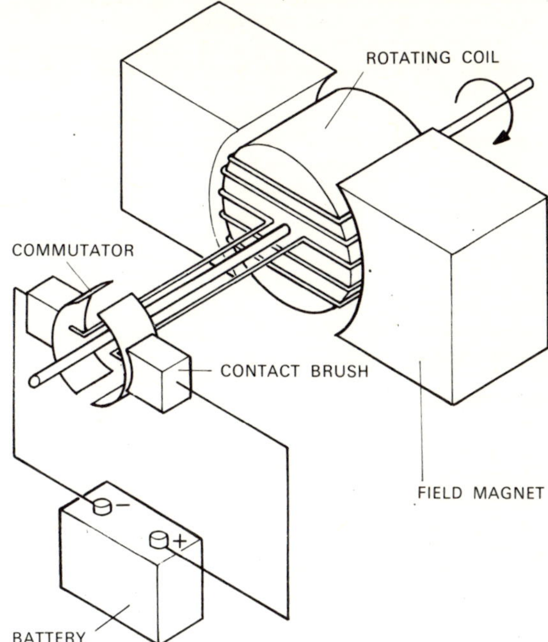

FIG 1:14 Simple electric motor

More powerful electric motors can be made by **1** increasing the numbers of individual coils rotating, **2** designing more efficient cores for the coils, **3** designing the coils to accept higher current flows, **4** using an electromagnet instead of a permanent magnet for the stationary field of the motor, **5** increasing the number of windings in the stationary magnet coils and in the rotating coils. Within these variables, motors designed specifically to develop adequate power for any application can be made. The starter motor is an obvious car application. Lower power motors can be very compact which makes them ideal for driving accessories such as windscreen wipers, windscreen washer pumps, heater blowers and cooling fans.

There is a common terminology applied to the parts of motors and generators (see **Section 1:11**):

Field windings: the coil(s) of the stationary magnet.

Stator: stationary magnet core.

Armature (or **Rotor**): the rotating winding and core, often composed of many thin sheets of soft iron bound or clamped together.

Commutator: the rotating switch which changes the current direction in the rotor.

Slip rings: used as rotating contacts when no commutating action is required.

Brushes: stationary contacts which are the means of electrical connection to the rotating coils through the commutator or slip ring.

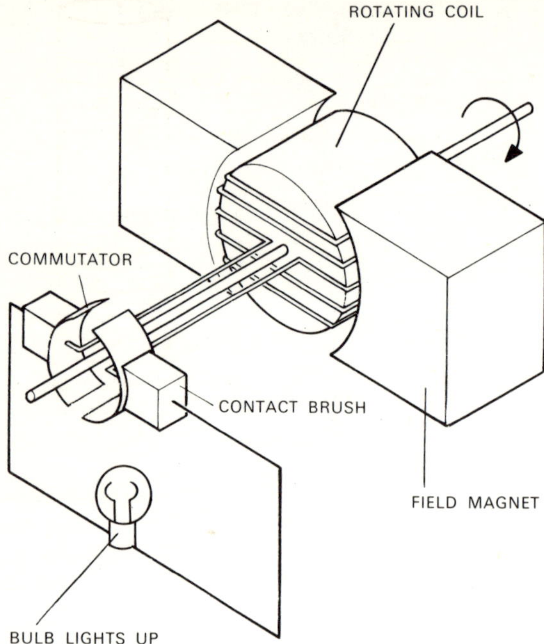

FIG 1:15 Simple electric generator (dynamo)

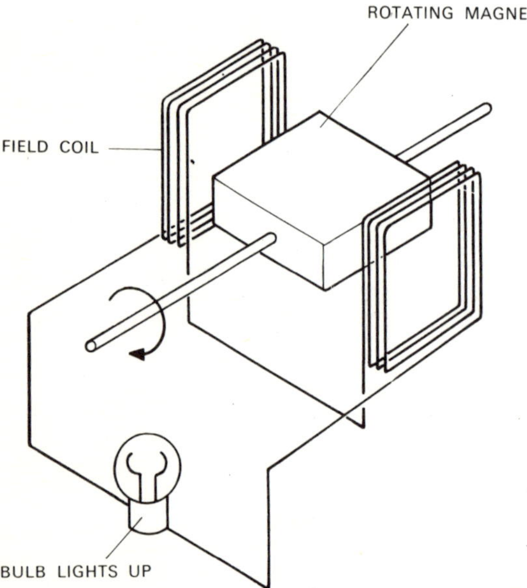

FIG 1:16 Simple electric generator (alternator)

1:10 Solenoids

The magnetism produced by electricity can be used to produce linear motion instead of rotary motion. The solenoid is a simple linear electric motor with several important applications in cars.

A solenoid consists of a cylindrical coil of wire inside which is a soft iron core, or plunger, free to move against the pressure of a spring. When the coil is energised by switching on the current the coil's magnetic field acts to shift the balance of the now magnetised plunger with the result that the plunger attempts to enter the coil's field against the spring pressure. Switching off the current causes the spring to return the plunger to its initial position. The restricted linear movement of the plunger can be used, for example, to operate a switch.

1:11 Generators

Not only does a current flowing in a wire create a magnetic field but moving a wire through the lines of force in a magnetic field produces a current flow in the wire. Once again the current produced can be increased by coiling the wire, increasing the number of windings and increasing the strength of the magnetic field.

Generators can be made in one of two basic ways. Either the magnetic field is stationary and the coil is rotated or vice versa (see **FIGS 1:15** and **1:16**). This is the simple difference between the dynamo (stationary magnet – rotating coils) and the alternator (stationary coil – rotating magnet). More important differences between these two types of generating device are discussed in **Chapter 3**.

Once again a generator has a rotor, a stator, and a commutator (or slip rings) and brushes which may collect the current generated or supply current to the field winding, depending on the type of device.

1:12 Transformers and the ignition coil

The ability to generate current by the movement of magnetic lines of force through the windings of a coil is used in one more, very important device, the transformer (see **FIG 1:17**).

A simple transformer consists of a non-magnetised iron core around which are wrapped two separate coils of wire. A magnetic field is created in the core by energising one of the coils, thus the second coil is surrounded and penetrated by magnetic lines of force. Switching off the current causes the magnetic field to collapse inwards to the centre of the core and results in a movement of the lines of forces through the windings of the second coil. Thus momentarily the conditions for current generation exist and a short burst of current flows. If the switching on and off of the current to the first coil is performed continuously in rapid succession an almost continuous supply of current can be obtained from the other coil.

The great advantage of this arrangement is that in common with the generator the more windings there are on the second coil the more efficient the transformer becomes. But you can't make something out of nothing – in other words the total amount of electrical power you can get out of a transformer can at best only equal the amount put in.

If the number of turns on the second coil is increased in relation to the number of turns in the energised coil, or primary winding, what are the characteristics of the electrical energy produced?

Simply, because more interruptions of the lines of force occur in the increased number of windings there is a greater pressure on the electrons in the second coil. Increased pressure means a higher voltage. Theoretically there is an increase in voltage proportional to the ratio of the windings in the primary and secondary coils.

But as the total power available cannot exceed the amount put into the primary coil the current flow in the secondary coil is decreased in the same proportion.

A hypothetical, completely efficient transformer supplied with a primary coil current of 10 amps at 12 volts and having a ratio of secondary to primary windings of 1000:1 would create a 12,000 volt (12 kV) current of 0.01 amps (10 milliamps).

Inefficiences in the magnet effect and other factors like the resistance of the coil windings prevent this perfect transformation of electrical energy. Simple transformers like the car's ignition coil are designed to take into account the energy losses inherent in the real situation. The actual characteristics of ignition coils are discussed in **Chapter 5**.

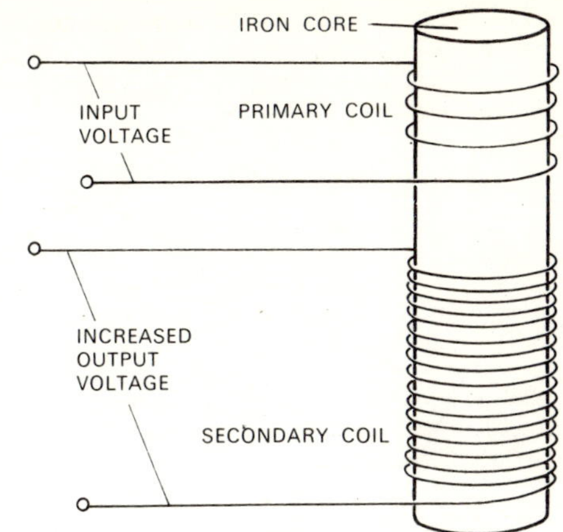

FIG 1:17 Simple transformer

1:13 Transistors and semiconductors

While it is true that for most applications of electricity, materials can be said to be conducting or non-conducting, there are some important exceptions. These are the materials which can be induced to carry current under certain conditions, the semiconductors. The discovery of this phenomenon in materials like silicon, beryllium, germanium and the compounds of these elements with other metals and non-metals, led to the invention of a device that has applications in every field of electricity use, the transistor.

The transistor is simply an electronic switch. It has no moving parts because it works on the principle that the application of a small electric current to the interfaces between three small chips of semiconductor material allows a much larger current to be conducted through the three pieces of material (see **FIG 1:18**).

The three pieces of material, called the base, collector and emitter, are sandwiched together, thus two distinct junctions are formed. Applying a small current to the circuit between the base and the emitter breaks down the internal resistance at the junctions so an even larger current can flow in a circuit connected across the collector and the emitter. So, very small currents can be used to switch on a circuit carrying very large currents. If the base circuit is then switched off, the junctions revert to their non-conducting state and the powerful current carrying circuit is broken.

Transistors are polarity conscious. Even momentary reversal of the current flow in either the base-emitter or the collector-emitter circuit can damage them irreparably. For several reasons, not least that a special heating and fusion process is used to make the junction, transistors are also very heat sensitive. Special care has to be taken in connecting them into circuits to ensure that heat from a soldering iron does not damage the junctions.

Their sensitivity to heat also means that precautions have to be taken to ensure that they do not heat up internally owing to the high current passing through them. To combat this heat build-up the transistor, which is really a very small component, is encapsulated in a special heat conducting can, up to half an inch in diameter. The can is often mounted on a very much larger aluminium component with cooling fins. The fins form a heat radiating and conducting surface that dissipate the heat generated in the transistor into the air around them. The finned mounting is called a heat sink.

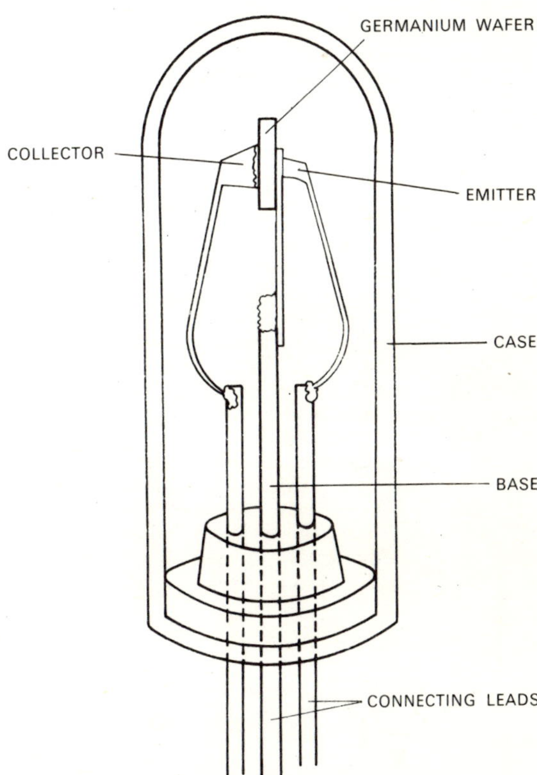

FIG 1:18 Simple transistor

A more robust kind of semiconductor device is found in some car electrical circuits, the diode. It is simpler in construction than the transistor as it normally only has one junction between two pieces of semiconductor material. The diode's virtue is that it will only allow current to flow in one direction in the circuit into which it is connected.

Special diodes can be designed that have additional characteristics. For instance the Zener or avalanche diode has a very high resistance to current flow at low voltage but as the voltage increases to above a predetermined level the device's internal resistance suddenly drops and allows current to flow. Applications of diodes are discussed in **Chapter 3**.

1:14 Electrical systems in cars

There is great and increasing complexity of types of electrical equipment used in today's cars but for simplicity the circuits which supply power to or collect power from these units can be separated into four main functional groups. These are **1** the charging system, linking the battery, generator and control box into the system; **2** the starter motor circuit, specially designed to handle the high current loads used to start the car; **3** the ignition circuits, designed to generate and synchronise high voltage pulses to spark off the internal combustion cycle; and **4** the auxiliary equipment circuits, supplying power to consumer units like horns, lights, radios and other accessories.

Each of these groups of circuits pose individual problems to the car electrician which will be dealt with in the following chapters. But first it is useful to understand the relationship between them.

The supply of electricity in a car starts with the battery, which acts like a reservoir, delivering power whenever the engine is stationary or idling at insufficient speed to obtain useful current from the generator. But when the car is on the road the generator supplies enough electric current to restore the batteries depleted stocks of electricity and to power the ignition system and the auxiliary equipment.

The third component of this system is the control box, a unit that is vitally important to the whole of the car's electrical system. The main functions of the control box are to prevent the battery's reserves of current leaking away through the coils of the generator. It also prevents the battery being damaged by receiving too much charging current from the generator and conversely protects the generator from being overworked and asked to supply too much current. The control box contains a voltage regulator which prevents the generator from supplying a current of too high a voltage, which could damage other components of the electrical system.

The control box is important to the other car circuits (except the starter motor) because in one sense or another they are all connected to it.

The starter motor is the exception because, first it uses more current than all other units on the car and secondly, its use is limited to a few brief seconds of life each time the car is started. This exceptionally heavy electrical load requires that the starter motor is connected directly to the battery via a special switch, the starter solenoid. After the car is started this simple circuit plays no further part in the car's electrical system.

The role of keeping the car going is borne by the ignition system which, as it is so crucial to the engine's operation, deserves the most maintenance, and, indeed, is the system which suffers the most faults.

The heart of the ignition system is the ignition coil which is a transformer, and transforms the ordinary working voltage of the car, 6V or more usually 12V, to the high electrical pressure of up to 30,000V (30kV). At this high pressure or voltage an electric current can jump a gap in an electrical circuit. This gap is provided at the tip of the spark plug. The current jumping across the gap between the plug's points makes a spark which ignites the mixture of petrol and air in the engine's combustion chamber.

But sparks have to be made at the right time in the combustion cycle, so the high voltage current from the ignition coil is switched on and off, as well as directed to the right cylinder, by a rotating switch called the distributor. The car's performance and economy depends on the adjustment of this switch, so considerable attention will be paid to its function in a later chapter.

The rest of the car's electrical system is composed of the individual circuits supplying current to the consumer units. There are separate circuits for each item like the lights, horn, wipers, instrument panel lighting, and accessories like fog lights, radio and tape-player. Each circuit is controlled by a switch in the supply lead and, as explained previously, the circuits are completed by the consumer unit's connection to a common earth, the car body.

The majority of the supply leads for all these circuits emanate from a single terminal on the control box.

This terminal is connected to the control box's current regulator and thus the unit is able to sense the total amount of current consumed by the car's electrical units, and therefore to control the load placed on the generator and battery.

CHAPTER 2

Practical aspects of car electrical work

2:1 Car wiring

Despite the fact that the car's body is used as the earth for car electrical circuits they still need a great deal of wire – over 200 feet of supply leads are used in the modern car. As many of these individual circuit wires run to and from units that are sited very near to each other it simplifies the potential tangle to bind the wires together into bundles called wiring looms or harnesses. Each loom – some cars have several, others only one or two – combines the wires supplying a section of the car like the engine compartment or the rear light clusters.

On older cars the wires themselves were insulated with rubber and fabric and the looms were bound with twine and fabric tape. On most recent cars the wires are insulated with polyvinylchloride plastics and bound together with adhesive plastics tape (see **FIG 2:1**).

Despite progress in automating most other operations in car construction looms are still handmade. To overcome the cost of this labour intensive operation a new type of car wiring loom is beginning to be used. Called Fabrostrip, this semi-automatically made loom consists of conventional plastics insulated wires heat-sealed onto a flat plastics strip (see **FIG 2:2**). The first car to have this new type of wiring was the BLMC Allegro – many more British and European manufacturers are expected to use Fabrostrip on their vehicles in the near future.

In the quantities used for car wiring looms, the cost of wire itself becomes very significant to the car manufacturers. Consequently they use the thinnest wire possible consistent with the current carrying requirements of the circuit (see **Section 2:2**). So several grades of wire are used to make up car wiring looms.

Thinner wires, or wires with fewer strands, are used in circuits like those for the interior lights, clock and other small accessories. Progressively thicker wires are used for higher current carrying applications like heater motors, headlamps and ammeter wiring. The thickest wire of all is used for the main battery lead and for the starter motor supply lead.

Three special types of conductor are also used on cars. Braided wire strap is commonly found connecting the earth terminal of the battery to the car body and earthing the engine block to the car body. A strap of this type is also used to ensure a continuous earth connection between panels that may be separated by hinges from the main body. This is a particularly important requirement in the suppression of radio interference (see **Chapter 9**).

Special leads are used for the high tension (high voltage) connections between the ignition coil, the distributor cap and spark plugs. Some high tension leads have a stranded copper conductor surrounded by extra thick plastics insulation. Radio interference suppression requirements have brought about the introduction of another type of high tension lead. This has a carbon impregnated rayon fibre conductor and, again, thick insulation.

The third type of special conductor increasingly found on modern cars is the printed circuit. Originally developed to facilitate the complex circuit requirements of modern transistorised devices, the printed circuit consists of thin sheet copper conductors etched into convoluted current pathways according to individual circuit requirements. The copper conductors are attached to a rigid resin impregnated board base or may also be fixed to a flexible plastics sheet. A common in-car application of printed circuitry, which cuts down on wiring clutter, is in the wiring of the instrument panel unit (see **FIG 2:4**).

A different type of printed circuit is used in the manufacture of heated rear windows. Special conducting

FIG 2:1 Conventional wiring loom

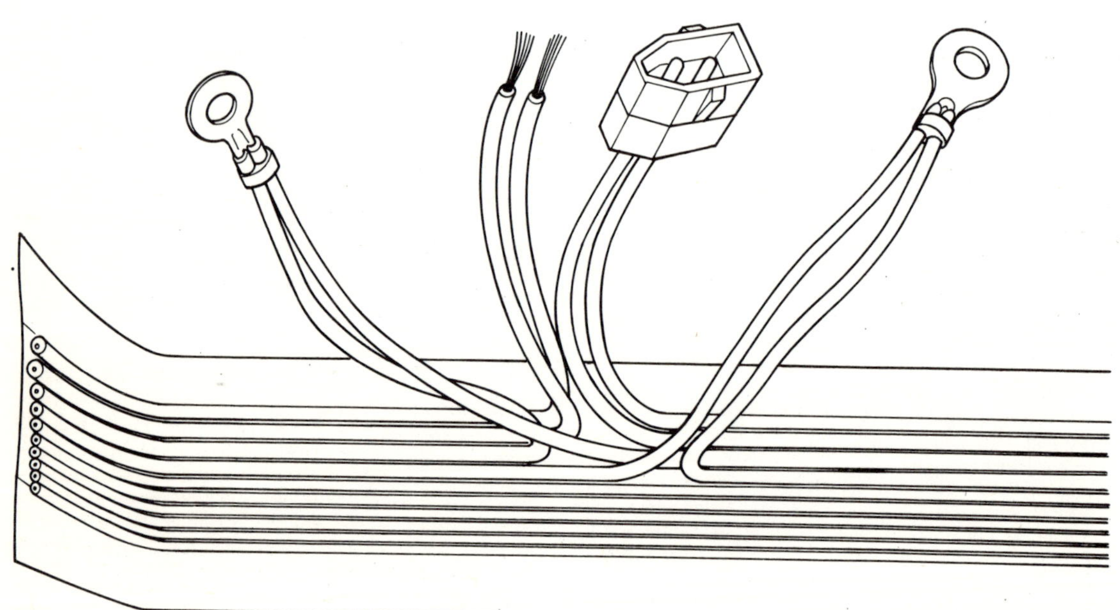

FIG 2:2 Fabrostrip loom

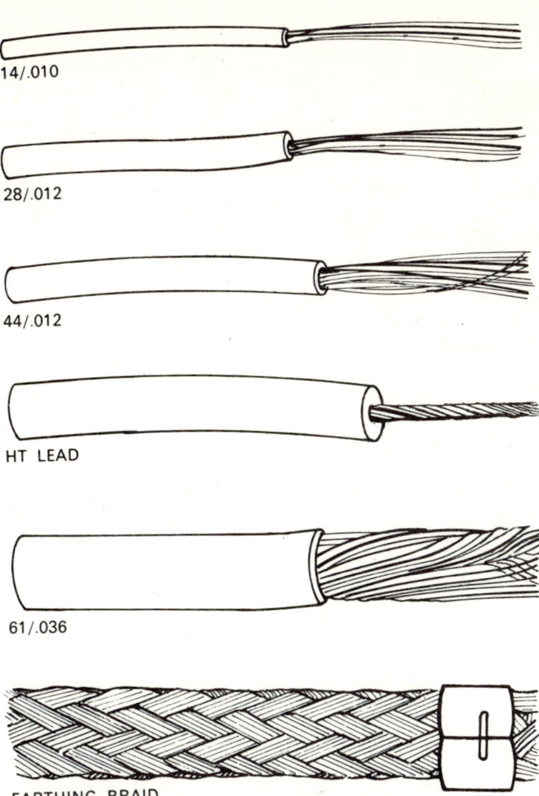

FIG 2:3 Different grades of wire

material is imprinted onto the inner surface of the glass and fused into the glass in a final heating process. The result is a very fine resistive heating filament which is actually a part of the window glass surface.

2:2 Using the correct wire grade

For rewiring purposes, repairing looms and fitting accessories the manufacturer's grades of wiring must be considered as the absolute minimum wire thickness to be used. If an existing circuit is to be used to carry the load of additional accessories it is wise to check that the original wiring is suitable for carrying the higher current.

Wires are graded by a number denoting the number of strands and the diameter of a single strand; 14/.010 wire has 14 strands with a diameter of 0.01 inch; 44/.012 wire has 44 strands each with a diameter of 0.012 inch.

Each grade of wire has a current carrying rating which is determined by **1** the total cross-sectional area of all its strands, thus its resistance; **2** as this resistance results in heating when current flows, the acceptable temperature rise in the circuit; **3** the acceptable voltage drop over the wire's length.

For example, a wire grade 14/.010 will carry a current of up to 6 amps with a very small rise in temperature and its resistance is such that at this current the voltage will drop by 1 volt over about 21 feet of wire. At lower currents this is acceptable for a single wire in a car where cable runs are usually considerably shorter.

However, wires in a loom cannot cool so well as when they are used singly. In the example above the 14/.010 wire should only be used for a maximum 4 amp current if it is bound in a loom and in use continuously, for instance in a rear or sidelamp circuit.

Table of wire grade applications:

Typical car wiring grade	Approximate current rating for continuous use	Typical applications
23/.0076 9/.012 14/.010	4 amps – 5 amps	sidelights, rear lights, interior lights, clock, radio, tape-player, anti-theft device
28/.012 35/.012	up to 15 amps	headlamps, wiper motor, heater fan, spotlamps and fog-lamps, heated rear window
44/.012 65/.012	25 amps – 30 amps	battery charging circuit, ammeter, horns, cigar lighter
97/.012	45 amps	main charging circuit on some cars with alternators
37/.036 to 61/.036	350 amps to 700 amps	main battery lead and starter motor supply lead

Current ratings are approximate and refer to continuous load condition with wires bound in loom.

The dimension used to identify wire grades in the metric system is the total cross sectional area in square millimetres. Approximate continuous current ratings for metric wire grades are as follows:

1 sq mm	3 amps	4 sq mm	20 amps
1.5 sq mm	6 amps	6 sq mm	25 amps
2.5 sq mm	15 amps	10 sq mm	40 amps

Heavier grades, up to 95 or 120 sq mm, are used for starter leads. The grades are often indicated on the wiring diagrams for Continental cars.

2:3 Colour coding

To facilitate the identification and tracing of car electrical circuits the wiring insulation is colour coded. The insulator is coloured a single main colour and usually has a stripe of a second contrasting colour. For some years now the wiring of most British cars (BLMC, Chrysler, Vauxhall) has been coded according to a British Standard Institution specification often referred to as the Lucas colour code.

European, Japanese and American manufacturers have different codes, detailed in the handbooks of each car. Ford have standardised the colour codes used for the wiring of their British and European made cars. It is expected that a European standard colour code will soon be introduced based on the British system.

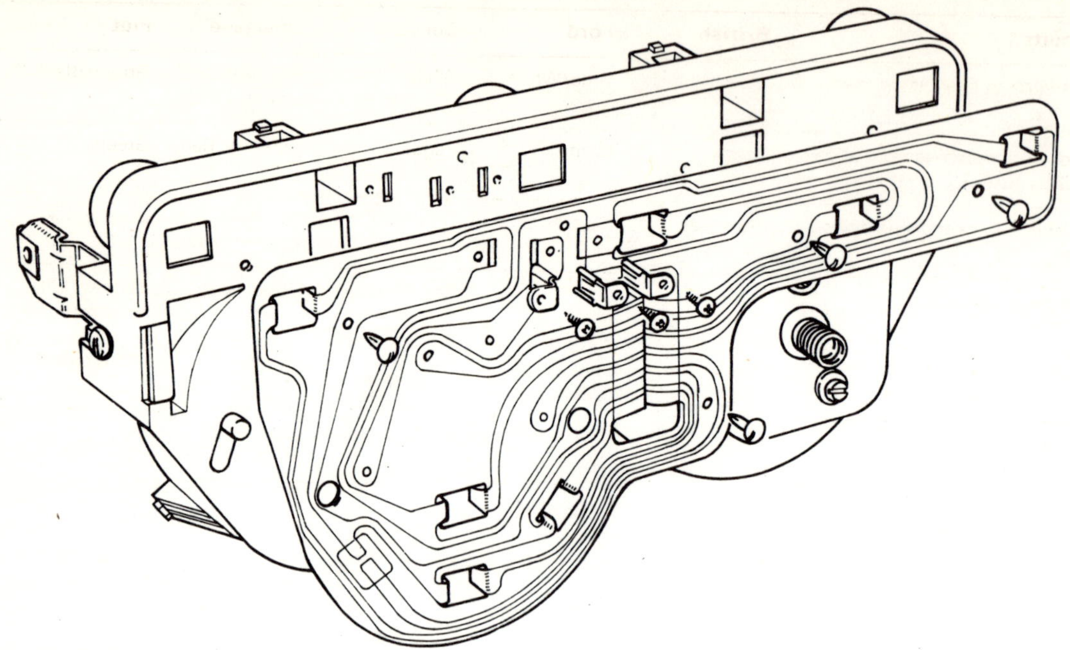

FIG 2:4 Printed circuit instrument panel

Circuits	British	Ford	German	Japanese	Fiat
Main battery feed to control box, lighting and ignition switches, equipment supplied direct from battery	Brown	Brown	Red	White	Pink
Feeds from ignition switch to ignition auxiliary fuse and unfused circuits	White	White	Black	Black/White or Black/Yellow	Black/Blue
Ignition switch to starter solenoid	White/Red	White/Red	Red	Black/White or Black/Yellow	Red
Distributor to CB on ignition coil	White/Black	White/Black	Green	Black or Blue	Black
Battery lead to ignition coil (SW) (ballast resistor systems only)	White/Blue or Yellow/Grey	Black/Yellow	Red	Black/Red	—
All feeds to accessories from ignition auxiliary fuse	Green	Varies	Varies	Varies	Varies
Control box (A1) to ignition switch (dynamos only)	Brown/Blue	Brown	Red	White	Brown
Control box (F) to dynamo field coil	Brown/Green	Brown/Green	Green or Black	White with another colour	White
Dynamo to control box (D) and ignition warning light	Brown/Yellow	Brown/Yellow	Red or Blue	Varies	Brown and Black
Light switch to headlamp dip switch	Blue	Blue	Varies	Red/Yellow or Red/White	Green

Circuits	British	Ford	German	Japanese	Fiat
Dipswitch to headlamps main beam	Blue/White	Blue/White	White	Red with another colour	Green/Black
Feeds to accessories from battery auxiliary fuse, e.g. horn feed	Purple	White	Varies	Green or Red	Green
Dipswitch to headlamps dipped beam	Blue/Red	Blue/Red	Yellow	Red with another colour	Grey/Black
Light switch to side lights	Red	Red	Grey/Red or Grey/Black	Green with another colour	Yellow (left), Brown (right)
Panel light feeds	Red/White	Red/White	Grey or Grey/Red	Red/Black	White/Black
Stoplight feeds	Green/Purple	Green/Yellow	Black or Yellow	Green with another colour	Red
Flasher unit to direction indicator switch	Light Green	Light Green/ Brown	Black/Green/ White (VW)	Varies	Violet
Direction indicator warning light feed	Light Green/ Purple	Light Green/ Purple	Blue	Varies	Light Blue/ White
Lefthand indicator light feeds	Green/Red	Green/Red	Black/White	Green with another colour	Black/Blue
Righthand indicator light feeds	Green/White	Green/White	Black/Green or Green	Green with another colour	Blue
Rear lights and number plate light feed	Red	Red	Grey/Red and Grey/Black	Varies	Brown and Yellow
Main beam warning light feed	Blue/White	Blue/White	Varies	Red/Yellow or Red/Blue	Green/Black

FIG 2:5 Wiring colour code conventions

The table in **FIG 2:5** gives some of the variations found in colour coding. Using wires of the same colour coding to replace wires in the car's loom may not always be expedient for the amateur car electrician as it may involve considerable expenditure on materials. However, it is good practice to bear in mind that a car's second or third owners may have difficulty tracing modified circuitry so it is a good idea to keep notes of any colour code changes made to the electrical system. This also applies to the wiring installed for fitting accessories.

2:4 Wiring diagrams and symbols

The most valuable collection of information to the car electrician is the wiring diagram which is to be found in the car's handbook. The diagram shows the wire connections between each electrical unit, usually giving the colour of the wire (or for some cars a number code), the numbers or other markings on the terminals of sealed units, and sometimes an indication of the loom into which the wire is bound.

To simplify all electrical diagrams, in cars and other electrical appliances, a simple shorthand of graphic symbols has been evolved. A few of these symbols cropped up in the simple diagrams in **Chapter 1** but the shorthand is more extensive than this. It covers all the possible components of an electrical system like light bulbs, switches, fuses, resistors and coils and transformers. Although there are some individual variations in the symbol used for each component, between manufacturers and from country to country (often according to the draughtsman's whim) each symbol is generally recognisable as referring to a particular unit (see **FIG 2:6**).

As well as a set of symbols covering the commoner and smaller components of a circuit, major units like dynamos, alternators, ignition coils, the control box and the complex switch which controls headlamps, direction indicators and, perhaps the horn, may be represented pictorially. In case of doubt it is usual for the manufacturer to give a numbered key to the diagram.

It is not the intention of a wiring diagram to give the exact position of components within the car. However, manufacturers tend to show closely associated groups of components, like the instrument panel cluster, in approximately the correct spatial relationship (see **FIG 2:7**).

2:5 Car electrician's tool kit

Working on car electrical systems becomes very much easier if a small range of specialised tools are bought for the tool box. Useful tools that may be bought in addition to the usual range of spanners, screwdrivers and sockets are:

10 mm and 14 mm plug spanners or sockets.
Small electrical screwdriver.
Small Philips screwdriver.
Long-nosed pliers.
Side-cutting pliers
Wire cutter and stripper.
Set of Allen keys.
Set of small spanners (Magneto spanners) in BA and Metric ranges.
Spark plug feeler gauges and setting tool.
Useful oddments for the tool box:
Selection of wires of various grades and colour codes.
Fabric or pvc insulation tape.
Selection of connectors (see **Section 2:9**).
Selection of rubber grommets of various sizes.
Crocodile clips.
Nail file or emery board.
Spare fuses, various current ratings.
A small 12 volt bulb and holder for use as a test lamp.

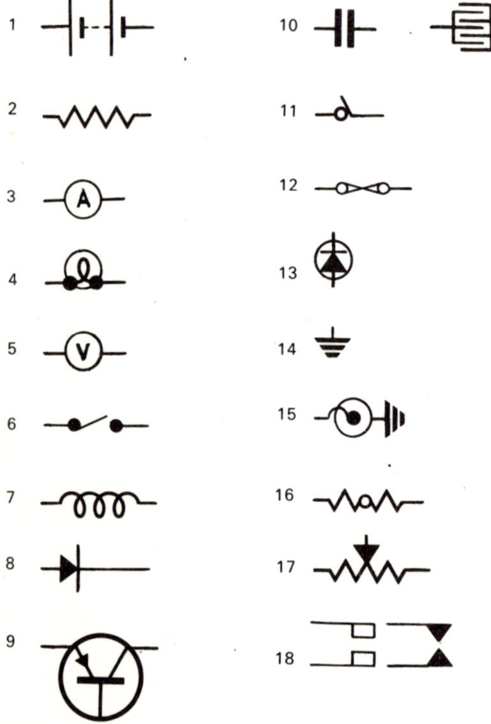

FIG 2:6 Wiring diagram symbols

Key to Fig 2:6 1 Battery 2 Resistor 3 Ammeter 4 Bulb 5 Voltmeter 6 Switch 7 Coil 8 Diode 9 Transistor 10 Capacitor 11 Brush contact 12 Fuse 13 Zener diode 14 Earth 15 Switch (courtesy light door switch) 16 Thermistor 17 Variable resistance (rheostat) 18 Contact points

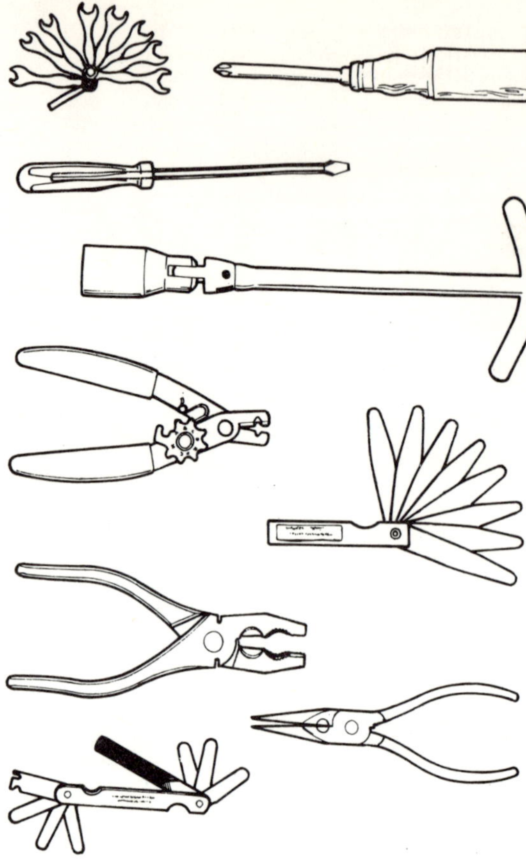

FIG 2:8 Tools for the electrical tool kit

FIG 2:7 (opposite) **Mini wiring diagram**

Key to Fig 2:7 1 Generator 2 Control box 3 Battery 4 Starter solenoid 5 Starter motor 6 Lighting switch 7 Headlamp dipswitch 8 Righthand headlamp 9 Lefthand headlamp 10 Main beam warning lamp 11 Righthand sidelamp 12 Lefthand sidelamp 13 Panel lamps switch 14 Panel lamps 15 Number plate illumination lamps 16 Righthand stop and tail lamps 17 Lefthand stop and tail lamp 18 Stop lamp switch 19 Fuse unit 20 Interior light 21 Righthand door switch 22 Lefthand door switch 23 Horn 24 Horn push 25 Flasher unit 26 Direction indicator switch 27 Direction indicator warning lamp 28 Righthand front flasher lamp 29 Lefthand front flasher lamp 30 Righthand rear flasher lamp 31 Lefthand rear flasher lamp 32 Heater fan switch 33 Heater fan motor 34 Fuel gauge 35 Fuel gauge tank unit 36 Windscreen wiper switch 37 Windscreen wiper motor 38 Ignition/starter switch 39 Ignition coil 40 Distributor 41 Fuel pump 43 Oil pressure warning lamp 44 Ignition warning lamp 45 Speedometer 64 Bi-metal instrument voltage stabiliser 83 Induction heater and thermostat (when fitted) 84 Suction chamber heater (when fitted) 94 Oil filter switch 105 Oil filter warning lamp

Cable colour code: **N** Brown **U** Blue **R** Red **P** Purple **G** Green **LG** Light green **W** White **V** Yellow **B** Black

When a cable has two colour code letters, the first denotes the main colour and the second denotes the tracer colour

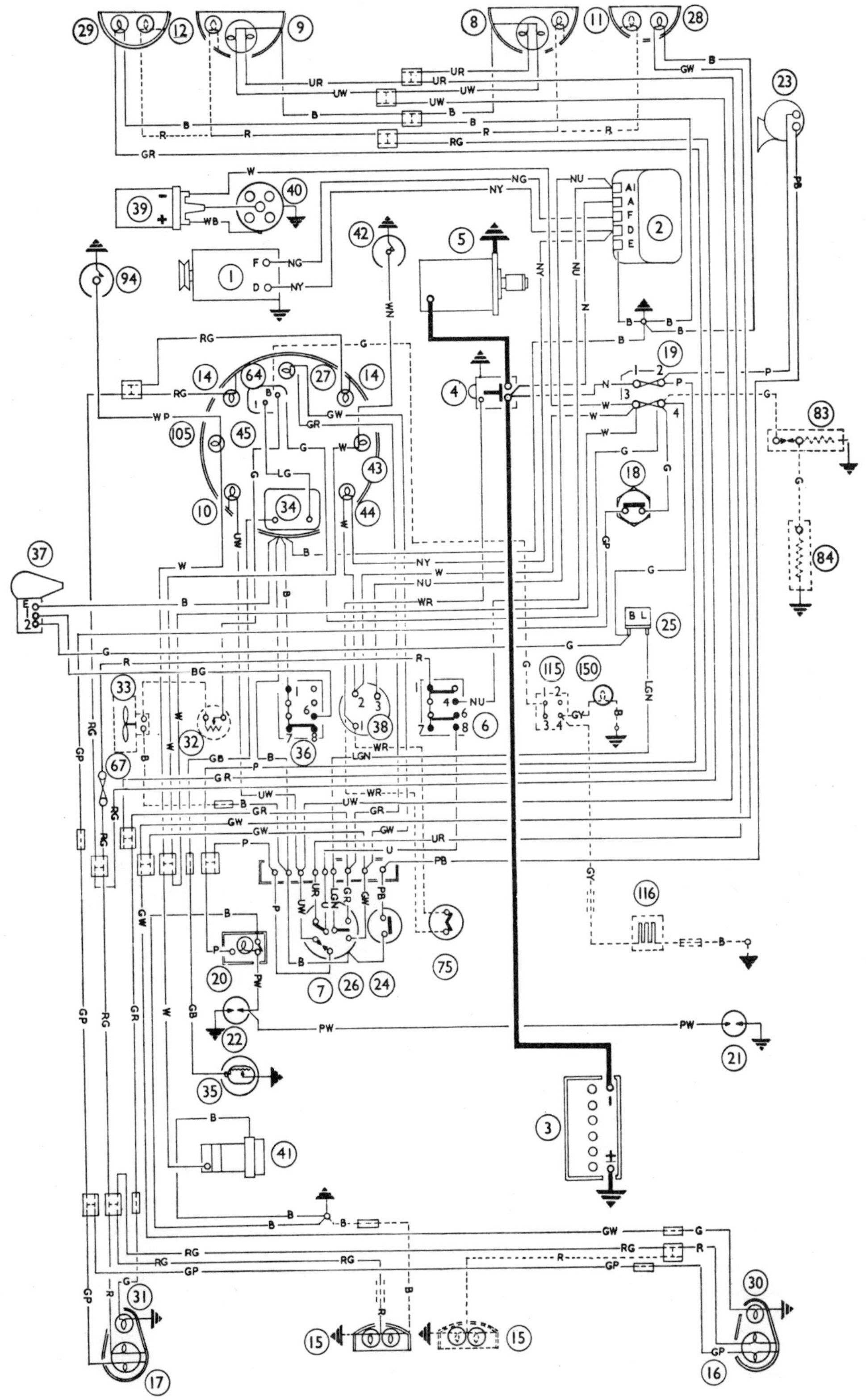

2:6 Useful equipment

Battery charger. There are numerous battery chargers on the market for home use. All of them consist of a transformer which reduces the domestic voltage of 230-250 volts ac to about 13-14 volts and a rectifier changing the current from ac to dc (see section on alternators, **Chapter 3**). The best type of charger to buy has a facility to charge 6 volt or 12 volt batteries, an ammeter showing the charging current (a dial showing from 0-4 amps or 0-5 amps), 4 amp or 5 amp fuse protection in the charging circuit and a lead for connection to the domestic supply that includes earth protection (a three-core lead). See **Chapter 3** on charging techniques.

Battery hydrometer. A hydrometer is a device used to check the specific gravity of fluids – in this case the battery electrolyte. The battery hydrometer consists of a glass or plastics tube containing the hydrometer float with a nozzle to facilitate drawing electrolyte into the tube by pumping a rubber bulb.

Electric soldering iron. The best size of soldering iron to buy for car electrics applications is one of about 50 watts power.

Stroboscopic timing light. A timing light enables accurate adjustment of ignition timing according to the manufacturers' specified timing marks found on the crankshaft pulley or the flywheel starter gear ring. The method is to connect the light so that its discharge tube flashes when a spark is supplied to No. 1 cylinder and direct the flashes towards the timing marks. The distributor can then be finely adjusted until the correct degree marking appears stationary against the manufacturer's fixed reference point. (For more detail on stroboscopic timing see **Chapter 5**).

Timing lights within the price range of the home electrician are of two types. The best has an independent source of current supply for the flashing light (the car's battery) and the pulses are timed by a lead sensing the high voltage impulses to the No. 1 spark plug. This kind of timing light has a bright flash and makes viewing of the timing marks very easy, even in daylight.

A much cheaper type of stroboscopic light utilises the spark impulse itself as the power source and the light produced is a lot weaker.

Instruments. More advanced diagnosis of car electrical circuits has to be carried out using instruments. The home electrician can obtain suitable instruments quite cheaply by hunting through the advertisements of electrical magazines.

The best instruments to buy are:

1 A moving coil ammeter with a full scale deflection of 0-50 amps dc.

2 A moving coil voltmeter with a full-scale deflection of 0-20 volts dc.

Or:

3 A cheap Multimeter type of instrument with voltmeter and ammeter capabilities within the same ranges as the separate instruments above.

It is most useful to have the two separate instruments when checking the characteristics of the charging system – otherwise the more expensive Multimeter type is suitable for car electrical applications. Voltmeters and ammeters which are sold as car accessories for instrument panel mounting are not accurate enough or sensitive enough for diagnostic applications.

Home-made equipment:

Jump leads. Useful for emergency starting of cars with flat batteries and for occasional use in tracking down battery circuit faults, jump leads can be bought as a set or simply made. To make jump leads, two lengths of at least six feet of heavy duty cable (minimum current rating 100 amps) should have large crocodile clips (or welding clamps) secured firmly at each end. The handles of the clips should be insulated as it is possible to experience painful electric shocks from the battery circuit of a car that is running. For details on use of jump leads see **Chapter 3**.

Low current jump leads. To provide connections between the separate halves of multiple pin connectors and to bypass loom wiring in emergencies and during circuit testing it is useful to have a small selection of jump leads for lower current carrying applications.

Some 3-4 foot leads should be prepared from wire with a current rating of up to 15 amps having a small crocodile clip at each end. Shorter leads can be made with a male spade connector at one end and a female Lucar connector at the other.

2:7 Emergency repair kit

As electrical faults which occur while motoring can be very inconvenient and sometimes potentially dangerous, it is as well to carry a simple emergency repair kit in the car for roadside use. The contents of this kit will have to be tailored to some extent to suit the individual vehicle, but a typical selection might be:

- Length of 15-25 amp rated wire (about 20 feet).
- Short length of high tension lead.
- Headlamp, side and tail light, indicator and stoplight bulbs (see car handbook for bulb types).
- Dynamo or alternator brushes.
- Insulating tape.
- Fan belt (belts if the car has more than one).
- Contact breaker set.
- Spark plugs.
- Distributor rotor arm.
- Fuses (various ratings to suit car).
- Assorted cable connectors, screws, nuts and self-tapping screws.

2:8 Workshop techniques

Like all maintenance and repair work on a car the key to the success of a job very often lies in the cleanliness and orderliness with which it is carried out. The only difference between electrical work and other car maintenance operations is that, generally speaking, the parts are smaller and more delicate.

Car electrical jobs may genuinely provide an excuse to work on the kitchen table. Even if this is not possible a bench area, well-cleared and free from dirt, should be used for all stripping down and assembly operations. Once the parts themselves have been cleaned (a good idea is to keep cleaned parts in small tins to avoid losing them) the bench or table can be covered with clean newspaper or cloth to prevent recontamination.

Before a unit is removed from the car to the work bench it is essential to label wires and connections, or note down the wire colour codes on a diagram of the unit's supply connection terminals, to ensure correct replacement. The same applies during the stripping down of the unit. Important things to note include the way thrust washers are assembled, the order of washers on a bolt (this may affect internal tolerances), the connected and unconnected terminals on switches, the use of similarly threaded screws of differing length, and so on.

Cleaning electrical parts:

Cars are a hostile environment to most electrical units which are able to operate most effectively and reliably only in a clean, dry, temperature-controlled atmosphere. Conditions under a car bonnet are far from ideal in this way, consequently only a short time after a car is made the electrical terminals become dirty, and grit, moisture and oil penetrate the various units, motors and generators. Corrosion also sets in. All these elements can be barriers to the passage of current and thus can reduce a unit's efficiency.

To clean grease off electrical units it is best to use a solvent. Petrol is the easiest to obtain and is the best all-purpose grease solvent. Large parts can be most economically cleaned by rubbing down with petrol soaked rag. Smaller more delicate parts can be immersed in a small bath of petrol and more inaccessible patches of dirt can be removed by gently brushing with a small paint brush. Methylated spirits are another useful solvent.

It is not advisable to immerse coils (such as motor windings) in petrol or any other solvent because abrasive particles may be carried into the spaces in the coil by the fluid's action. Accumulations of dirt on coils are best dealt with by gentle brushing or by puffs of air from a photographer's lens brush with rubber bulb squeezer. Modern coil windings are made from lacquered wire – the lacquer is the insulator and it is very easily scratched and rendered ineffective unless cleaning is carried out with care.

Corrosion and dirt on terminals can be abraded away. A useful tool for the cleaning of terminals is a nail file or emery board (which has the additional advantage of being flexible). For more delicate work slivers of glasspaper can be used. When using an abrasive ensure that metal filings or grit from the emery board or glasspaper cannot accidentally enter the moving parts of a unit. A thin hacksaw blade is useful to clean the gaps between commutator segments.

Never use emery paper in electrical work – small metallic particles from the paper can cause damage. (Emery boards, in spite of the name, are faced with glasspaper.)

2:9 Making good connections

The aim in connecting electrical units up to a source of supply, is to provide as easy a pathway as possible for the current. This means reducing the resistance of the connection – a bad connection with a high resistance adds to the overall resistance of the circuit and lowers the voltage of the supply available to the unit. A good connection needs as great an area of contact between the metal of the supply wire and the metal of the connecting terminal as possible.

The following paragraphs deal with a number of ways of making good connections. The advice that applies to all of them is to ensure that all mating surfaces are clean; grit and dirt can physically separate the connection and corrosion can add to the resistance of the joint. Grease, too, is an insulator and although it may not prevent the two metal parts connecting it attracts other dirt and may cause future connection problems – clean it off.

Car electrical connectors:

For speed in assembly and reliability in service, car manufacturers have developed a number of connecting devices, both for jointing wires and for making electrical contacts with the various units in the car. Car parts shops and garages can supply these tiny devices and a selection of them is a useful addition to the supplies box.

The commonest connector found in cars is the bullet type. The bullet is a tiny metal tube soldered to the bare end of the wire. The bullet fits into a crimped metal tube and is secured by the crimped restriction mating with a neck on the bullet. The tube takes a bullet in each end and is insulated by a plastics or rubber cover. Thus, when the two bullets on the wires to be joined are pushed firmly into the tube the insulation is continuous. Multiple bullet connectors with several tubes are used when connecting a number of wires together.

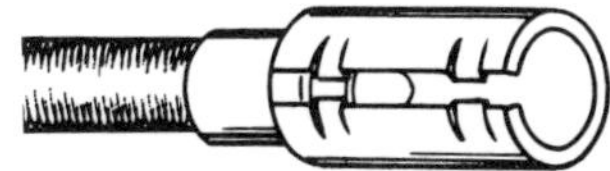

FIG 2:9 Bullet type connector

Although this type of connection is widely used and it is extremely reliable, the insulating sleeve can hide a bad case of corrosion so it is always wise to look at the condition of the bullet connectors in a circuit if there is any doubt that a good connection exists.

Fit bullet connectors by baring a $\frac{1}{4}$ inch of wire, tinning it and then inserting it into the bullet. Heat the bullet until the solder has flowed properly around the joint and trim off any excess bare wire. If solder is not available a good connection can be made by folding back the bare wire emerging from the bullet nose and pushing the bullet into the tube so the wire is tightly trapped. A special tool is available for inserting bullets into tubes – since it is sometimes difficult to apply enough pressure to this tiny part the tool is a good buy especially if a major job like rewiring the car is being attempted.

The flat interlocking spade connector – often called the Lucar connector – is the most common way electrical components are attached to leads. The spade, or male, part of the connector is riveted or moulded to the unit and the female part is crimped, soldered or resistance welded to the supply lead. There are two sizes of Lucar connector – the larger is for high current carrying applications such as the generating circuit, and the smaller connector is used for almost every other purpose. A specially moulded plastics insulator covers the finished connection.

Lucar connectors are occasionally used as joints between wires in which case a special double-ended spade is used between two female parts. For connecting other accessories to existing circuits it is possible to buy three-way Lucar connectors.

Fit female Lucar connectors by stripping the insulation

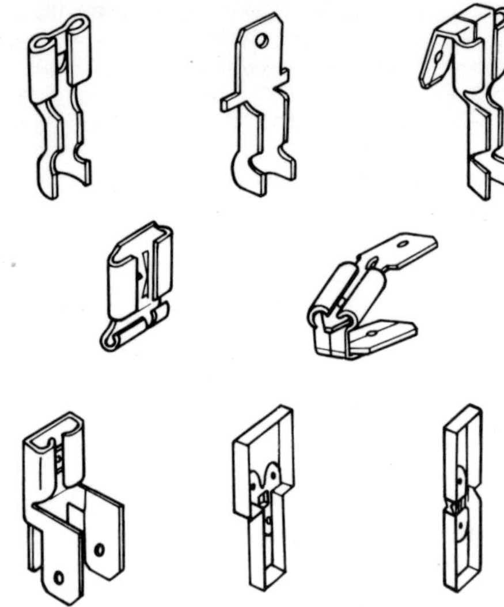

FIG 2:10 Lucar connectors and junctions

Tag connections should always be used to connect wire to screw terminals or when connecting a lead to the car body. The tag is a metal eye or slotted spade which can be crimped or soldered to the wire in the same way as Lucar connectors.

It is very important to ensure that both surfaces of a tag connector are clean before connection. Rubbing them with a nail file or emery board every time the connection is dismantled ensures satisfactory connection.

Another type of connector, the Scotchlok, often supplied with accessories as the means of connecting them into an existing circuit, consists of a plastics insulating cover and a small slotted metal plate specially designed to cut wire insulation without actually breaking the wire.

This type of connector is used to connect a supply lead direct to an insulated wire. It is fitted by pressing the supply wire into one of the grooves in the insulator, slotting the connecting wire into the other groove, pressing together the hinged halves of the connector, ensuring the metal plate is driven home (using pliers) and locking the device with its snap-round insulator. Never use this type of connection for high current carrying applications or in instances where it may by necessary to disconnect the unit at a later date.

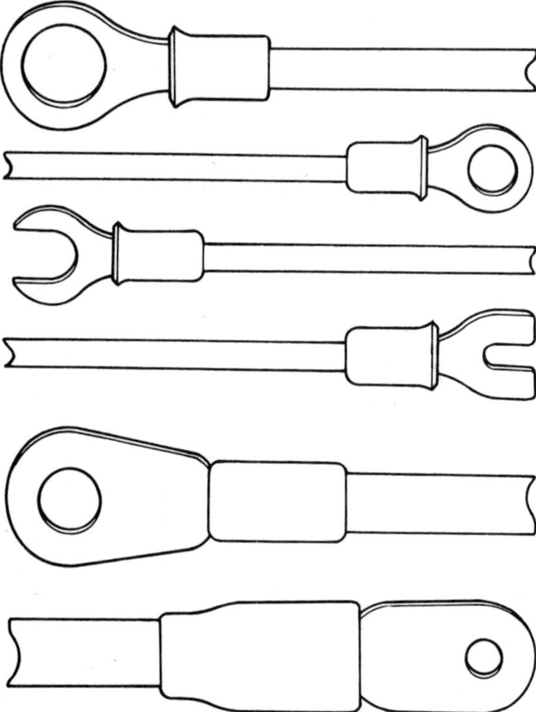

FIG 2:11 Tag connectors

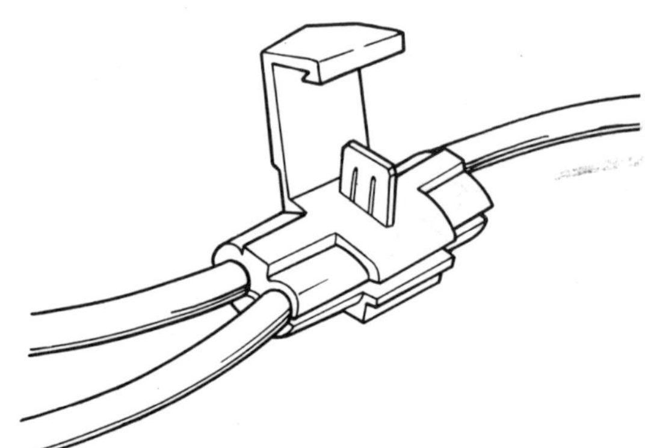

FIG 2:12 3M Scotchlok connector

off $\frac{3}{8}$ inch of wire; tin the bare end and solder into place on the connector shank crimping the lugs down on top of the solder joint. If no solder is available tightly crimp the small lugs down onto the wire end. A special crimping tool can be bought but it is unnecessary to use it if the joint is soldered. Always remember to slide the insulator over the wire before fitting the Lucar connector.

There is another design of connector that is actually bent round an insulated wire. During bending two pointed projections pierce the insulation and make the electrical contact. The same warnings apply about the use of this device as for the Scotchlok connector.

While there are all these connectors that are used specifically in car wiring applications it is on occasions useful to use the conventional screw barrel connector which can be purchased in multiple blocks at any electrical shop. The use of this type of connector is discussed in the chapter on fitting accessories.

An obstacle presented to the car electrician by the manufacturer is the multiple or block connector. Used to connect up electrical units having multiple spade or pin terminals, the block connector consists of a number of female Lucar type connectors or small pin sockets combined in one large plastics insulator. The same kind of device is used for interconnections between looms, the passage of wires through bulkheads on some especially well sound-proofed cars, and for the connection of multiple switches such as the headlamp dipswitch–indicator switch–flasher–horn stalk on the steering column.

It proves an obstacle because the plastic body of the insulator often prevents the ingress of a probe for circuit testing. To overcome this problem the low current jump leads described in the equipment section can be used. These short links of wire with a female Lucar connector at one end and a spade terminal at the other can be placed between the halves of the block connector and thus provide plenty of space for probe access or for other emergency wiring.

Finally, a word of warning. Never be tempted simply to twist wires together to make a connection. This is not an effective or enduring method of joining wires.

2:10 Good wiring practice

In fitting accessories and replacing loom wires there will be many occasions when it is necessary to run a wire between two points in a car. Fit a few accessories and rewire various circuits and the clutter of wires in the engine compartment alone could become a mare's nest. For neatness, accessibility during subsequent circuit tracing and to provide adequate electrical safety and reliability it is wise to observe a set of rules when wiring a car.

1 Where possible use wires of differing colour code to those in the looms and other circuit wires.

2 Use Lucar or bullet connectors where possible for circuit connections–tag types should be used for earthing. Where electrical units have no spade terminals or other means of firmly attaching the wires use solder joints.

3 Even if it means using a great deal more wire, route new wiring along the existing looms–very often there are clips on the body which will accommodate a lot of extra leads. Tape new wiring neatly to the existing loom to ensure that it stays in place.

4 Avoid placing loose wires near moving parts like the fan belt pulleys, starter motor end shank, wiper arm cranks, bonnet hinges etc. Even if the wires do not interfere with the operation of moving parts, slight catching could cause chafing and eventual severing or short circuiting of the wire.

5 Although modern insulating materials can withstand quite high temperatures it is best to avoid routing wires over hot surfaces like the ignition coil, radiator and oil feed pipes. The heat softening of the insulation might aid chafing and eventual wearing through of the wire. Keep wires well away from the exhaust pipe and manifold–this kind of temperature will burn insulation.

6 Try to fit connectors (like in-wire bullet connections) away from points where moisture and dirt can penetrate to the conducting surfaces. If this is unavoidable, say in the case of spotlight connections behind the radiator grille, give the connector additional protection against the environment by wrapping it up well in plastic insulating tape.

7 Avoid drilling additional holes in bulkheads or other body panels for the passage of new wiring–this can let in water, dirt or noise. Instead try to find existing holes in the cable's path and slot the wire in with the other wires or hoses. If drilling a new hole is unavoidable always use a rubber or plastic grommet in the hole to prevent cutting or chafing of wires against the sharp metal.

8 It is sometimes necessary to run wires across panel areas like the floor of the car or the boot floor where heavy weights and grit and stones can damage them. Avoid using this route if possible–if not, ensure that the wire is fixed to the surface with clips or wide tape and provide some additional protection to the wire. One way is to tape strips of metal or wood over the wire at all the points where it may be exposed to accidental damage.

2:11 Simple circuit testing

Using a basic home-made or commercial circuit tester:

A good basic circuit tester can be made from a 12 volt (or 6 volt if the car to be tested has this type of system) low-powered (5 watts or less) light bulb in a small bayonet or Miniature Edison Screw lamp holder. Connect to one terminal of the lamp holder a long lead (4 ft-5 ft) with a small crocodile clip at the other end. To the lampholder's other terminal connect a much shorter lead (about 1 ft or less) the other end of which is attached to a sharp-pointed probe.

A good probe can be made from a knitting needle or a

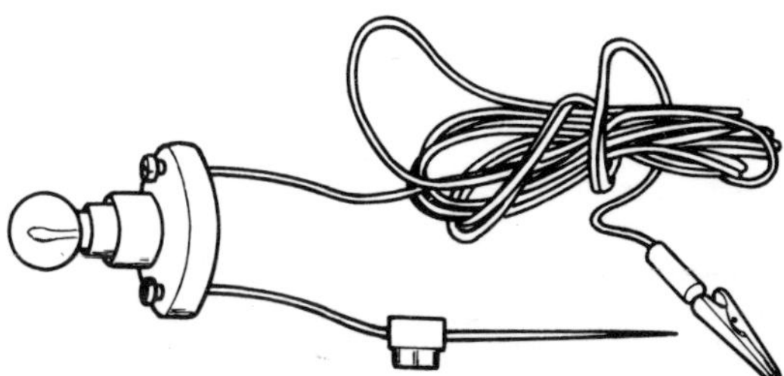

FIG 2:13 Home-made circuit tester

piece of copper rod up to $\frac{1}{8}$ inch diameter. The probe should be about 6 inches long and the point should be sharp enough to pierce the plastic insulation of a wire without too much force. An easy way to connect the probe to its lead is to use a plastics insulated barrel connector.

The probe should be insulated, leaving only the pointed tip bare. Plastic insulating tape can be used for this although a neater, more permanent, job is made by shrinking thin plastic tube onto the probe–detergent and water will make the tube easier to slip onto the metal rod. The rest of the connections on the circuit tester should also be well insulated to guard against the possibility of a short circuit.

Commercial circuit testers are designed on similar lines.

A typical example has the probe and lamp integrated with a convenient hand tool like a screwdriver. The lamp may be a tiny neon discharge type. The neon bulb has the advantage that it can be used for both 12 volt and 6 volt systems.

Check that the tester is operating, before starting any circuit test, by fixing the crocodile clip to a bare metal part of the engine or car body. Touch the probe to the non-earth or 'live' post of the battery or any terminal in permanent connection with the live side of the battery such as the starter solenoid battery terminal. The bulb will light up if the tester is working correctly.

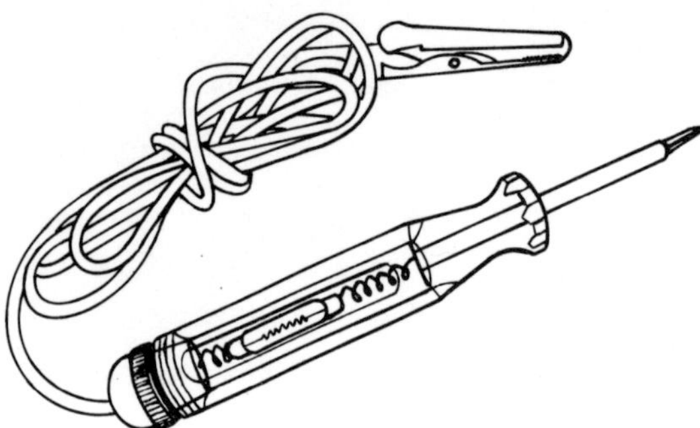

FIG 2:14 Commercial circuit tester

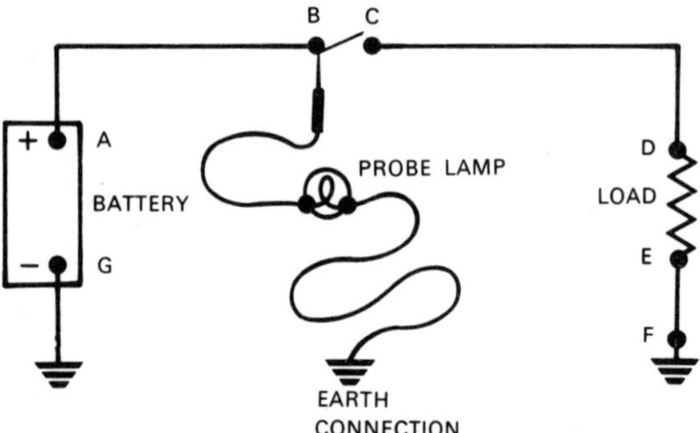

FIG 2:15 Using a circuit tester

In the circuit shown in **FIG 2:15**, with the crocodile clip connected to the earth side of the system, the probe position **A** checks the tester bulb is working. Moving the probe to position **B** tests whether the live supply is getting as far as the switch. As the circuit is drawn with the switch open, moving the probe to **C**, the other switch terminal, should result in the bulb failing to light. The switch's operation can be checked by switching on – the bulb will light if it works properly. If the bulb lights with the probe at **D** the supply to the load is operating correctly.

To check that the load is properly connected to earth

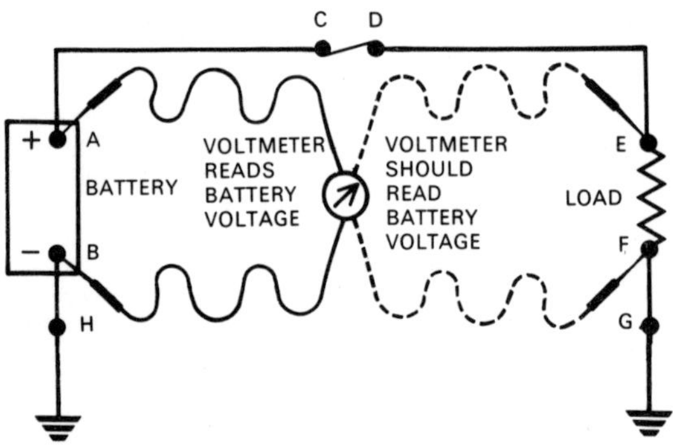

FIG 2:16 Using a voltmeter to test a circuit

(testing earth continuity) the crocodile clip has to be fixed at **A**. If the bulb lights when the probe is touched at points **E**, **F** and **G** in the circuit earth continuity is proved.

What deductions can be drawn from this process?

1 If the load is still refusing to operate and the bulb lights during all the checks the fault lies in the load.

2 If the bulb does not light at any point in the circuit the fault or interruption of the circuit lies somewhere between this point and the last probe position where the bulb lit up.

These are the two principles of circuit checking with a simple tester.

Occasionally it is difficult to see a point where the probe can be touched onto the circuit. This is where the sharp point comes in – the probe can be pushed through the insulation of a wire to contact the conductor without causing too much damage. Another obstacle is the multiple block connector, as described already. Sometimes this can be separated enough to allow probe access but for extensive testing use the short jump leads described in the equipment section and pierce the wires to make probe connections.

Using a voltmeter for circuit testing:

A voltmeter can be used in exactly the same way as the simple circuit tester above but, in addition to the normal checks for circuit continuity, it can be used to find bad circuit connections or resistances. In other words the voltmeter can find the voltage drop over a resistance described in **Chapter 1**.

In the circuit in **FIG 2:16** the reading with the meter connected across points **A**-**B** should be exactly the same as the reading when the meter is connected across **E**-**F** and should be the voltage of the battery, about 12 volts. If the needle of the voltmeter reads anything significantly different there may be a resistive connection in the circuit.

To track down this resistive connection, which may only be causing a voltage drop in the order of 0.2 volts, voltmeter readings should be taken between points like **A**-**C**, **C**-**D**, **D**-**E**, **F**-**G** and **B**-**H**, all the possible places in the circuit where a break or resistance can occur.

The first voltmeter test – checking that there is a voltage drop at the load – will indicate the size of voltage drop that the meter will show at the faulty connection. If the drop is very small the meter needle may only kick slightly as the voltmeter probes are connected. The 0-20 volt voltmeter will only begin to show an accurate steady reading when the voltage drop is over about 1 volt. (Multimeters with a millivolt scale should only be used for this job if adequate protection against higher voltages is built in – accidental connection to earth, a full 12 volts, could damage the instrument.)

Voltage drops in the circuit may arise as the result of a series of bad connections. In this case the voltmeter should be used to diagnose each one, a repair should be made, the next fault can be found and repaired and so on round the circuit.

Voltmeter checking of this kind can only be carried out with the circuit switched on.

A rule to observe in the use of a voltmeter is that it must always be connected in parallel with the part of the circuit to be tested.

If an ammeter is used in circuit testing, always connect it in series with the circuit load.

CHAPTER 3

The battery and the generating circuit

3:1 The lead-acid battery

All today's cars are fitted with a lead-acid battery. Most cars have a 12 volt battery although, until recently, a common exception was the Volkswagen Beetle which had a 6 volt electrical system and battery. Some commercial vehicles have a 24 volt battery (or two 12 volt batteries connected in series).

A battery provides a chemical means of storing and regenerating electricity hence its old-fashioned name, the accumulator. The battery is made up from a number of cells packaged together but functioning separately. Each cell consists of a number of battery plates – plates connected to the cell's positive terminal are interleaved with plates connected to the negative terminal. The cells, each having a nominal voltage of 2 volts are connected in series, thus there are six cells to a 12 volt battery. The plates, there may be 7, 9 or 11 to each cell (always one more negative plate than positive), are immersed in an electrolyte, a dilute solution of sulphuric acid. They are separated by porous ceramic spacers.

A plate is made by coating an antimony and lead alloy grid with an active paste. When the battery is charged a positive plate consists of lead peroxide (PbO_2) and a negative plate consists of pure lead in an active form known as spongy lead (Pb). When a pathway for electrons to flow is opened up by connecting the battery into a circuit the acid reacts with the lead in the plates and progressively turns the substances in both plates into lead sulphate ($PbSO_4$). In the process water is formed at the positive plate which weakens the acid as the battery discharges.

The process is reversed by applying a current across the battery terminals and thus charging the battery. During battery charging the oxygen element of water is recombined and some of the hydrogen element is given off in the form of gas bubbles. The acid also regains its strength.

The capacity of a battery to supply current is dependent on the number of plates in each cell. The capacity is measured in amp-hours. For instance a new, fully charged 56 amp-hour battery will theoretically deliver a current of 1 amp for 56 hours – thus it will deliver 8 amps for 7 hours and a 100 amp starter motor current for about 30 minutes (in theory). Sometimes it is more useful to quote the battery's capacity related to a specific time such as the 20 hour rate. An example is the Lucas Pacemaker A7 (seven plates per cell) battery which has a 20 hour rating of 30 amps – the larger A9 battery (nine plates per cell) has a 20 hour rating of 40 amps.

Because the battery is a chemical device it is affected by the temperature at which it operates. Winter temperatures cause it to be a less efficient regenerator of current – in fact at freezing point a battery becomes approximately 40 per cent less efficient than on a hot summer's day. Also, at lower temperatures the battery has to do a lot more work in starting the car because the engine oil is considerably thicker. The extra effort required of the battery on a cold day could be as much as 75 per cent more than in the summer.

The battery's performance deteriorates slowly throughout its life. The car is not the best environment for a battery – the vibration alone can damage the plates, gradually causing loss of the active material. But the greatest cause of deterioration is neglect and misuse. Failure to top up the battery cells with distilled water (to replace loss by evaporation and chemical reaction) may leave the top of the plates dry and render that portion inactive. Overfilling may cause acid loss, with consequent damage to the car body or battery mounting, and leave the electrolyte depleted in strength.

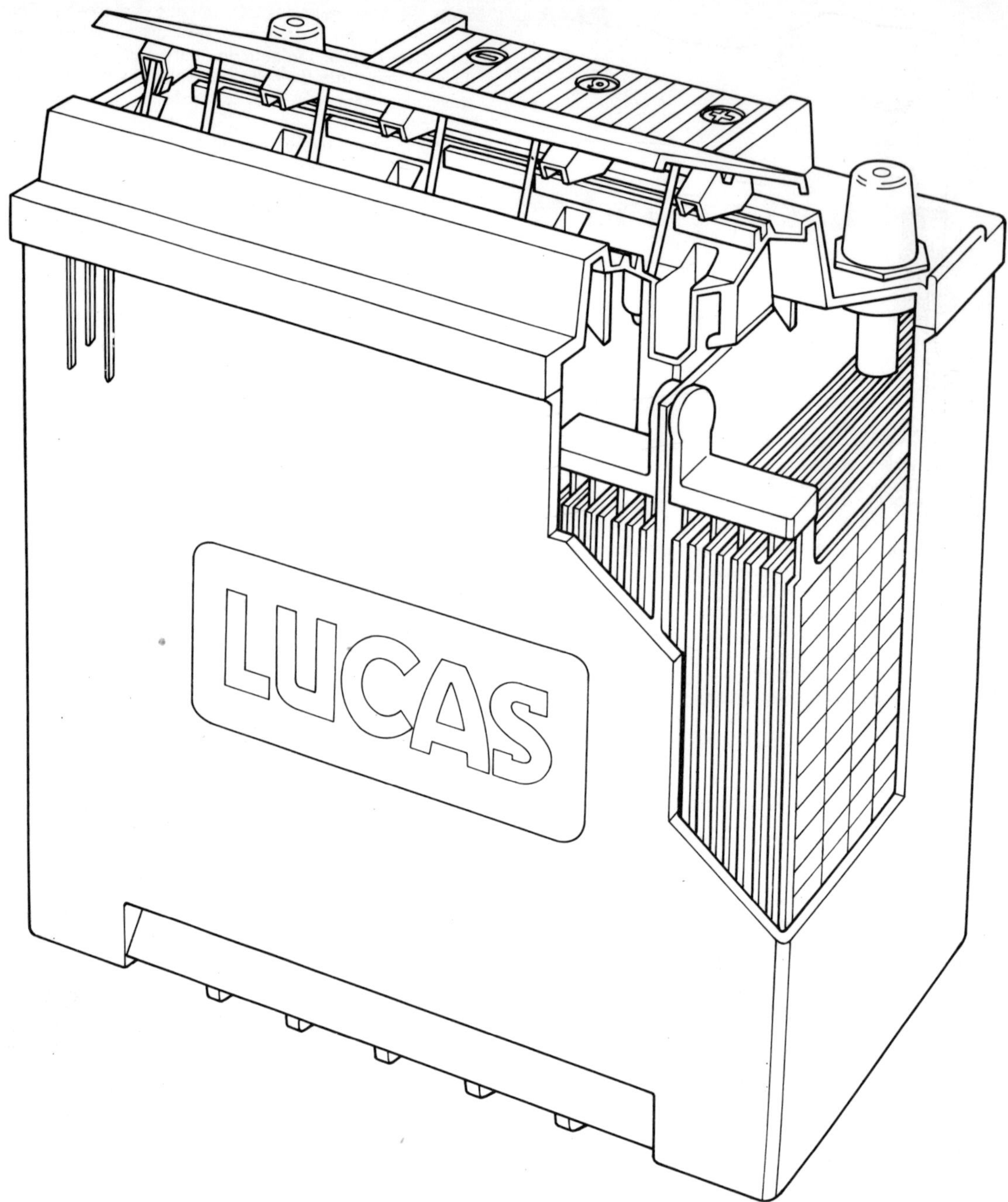

FIG 3:1 The construction of a lead acid battery

Leaving the battery in a poorly charged state allows a deleterious process called sulphation to take place. Lead sulphate coats the plates and fills in the pores of the ceramic spacers thus reducing their ability to allow the free passage of electrolyte in the cells. Attempts to charge a heavily sulphated plate may physically split the cell apart.

Cycles of heavy starter motor discharge, for example when the car is starting poorly, and frequent need for a high current boosting charge from a garage battery charger is another cause of battery deterioration.

Maltreatment like this can reduce the life of the battery from what may be a fully effective term of over two years to a matter of weeks.

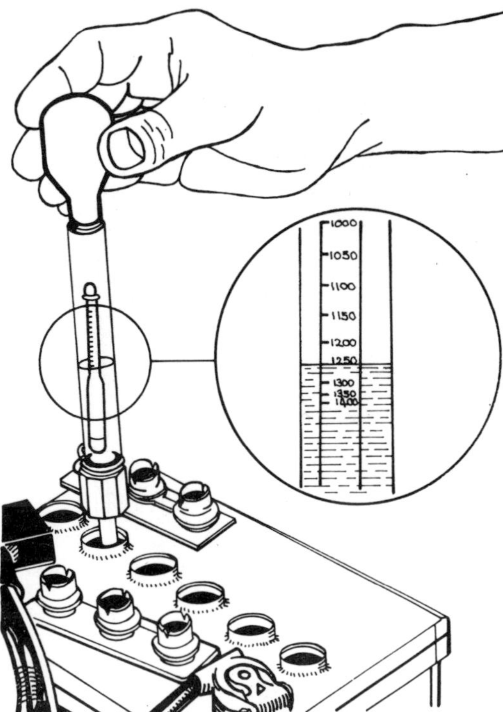

FIG 3:2 Using a hydrometer to test the battery

3:2 Battery testing

All electrical testing of a battery's capacity (in effect its remaining ability to provide adequate current for starting requirements) and its charge retaining ability should be done by a specialist vehicle electrician. The equipment required and the techniques used are beyond the scope of the home electrician and most garages. Battery manufacturers have also made the job of battery testing much more difficult by enclosing the connections between cells inside the sealed battery case. It is thus difficult, even for the professional, to spot internal short circuits and other faults.

There is, however, one very important test that the car owner should perform as part of a regular weekly maintenance schedule. It is the use of a hydrometer to check the specific gravity or strength of the battery acid which, as explained above, varies with the battery's state of charge.

A hydrometer is an instrument which compares the specific gravity (s.g.) of liquids to that of water with an s.g. of 1. Special battery testing hydrometers are inexpensive and can be bought at motor accessory shops.

To use a hydrometer correctly:

1 Top up each cell of the battery to the correct level and either charge the battery for a period of about one hour or leave the battery several hours. This procedure ensures the electrolyte is evenly mixed throughout the cell.

2 Withdraw a quantity of electrolyte from one cell at a time. The quantity withdrawn should be sufficient to allow the float inside the instrument to float freely. Read the scale on the float at the point where it breaks the electrolyte surface and note down the reading. Discharge the electrolyte into the cell from which it was withdrawn and proceed along the battery repeating the process on each cell.

3 Wash out the hydrometer with tap water after use.

Interpreting the readings:

The readings from each cell should be approximately the same – any variation indicates a faulty cell.

Hydrometer reading	State of battery
1.270-1.290	Fully charged
1.190-1.210	About half discharged
1.110-1.130	Discharged

(these readings are true for a temperature range of approximately 55 deg F-65 deg F (13 deg C-18 deg C).

A battery should never be left for any period with a s.g. of lower than 1.150 (equivalent to being about 75 per cent discharged).

3:3 Battery maintenance

Checking battery security:

It is most important that the battery be firmly mounted in the battery carrier. Ensure the battery clamp bolts are done up tight enough to prevent movement under vibration or other car movements. A loose battery may move enough to cause gradual plate damage.

Checking for battery leaks:

Battery cases can be fragile (especially at lower temperatures) and periodic checking for leaks is useful. Leaks occur most frequently around the terminal posts where the case is subjected to the strain of terminal removal and around the top rim of the battery where the lid is sealed to the battery case. The leak may be betrayed by a white crystalline substance forming a thin deposit over the crack – clean off the white deposit with a wet rag before making a repair with either hot sealing wax or a proprietary brand of battery sealer.

It is not possible to repair a leaking case permanently if the crack extends below the electrolyte level. It may be possible to make a temporary get-you-home repair by running a hot soldering iron over the crack so its edges are fused.

Acid spillage and leaks from cracked batteries can be cleaned up by immersing affected parts in a solution of household soda for up to 15 minutes. Washing the parts in water and then renewing anti-corrosion and paint protection should prevent further acid attack.

Care of battery terminals:

Two types of battery terminal connection are in common use on cars. One is a lead alloy cup which fits over the battery terminal post and is secured by a screw. The other is a thick metal clamp pinched on to the battery posts by a bolt.

There is a temptation to use too much force on both types of connection to remove them from the battery post. The result can be damage to the connection and loosening

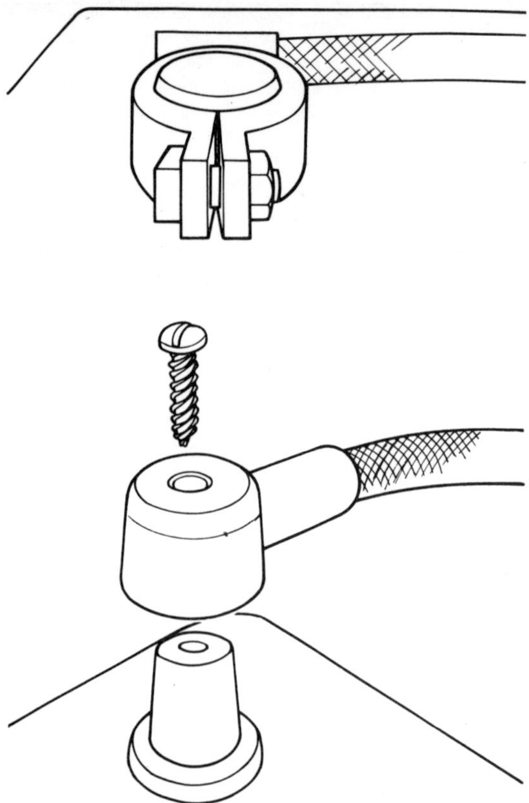

FIG 3:3 Two types of battery lead connector

of the battery post – so always take care to use the minimum force necessary to remove terminal connections after loosening off the clamp or undoing the screw as far as possible. It is best to lever a little at a time around the circumference of the terminal.

Both types of connector must be cleaned on the surfaces which mate with the battery terminal. As this is a common site for corrosion of a particularly hard crystalline nature, a coarse file is the best way to make sure the surfaces make good electrical contact. The battery terminal posts should be cleaned with glass paper. Over enthusiastic and too frequent cleaning of posts and terminals should be avoided – the connections might not fit tight enough.

To avoid further cleaning it is wise to smear terminal posts and connectors with Vaseline, both for protection and for ease of subsequent removal.

When checking battery connections don't neglect the security of the wire connection (usually crimped, or pinched by a separate screw to the connector) or the cleanliness of the mating surfaces on the earth strap's connection to the car body.

Filling the battery:

Only distilled water or de-ionised water should be used for battery filling. A special dispenser that only allows a little water at a time to enter the battery should be used to guard against overfilling.

Each cell should be filled so the electrolyte is about $\frac{1}{4}$ inch above the top of the plates. Some batteries have a trough, designed so that water poured anywhere in the trough will be distributed evenly to each cell. Water spilt in filling the battery should be wiped up.

During the winter monthly battery topping up should be sufficient but more water will evaporate in the heat of summer so weekly checks are advisable. Undue water loss can mean the battery is overcharging (see control box faults, **Section 3:9**).

Never use a naked flame to examine the electrolyte level – the hydrogen gas given off during battery charging is highly inflammable. Avoid causing sparks when connecting or disconnecting the terminals for the same reason.

Charging the battery:

Do not use anything other than a properly designed battery charger to charge a car battery (see **Chapter 2, Section 2:6**). With the charger switched off, it must be connected with the positive lead (usually red) to the positive terminal of the battery and the negative lead (usually black) to the negative terminal of the battery. If the car has an alternator disconnect the battery before commencing charging – delicate devices in the alternator control box can be damaged by the application of a charging current.

Before switching the charger on ensure that it is mounted free of damp wall or floor patches and that its ventilator grilles are not obstructed. Loosen the battery filler caps to allow the escape of gas and to prevent gas discharge blowing electrolyte out of the cells. On the Lucas Pacemaker type the lid must be closed during charging. The charger can now be switched on.

The charger's ammeter will initially register a high charge of up to 4 amps but after a while this falls to a 'trickle' charge of about $1\frac{1}{2}$ amps. Charging of a completely discharged battery should be complete after about 10 hours – hourly checks with a hydrometer can be made towards the end of the charging period. When an electrolyte s.g. of between 1.270 and 1.290 has been reached the battery is charged.

To avoid a spark which might ignite any inflammable gas residue after charging always switch off the charger at the mains before disconnecting the charger leads from the battery.

FIG 3:4 Generator mounted on engine

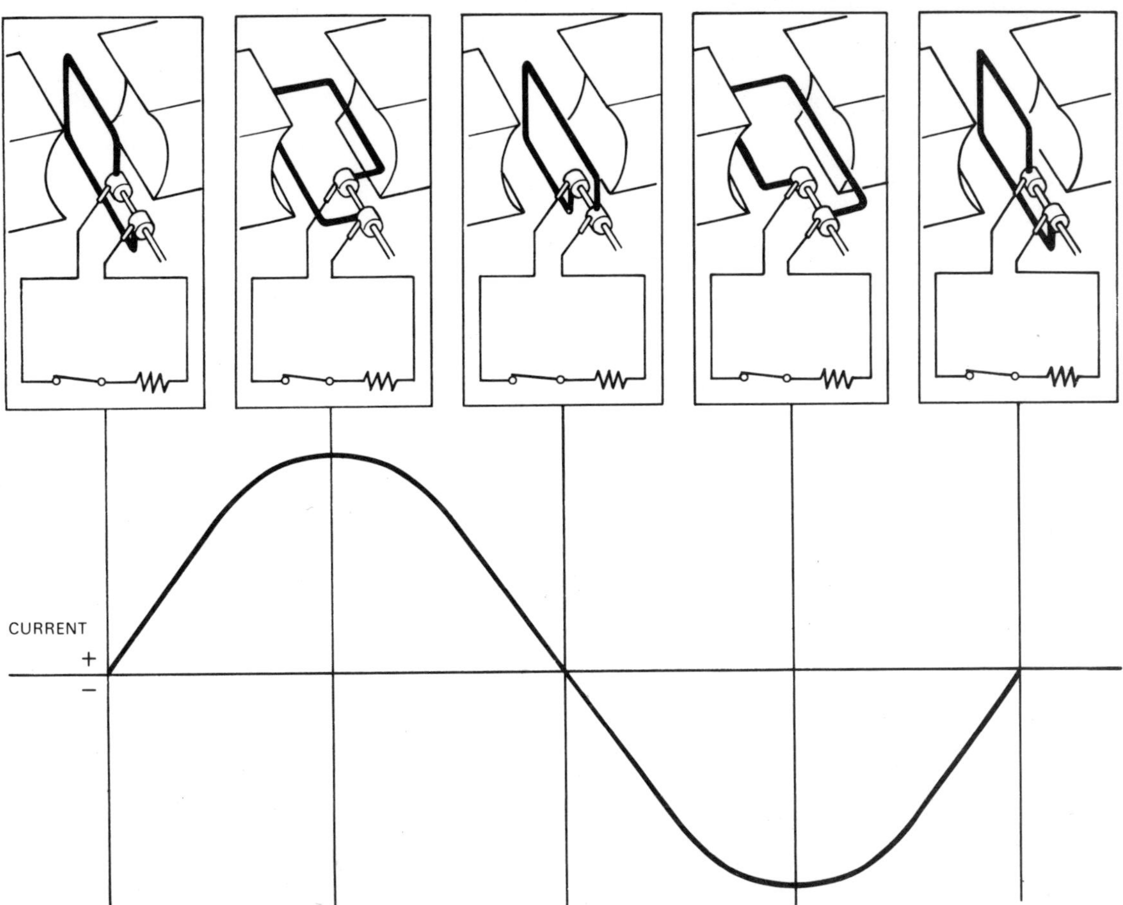

FIG 3:5 Simple generator producing alternating current

3:4 Dynamo systems

The dynamo is an electromagnetic generator which (as described in **Chapter 1, Section 1:11**) produces current by the principle that the movement of magnetic lines of force across a coiled wire induces electron movement. Car dynamos consist of stationary field windings mounted inside a heavy duty outer case – these create the magnetic field. Rotating inside the field coils is an armature with multiple windings in which the current is generated. The armature is driven by the engine crankshaft pulley via the fan belt and a pulley on the armature shaft. (Note that the dynamo generates current by moving the wire coils through the magnetic lines of force – the alternator (described later) generates by moving the lines of force through the wire coils).

Current flows from the rotating windings via two brushes bearing on a drum commutator consisting of many copper segments connected to the rotating windings. To understand the commutator's action it is necessary to consider the case of the simplest generator – a coil of wire rotating between a north and a south magnetic pole (see **FIG 3:5**).

At 0 deg the coil is travelling parallel to the lines of force. It is not cutting them so no current is produced. But as the coil continues rotating to the 90 deg position the number of lines of forces intersected increases to a maximum. The maximum current now flows in the coil but a quarter turn further on (at 180 deg) the current again diminishes to zero. The cycle is repeated between 180 deg and 360 deg but the current generated flows in the opposite direction to that generated in the first half of the cycle. The graph of the current's polarity (or direction) with regard to the position of the rotor is of the type known as a sine curve. The type of current generated is called an alternating current (ac) because its polarity alternates between positive and negative.

But the rest of the car's system is of constant polarity (current flow in a single direction), a type of current known as direct current (dc). It is the commutator that changes (rectifies) the dynamo's ac to the dc required by the car's system.

The simple generator in **FIG 3:5** is connected to the external circuit by slip rings – by arranging that one end of the coil is connected to a contact that forms a segment of a circle and the other end is connected to the contact forming the other segment of the circle a commutator is formed (see **FIG 3:6**).

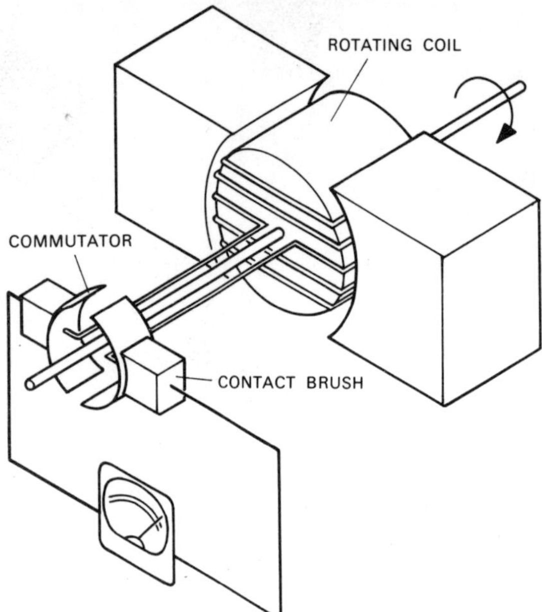

FIG 3:6 A commutator rectifies the generator output

Its operation is very simply that the fluctuating current direction in the coil is rectified to a unidirectional flow in the external circuit by the rotary switching from one brush to the other of the commutator segments. The resultant current flow from this single coil generator looks like **FIG 3:7** in graph form. This is known as half-wave rectified dc.

By increasing the number of coils rotating and spacing them round the diameter of the rotor, thereby increasing the number of segments in the commutator, the dynamo can supply a current of almost constant voltage equal to the peak's in each coil's cycle of generation. The graph of the current produced from multiple coils looks like **FIG 3:8**.

Current to energise the field windings and create the magnetic field is supplied by the dynamo itself. But without a magnetic field to start with a dynamo would produce zero current. This problem is overcome by designing the field winding cores to have a residual magnetism which is sufficient to start the generation process. Dynamos of this kind are called self-exciting.

The weight and construction of the dynamo armature, and problems of cooling the armature windings place a limit on the speed of armature rotation. The safe limit is about 6000 rev/min. Cars with engines capable of exceeding this speed may have a dynamo pulley slightly larger than the crankshaft pulley. However, on most cars the dynamo armature revolves at engine speed.

Car dynamos can produce a current of up to 30 amps and an electrical pressure of up to 30 volts. The voltage is considerably greater than that used by the car's electrical system so an external voltage regulator is required. This forms part of the control box described later, and drops the voltage to about 14 volts – the extra 2 volts pressure is required for efficient charging of the battery and it does no harm to the rest of the units in the car.

The dynamo's most unfortunate characteristic is that it does not produce enough current to charge the battery at below 1200 rev/min. Thus at engine idling speeds (about 600-800 rev/min) the battery bears the car's full electrical load.

Modern cars have more ancillary units, like the heated rear window, with relatively large current demands. So the battery can become discharged very rapidly if the car idles for any length of time – for example, during short, stop-start, shopping runs in a busy town. For this reason, the alternator is being used for more and more modern cars. The alternator's advantages and characteristics are discussed later.

3:5 Dynamo maintenance

The dynamo is a reliable unit and provided two maintenance operations are carried out at the specified intervals it will perform adequately for over 50,000 miles.

1 Every 3000 miles check the fan belt tension. The fan belt is tensioned by pivoting the dynamo on its two upper mounting bolts and the required position is maintained by

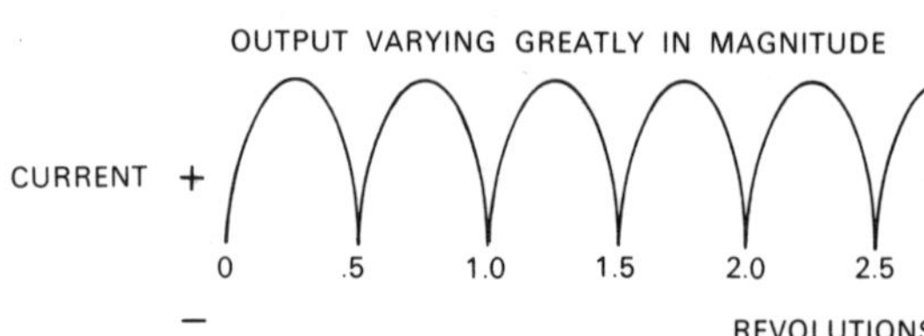

FIG 3:7 Half-wave rectified current

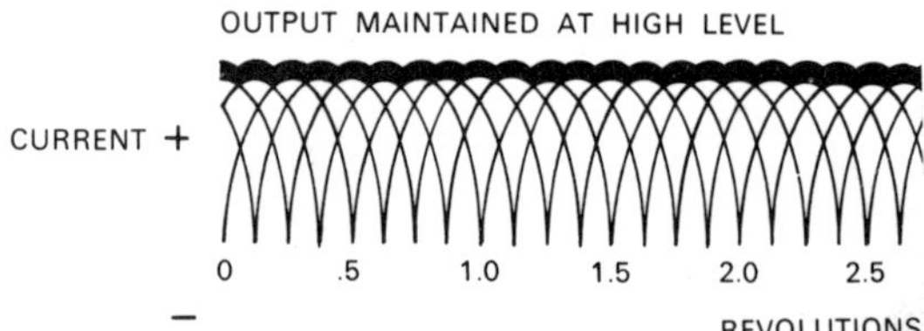

FIG 3:8 With more coils the output is more constant

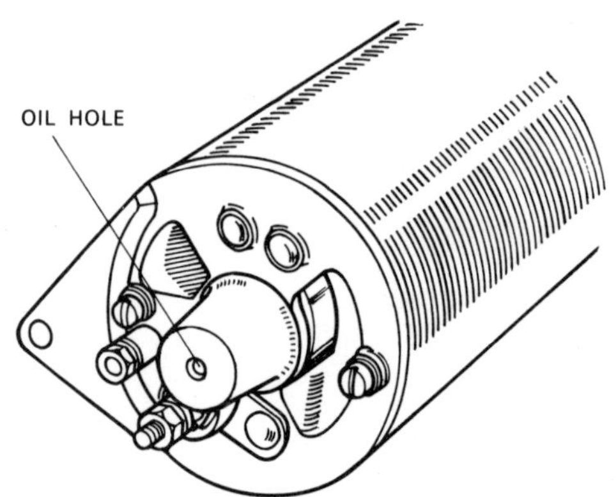

FIG 3:9 Dynamo rear bearing lubricator

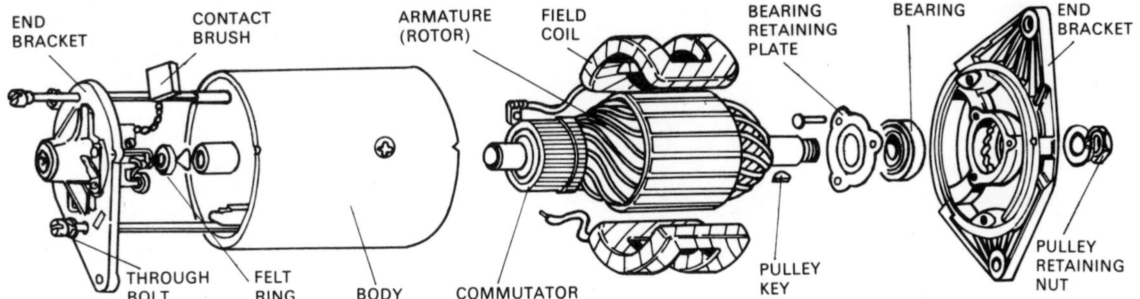

FIG 3:10 Exploded diagram of a Lucas generator

the clamp bolt which locks onto a slotted bracket mounted at the front of the engine (see **FIG 3:4**).

To tension the fan belt slacken off the clamp bolt and the two upper mounting bolts. Pull the dynamo out away from the engine until the desired belt tension is achieved. Holding the dynamo in this position, tighten the clamp bolt and then the two mounting bolts.

There may be precise belt tension recommendations in the car handbook but a good rule of thumb is that there should be between $\frac{1}{2}$ inch and $\frac{3}{4}$ inch play in the middle of the longest belt length between two pulleys – this is usually the length between the dynamo and crankshaft pulleys.

Overtightening of the fan belt causes damage to the dynamo front bearing and the water pump bearing. A loose fan belt may cause loss of generated current due to the inability of the belt to drive the dynamo at a sufficiently high speed.

2 Every 12,000 miles apply two or three drops of ordinary engine oil to the dynamo rear bearing. The dynamo's rear bearing is a porous bronze bush in contact with a small absorbent felt disc. An oil hole is provided for lubrication (see **FIG 3:9**). Over-lubrication should be avoided as excess oil may be shed onto the commutator.

3:6 Removing and dismantling the dynamo

The dynamo is such a simple piece of equipment that there are few variations in design between various manufacturer's models. Disconnect the battery before removing the dynamo.

Remove the dynamo from the engine by loosening the clamp and mounting bolts, releasing the fan belt from the dynamo pulley and detaching the two Lucar type connectors from the terminals at the rear of the unit. Note that one connector is larger than the other – the big one (D terminal) carries the charging current. Remove all three bolts and the dynamo can be lifted free of the engine.

Clean off grease and dirt from the body of the dynamo before taking it to the clean work-bench.

The dynamo is held together by two long retaining bolts running the length of the casing – unscrew and withdraw them from the rear of the unit. Gentle tapping on the rear end plate with a soft mallet or block of wood will loosen it enough for its removal.

This end plate carries the carbon brushes which are held in guides and sprung against the commutator by coiled clock springs. The brushes should be replaced if they are shorter than $\frac{1}{4}$ inch. Brushes are connected by tags – one connection is made to the end plate (earth) and the other via the brush guide to the larger insulated terminal (D).

Gentle tapping on the front end plate will loosen it sufficiently for the armature to be carefully withdrawn from within the field windings.

It is possible to remove the dynamo pulley from the armature if the dynamo is being replaced or if a new pulley is required. Undo the retaining nut until it is almost off the shaft. Holding the pulley in one hand and striking the nut firmly and squarely with a hammer will release the pulley from the shaft and the nut and pulley can then be removed. (Sometimes a Woodruff key, a small wedge of metal slotted into the shaft, is used to locate the pulley firmly – ensure it is not lost when the pulley is removed).

Removal of the pulley and end plate is not necessary for normal inspection and care of the commutator and armature.

When inspecting the commutator look for burn marks – these can be removed by careful use of a strip of glass-paper. If there are signs on the dynamo casing and armature of burnt insulation lacquer and splattered solder the dynamo is beyond repair. Gaps between commutator segments can be cleaned out with a hacksaw blade to a depth of about $\frac{1}{16}$ inch. Clean the commutator and armature with a brush or clean rag.

Check that there is no play between the bearing bush in the rear end plate and the commutator end of the armature shaft. It should be free to revolve with no appreciable side to side movement.

A worn rear end bearing can be replaced. Chip out the old bearing very carefully with a small cold chisel (or an old screwdriver). The new bearing insert must be soaked in cold oil for 24 hours (or oil heated to 100 deg. C for 2 hours) before it can be inserted in the plate and tapped home gently using a wooden dowel drift. Bearings can also be pushed home between the jaws of a vice provided a block of wood is used to protect the new bush.

Field windings are retained by two large cross-head screws – these should not be removed. Clean the inside of the casing as well as possible using a clean rag.

Commence reassembly of the dynamo by carefully feeding the armature back inside the field windings and locating the front end plate correctly on the positioning stud. Tap the end plate home.

Lodge the clock springs on the side of the brushes so that they are held clear of the commutator for replacement of the rear end plate. The plate is located both by a positioning stud and the insulated field terminal (F) which is attached to the main casing and feeds through a slot in the end plate.

Replace the long retaining bolts and tighten them. Using a small probe or screwdriver inserted through the ventilation holes in the end plate the clock springs can be relocated to bear upon the brushes in the correct manner. The dynamo can now be remounted to the engine.

Polarity correction:

If a dynamo has been left in its stripped down condition for any length of time it is possible that there is no residual magnetic field in the field winding cores. Exchange dynamos, new units and units bought from a scrapyard may have no residual magnetism or the polarity may be opposite to that required for the car. The result of using an incorrectly polarised dynamo is that current will be generated in the opposite direction to that required by the car causing damage to the control box. There is a simple procedure to correct the dynamo polarity.

1 Mount the dynamo in the car in the correct manner and reconnect the battery. Connect up the lead to the D terminal but leave the F terminal (the smaller one) lead unconnected.

2 Use a jump lead connected to the battery's live side (non-earthed battery post) or the live terminal of the starter solenoid. Touch the bare end of this jump lead onto the dynamo's F terminal momentarily – a good connection will be signified by a blue flash as the lead is removed.

The short flow of current from the battery will have ensured the build-up of a small magnetic field in the field core with its poles oriented in the correct sense for current generation.

3:7 Changing a car's polarity

Many older British cars have a positive earth system. Owners may find the choice of accessories (particularly radios and tape-players) available for positive earth fitting very restricted as most of the world's cars are now produced with negative earth systems.

In some instances it is possible to change a car's polarity. However, the first thing to check is that the change from positive to negative will not involve replacement of units like electric fuel pumps, heater motors, and windscreen wiper motors. These units may be polarity conscious. Manufacturer's service departments will be able to advise on the units that will be affected by the change.

WARNING: Do not attempt to change the polarity of cars fitted with alternators, transistorised ignition equipment or a radio or tape-player with positive polarity (unless it is intended to change the unit or it has a polarity change switch – see **Chapter 9**).

Provided that all these checks have been made polarity changing should be carried out in this sequence:

1 Disconnect both terminals of the battery.

2 Remake the connections to polarity conscious units like the clock and ammeter in the opposite sense.

3 Ensuring that on those batteries with terminal posts of differing size the earth strap and main lead have new connectors fitted, reconnect the battery with its negative terminal to the earth strap.

4 Carry out the dynamo polarisation procedure described earlier.

It is good practice to affix a notice of the changed polarity in a position that garage mechanics cannot miss. Also make a note of the change on the car's service coupon book and in the car's handbook – this will aid subsequent owners.

3:8 Dynamo control boxes

The dynamo control box is one of the most complex units fitted to the car, it is sensitive to dirt and temperature, performs key tasks in the charging system and yet it is quite a reliable piece of equipment provided it is not tampered with by persons without the requisite level of electrical knowledge.

Three jobs are performed by the control box:

1 preventing the battery discharging through the dynamo when the engine is idling or stationary;

2 sensing when the dynamo is producing a high enough voltage for battery charging;

3 controlling the output current and voltage of the dynamo to prevent it damaging itself or other units connected to it.

Underneath the clip-on lid of the control box (this vital part ensures accurate temperature control) are two or three magnetic relays. A relay is similar in operation to a solenoid except that the core of the coil is fixed and the switching movement is performed by an iron flap hinged above the core and controlled by an adjustable return spring – usually a strip of spring steel.

For many years the commonest type of control box was the two-bobbin (relay) like the Lucas RB106. Some cars now have a three-bobbin control box, a sealed unit which can be simply checked like the two-bobbin type. However, if it is faulty the entire unit has to be replaced. Minor differences between the operation of two- and

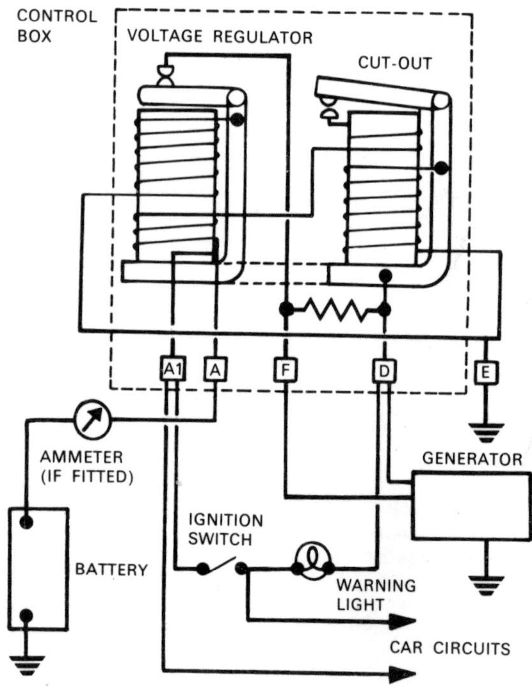

FIG 3:11 Circuit of two bobbin control box

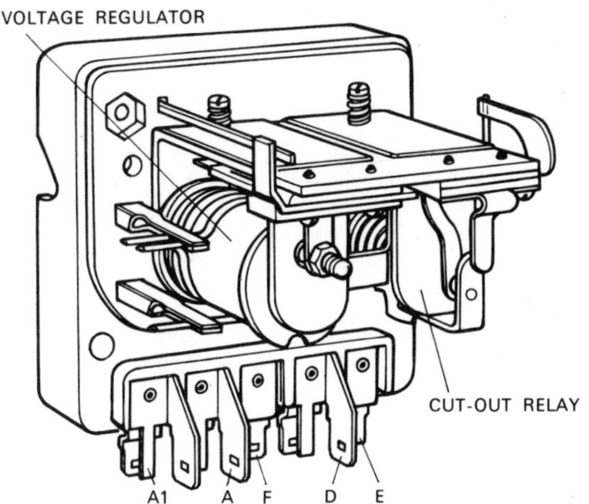

FIG 3:12 **Two bobbin control box with cover removed**

three-bobbin types will be discussed later but it will suffice to examine the operation of the two-bobbin type only as a guide to control box functions (see **FIG 3:12**).

When the car's ignition is switched on current is supplied to the ignition warning light which glows brightly because its circuit is completed via terminal D on the control box which is connected through the brushes and commutator of the dynamo to earth.

Running the engine turns the dynamo and due to the residual magnetic field it begins to generate current. This is fed to the control box via terminal D which is connected to the frame of the box and thus to the iron flaps of the relays. The current flows through the closed voltage regulator contacts and out via terminal F to the dynamo's field windings.

Supplied with this current the field windings become progressively stronger so more current is generated. The amount of current is also increasing due to the rising speed of dynamo rotation.

Simultaneously, some of this current is fed through the thin wire shunt coils wound on each bobbin so the cores are becoming stronger and stronger magnets.

When the dynamo output approaches 12 volts the ignition light begins to dim because the back pressure of the generated current opposes the 12 volt battery pressure until at a generated voltage of 12 volts the ignition light is extinguished.

At a dynamo output of about 13 volts the core of the cut-out relay is a strong enough magnet to attract the iron flap downwards to close the points and connect the dynamo to the battery via the thick outer windings linking the two relays and control box terminal A. This flow of charging current also reinforces the magnetic field of the cut-out relay and holds the points closed.

If the dynamo now slows down so its output is less than the battery voltage the magnetism in the cut-out relay diminishes. Current also begins to flow in the opposite direction through the heavy windings creating a magnetic field of opposite polarity. The resulting rapid diminution of the magnetic field allows the tensioned iron flap to spring back and disconnect the dynamo from the battery. In this way the cut-out prevents battery current draining away through the dynamo.

The points of the voltage regulator are normally held together by the spring tension on the iron flap. The spring is tensioned with a screw so that it is not until the dynamo output reaches 16 volts that the regulator core becomes sufficiently magnetised to attract the iron flap. With the regulator points parted no current is supplied to the dynamo's field windings except through the shunt resistor connected across the D and F terminals. This resistor (about 60 ohms) provides a minimal current to the field windings so there is a drop in the output voltage from the dynamo. The result is that the voltage regulator shunt windings exert less magnetic effect and the points close again under the pressure of the spring. In fact this voltage control cycle occurs with such rapidity that the points open and close like the points of a buzzer when the dynamo is revolving at top speed.

The control box's current control function is performed by the heavy windings on the voltage regulator bobbin. These are connected to the heavy windings of the cut-out and thus carry the full charging and electrical supply current from the dynamo. The windings on the regulator coil have a magnetic effect which supplements the shunt windings. In other words as the current demand on the dynamo rises they increase the ability of the shunt windings to open the voltage regulator points, in effect opening them sooner, and reduce the generating ability of the dynamo.

If the current demand on the dynamo were not limited in this way overheating of the dynamo armature windings would result. By heat transference the commutator segment solder would become molten and spatter over the inside of the dynamo.

The difference between a two-bobbin and three-bobbin control box:

The extra bobbin (relay) in a three-bobbin control box like the Lucas RB340 is a separate current control relay.

Terminal coding of the three-bobbin type is also different. The two B terminals are equivalent in their connections to the A1 and A terminals of a two-bobbin type. An extra terminal WL is in fact connected to the D terminal. It may be used for the warning light connection, but is more often a spare testing position on the box.

Three-bobbin control boxes are factory set, the seals must not be tampered with during the car's warranty period and the possibilities of setting adjustment are so limited it is unwise to remove the cover at all. If a faulty unit is indicated a complete replacement should be made.

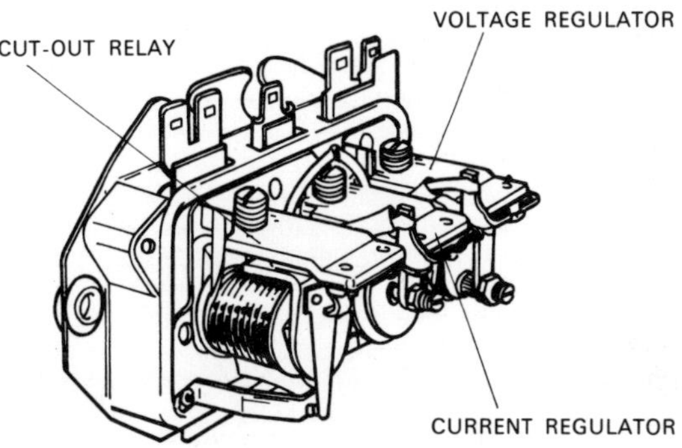

FIG 3:13 **Three bobbin control box with cover removed**

Temperature sensitivity of control boxes:

The control box is designed in such a way that the relay coils heat up at the same rate as the windings of the dynamo. An important part of this temperature regulation is the control box lid – if it is cracked it must be replaced or the correct temperature environment for the relays will not be maintained.

Why is temperature so critical to the control box's operation? The principle reason is the varying ability of the dynamo to produce current at different temperatures. Unlike the battery the dynamo can produce more current when it is cold because at lower temperatures the resistance of all its windings are lowered – so current flows better and stronger magnetic fields are created. This is a useful characteristic because at low temperatures it enables the dynamo to replace current lost from the battery more efficiently.

However, it also means that the dynamo could be called upon to do more than it is designed to do. So some temperature control to compensate for this has to be made in the control box.

Temperature control is effected by bi-metallic strips which increase and decrease the spring tension on the iron flaps. The bi-metallic strip acting on the voltage regulator flap has the effect of closing the points earlier so that, like the current regulator, it cuts down dynamo output. On the cut-out relay it acts to ensure that the cut-out voltage remains constant over a wide temperature range.

3:9 Dynamo system fault-finding

Symptom	Causes
Ignition light glows continuously with engine revving	a broken or very loose fan belt b fault in dynamo or control box field connections c faulty dynamo earth connection d short circuit to earth on control box D or F terminals or on ignition light lead
Ignition light extinguishes late or glows dimly	a slipping fan belt b fault in lead from dynamo (F) to control box (F) c burnt or scored commutator d control box fault
Ignition light fades then begins to glow dimly or brightly with increased engine speed	a burnt or faulty cut-out contacts b broken shunt coil connections in control box c incorrect setting of cut-out points d fault in cut-out connections
Ignition light does not glow at all	a faulty bulb or ignition light lead b dynamo disconnected at D and F terminals

Control box maintenance and repair:

The most frequent causes of control box failure are tampering and damage to the control box lid. It is not necessary to carry out any regular maintenance of the control box except to inspect it occasionally for ingress of moisture and dirt.

If the control box lid is removed for inspection take care not to touch the iron flaps on the relays. When the lid is replaced, start the engine and rev up hard for a few seconds. This will ensure that, if the cut-out points have accidentally been closed, the fall-off of current generated will open the points.

Also occasionally remove the control box from its bulkhead or flitch panel mounting to ensure that there is no dirt or moisture affecting the resistors underneath the control box base plate.

Corrosion and dirt can affect the connections made to the control box terminals – check that these are clean, especially the earth (E) terminal.

Resetting or adjusting the control box is an operation that should be left to a skilled vehicle electrician equipped with the necessary test gear. Apart from the risk of harming the control box itself, extensive damage can be caused elsewhere in the system if the adjustments are incorrectly carried out. And in practice the control box very rarely needs resetting.

Although it is possible to save money by obtaining a control box lid from a scrapyard to replace a cracked or broken one, never replace the control box itself with a scrap part unless; **1** it is in almost new condition from an exactly similar model of car; **2** it is checked by a vehicle electrician after fitment.

Testing a dynamo with circuit tester and instruments:

1 Disconnect dynamo D and F terminals and connect circuit tester or voltmeter between D and earth. Start the engine. As the engine is revved up the test light should glow dimly – a voltmeter should show a reading between 1 and 3 volts. If the test is negative there may be a brush or commutator fault, for example, a brush jammed in its guide.

2 Connect a light or voltmeter between dynamo D terminal and earth and try the test with a jump lead between the F terminal and earth and then with a jump lead between the F and D terminals. (Both should be tried as some dynamos are earthed internally – others through the voltage regulator points of the control box).

On revving the engine the test lamp should increase in brightness with engine speed (do not exceed 1200 rev/min) – the voltmeter reading should rise to 12-14 volts. This test shows the dynamo is working correctly – a negative result means the dynamo needs repair. A fluctuating voltage or flickering lamp indicates commutator or brush trouble.

3 In the above test an ammeter can be used to earth the F terminal (or connect it to the D terminal). Following the procedure in test **2** the current reading should be about 2 amps. No current reading means a break at the F terminal connection. A current of about 4 amps indicates one of the field coils is short circuited to earth.

If there is still a fault in the charging system, battery and dynamo faults having been eliminated, the trouble lies in the control box. There are two other clues to control box faults:

1 rapid battery discharge, possibly to the extent that the battery overheats or the D terminal lead becomes warm, means a cut-out fault – the points are failing to open;
2 gassing and heating of the battery means overcharging and thus a fault in the voltage or current regulator section of the control box. Overcharging may also be spotted if the battery needs frequent topping up, provided the possibility of a leak has been eliminated.

3:10 Alternator systems

In a dynamo current is generated by moving coils through the lines of force in a stationary magnetic field. The alternator differs fundamentally from this principle. In the alternator current is generated by creating a rotating magnetic field – the lines of force intersect stationary coils placed very close to the magnetic poles of the rotor.

Alternating current is generated in the stationary windings and this is rectified to direct current by a system of semi-conductor devices called diodes. The diode rectifier pack is built into the alternator body. The diode's most important property is that it only allows current to flow in one direction so the existence of the diode rectifier between the battery and the alternator means that no cut-out is needed. The alternator is also designed to be self-limiting in current output so the remaining alternator control requirement is for a voltage regulator.

Alternator voltage regulation is carried out by a transistorised unit. On early systems this was a separate unit mounted away from the alternator like the dynamo control box. However there are considerable advantages to be gained by mounting a transistorised voltage regulator alongside the diode rectifier inside the alternator body. The whole system becomes very compact and the voltage regulator can be cooled by the air current induced by the alternator fan in the same way as the diode rectifier.

Today's alternators offer many benefits to the motorist. An alternator is compact and its simple rotor design, with slip rings instead of a commutator, make rotation speeds of up to 12,000 rev/min possible. The higher speed is achieved by using an alternator pulley of a smaller diameter than the crankshaft pulley. The result is that the alternator can produce more current at a given engine speed than the dynamo – in fact it produces a battery charging current at engine idle speed. An alternator system is thus capable of protecting the battery from undue discharge during stop-start running.

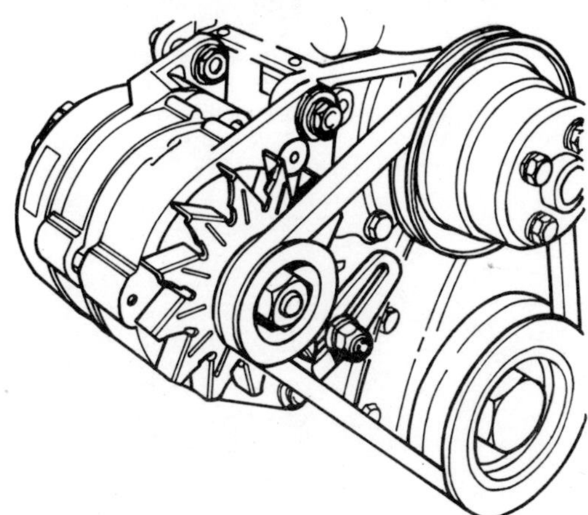

FIG 3:14 Alternator mounted on engine

Even though higher speeds are used in an alternator, wear of various components is reduced. Slip rings do not wear out brushes as fast as commutator segments (another factor is that the current carried by the alternator brushes is very small) and the shorter rotor length cuts down on bearing wear.

Semi-conductor devices like the diodes and transistors in the voltage regulator are generally much more reliable than the complex mechanical control box apparatus.

A typical alternator (see **FIG 3:14**) consists of a stator core clamped between the two halves of the generator body. The stator windings in which the current is generated are arranged round the circumference of the stator – they are connected in such a way that three phase alternating current is produced. Simply, this is current with a waveform of three sine curves each separated in phase by 120 deg of magnetic field movement.

The field winding consists of a single coil clamped between two plates. The edges of the plates are turned in over the winding and are designed in the form of interlocking claws. A typical alternator rotor has six claws on each plate – each claw is a pole piece, thus there are six combinations of north and south magnetic poles around the circumference of the rotor.

The windings terminate at two slip rings built into the rear face of the rotor. Slip ring design is of two main types. One consists of two concentric rings of metal – in the other there is a round central disc and a concentric ring. Brushes mounted in a plastics carrier on the rear half of the alternator casing bear on the slip rings.

The rotor revolves in bearings inserted in the two halves of the casing. The front bearing is usually a ball race while the rear bearing is often of the needle roller type.

A protective plastics end cap mounted on the rear end of the alternator houses the diode rectifier pack and, on modern units, the transistorised voltage regulator as well. Connections to the alternator are via terminal spades in the end cap – a multiple Lucar connector block is the usual way of making contact.

Alternator cooling is by a fan mounted behind the pulley. It draws air through the alternator casing via the cooling slots in the rear end cap.

3:11 Operation of the diode rectifier

As explained already, a diode is a device which acts as an electrical one-way valve. Current will only flow through it in one direction – in a circuit diagram that direction is shown as the way in which the arrow forming part of the diode symbol is pointing (although this indicates the true negative-positive electron flow direction).

From **FIG 3:15** it is possible to see that in whatever direction the current fluctuates within the stator coils of the alternator, electrons can only emerge from the diode rectifier travelling in one direction. The current path is only shown for two pairs of the six diodes employed – a type of diode connection called a rectifier 'bridge'. The third diode pair plus the central pair form another rectification bridge complementary in action to the first

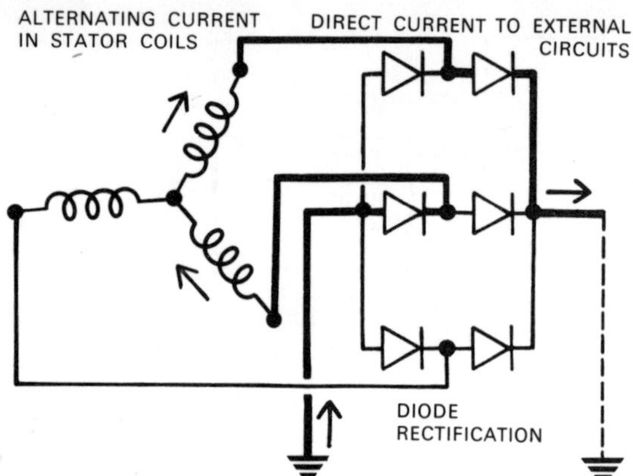

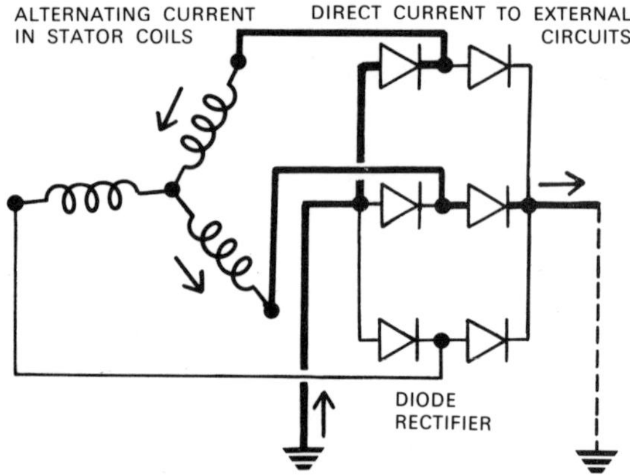

FIG 3:15 Three phase diode rectification

two pairs. Similarly the two end pairs form the third 'bridge' of connections.

There are two main types of diode rectifier found in alternators (see **FIG 3:16**). In one type there are six diodes of two types, those that conduct from can to lead and those that conduct from lead to can. The three diodes of each type are mounted on separate strips of metal which act as heat sinks and as the output connectors. The two metal strips form a circular yoke round the inside of the alternator casing.

The second type of diode rectifier has nine diodes all of the same type soldered in a complex pack consisting of heat sink plates spaced side by side with insulating washers. The three extra diodes are necessary to provide an independent current supply for field excitation. A rectifier of this kind is fitted to a self-exciting alternator.

A six diode rectifier is fitted to an alternator which is excited by current fed from the battery. This earlier type of alternator needs two additional electrical units besides the voltage regulator. They are both relays – one is the warning light control and the other the field isolating relay.

3:12 Alternator excitation

Both self-excited and battery excited alternators derive their initial field excitation current from the battery. This is the reason why alternator fitted cars with a very flat battery cannot be pushed or tow started. There is simply not enough current available to begin the current generation cycle.

In the self-excited alternator (see **FIG 3:17**) the three additional rectifier diodes feed current generated in the first few revolutions of the field coil back to the field via the voltage regulator. This increases the field and progressively raises the amount of current generated. The initial field current is supplied from the battery via the ignition warning light (or the parallel resistor designed as a back up in case of bulb failure) and via the voltage regulator. The warning light extinguishes in the same way as a dynamo warning light – when the back pressure of generated current equals 12 volts.

Battery excited alternators (see **FIG 3:18**) rely on a direct supply from the battery or a point in the main battery supply lead, like the starter solenoid. The field coil is connected via the field isolating relay which is necessary to prevent battery current draining away when the ignition is switched off. The relay is energised to switch on the alternator field current by a separate feed from the ignition switch.

As there is no way of connecting the warning light into the generating circuit in such a way that it would react to the build-up of generated current a separate circuit is required. This is arranged from the ignition switch via the warning light control relay, a thermal device to earth. The relay's thermal resistor is connected to a separate

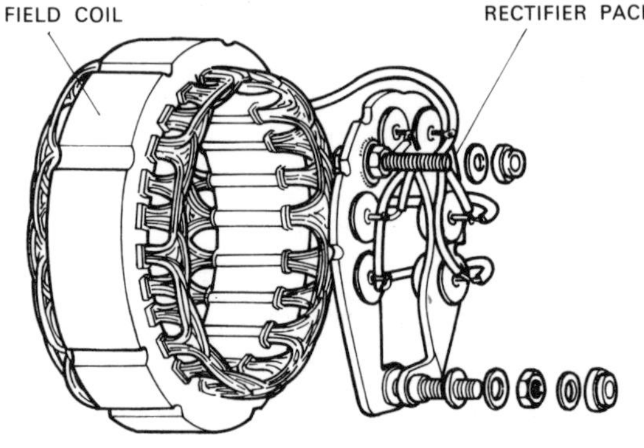

FIG 3:16 Two types of diode rectifier pack

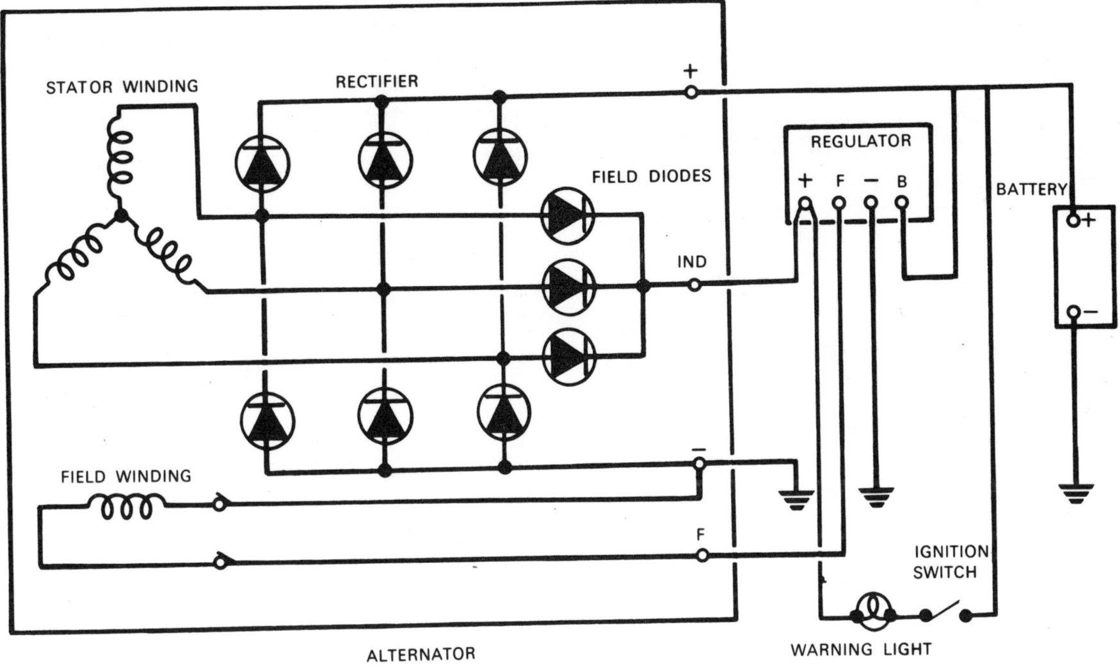

FIG 3:17 Circuit diagram of self excited alternator

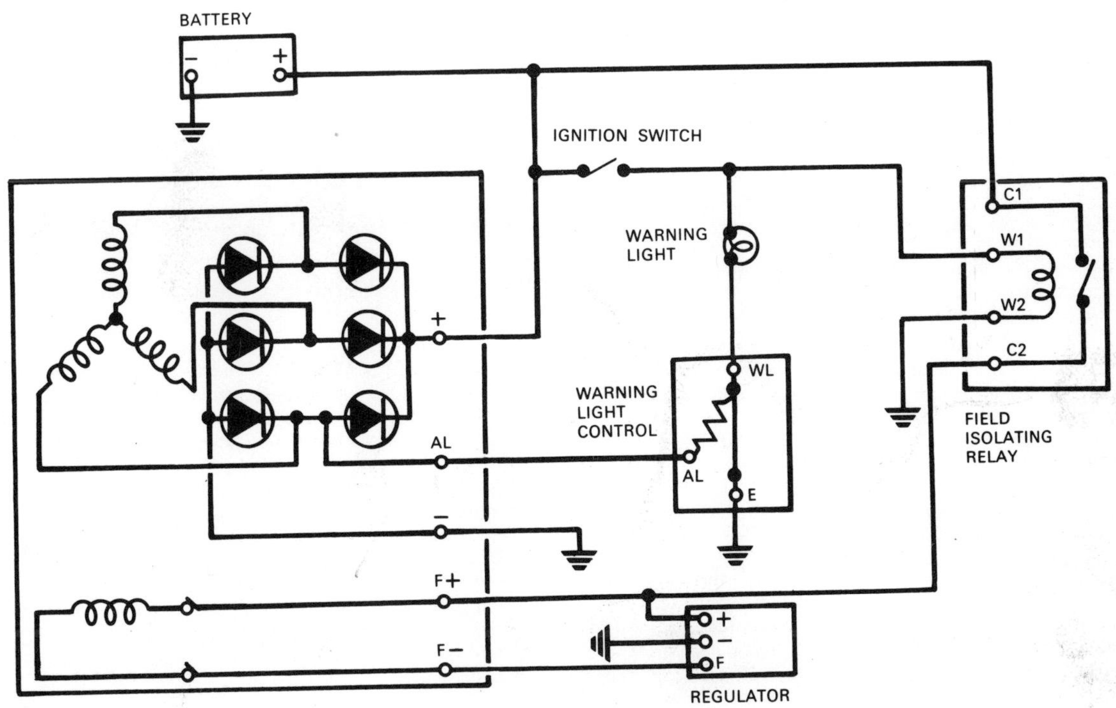

FIG 3:18 Circuit diagram of battery excited alternator

alternator terminal (AL) which is a lead from the rectifier pack. When the alternator generates sufficient current the resistor heats up and separates the relay contacts, thus switching off the ignition light.

3:13 Transistorised voltage regulation

As explained in **Chapter 1, Section 1:13**, a transistor is an electronic switch which, by the application of a current to its base (B) and emitter (E) connections, allows a larger current to flow across its collector (C) and emitter connections.

Many alternator voltage regulators have two transistors connected in a manner known as the 'Alpha couple'. In practice this means that the collector of transistor 1 (TR1) is connected to the base of TR2. The effect of this couple is that a small current applied across B-E of TR1 allows a current to flow across C-E of TR1. This switching of the current deprives the B connector of TR2 of a supply and thus 'switches' TR2 off, so no current can flow between C-E of TR2.

In the Lucas 4TR voltage regulator, now superseded but still nevertheless typical of most voltage regulator circuits, this effect is employed in the following manner (see **FIG 3:19**):

1 Switching on the ignition allows a current to flow through R1, switching TR2 on and enabling a current to flow across C-E of TR2 – battery voltage is applied to the alternator field winding.

2 The rising voltage generated as the alternator speeds up is circuited through R3, R2 and R4 – note, there is a drop in voltage between each resistor. The Zener diode is tapped off R2 at a point where the voltage is a proportion of the desired output voltage equal to the breakdown point of the diode: at its breakdown point a Zener diode conducts both ways (as explained in **Chapter 1, Section 1:13**).

3 When the voltage at the tap on R2 reaches about 10 volts the Zener diode 'avalanches' and applies a current to B-E of TR1.

4 This switches TR1 on, allowing current to flow between C-E of TR1. This current is diverted from the B connection of TR2 so this transistor is switched off.

5 Current can no longer flow through C-E of TR2, thus the field winding becomes de-energised and output voltage drops.

6 As the output voltage drops the voltage at the tap on R2 falls below the avalanche point of the Zener diode and it no longer conducts current to TR1.

7 As TR1 switches off TR2 switches on again and the field coil is energised.

This oscillating switching action of the transistor pair, which can occur at up to 1000 times a second when the alternator is at peak revolutions, controls the alternator output voltage to between 14 and 14.4 volts.

Of course, the circuit is a little more sophisticated than that. R5 and capacitor C2 are connected in circuit with the Zener diode carrying current to B-E of TR1 – this ensures a clean on-off switching action. The surge quench diode is designed to prevent damage to TR2 which could be caused by a back emf if there were a rapid collapse of the alternator's magnetic field. Capacitor C1 prevents the rapid oscillation of the transistor pair giving rise to radio interference, R6 drains away any current that might leak through the Zener diode at high operating temperatures

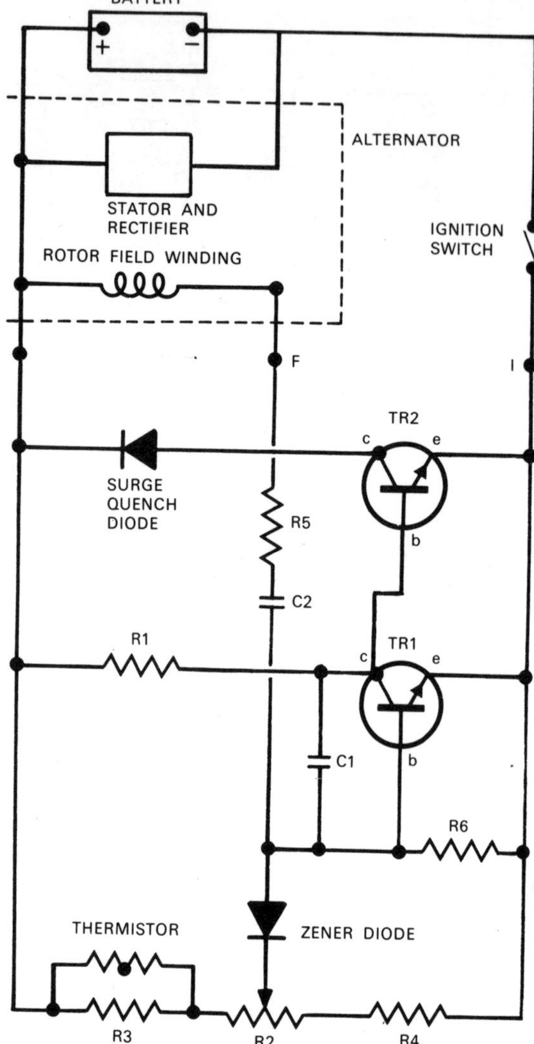

FIG 3:19 Circuit of Lucas 4TR voltage regulator

and the thermistor (a resistor in which the resistance **decreases** with temperature) connected parallel to R3 compensates for changes in operating temperature.

WARNING: Because of the semi-conductor devices which rectify and control current and voltage in alternator charging circuits, all units are polarity conscious. Observe the following precautions when testing or working on the alternator circuit:

1 Never charge the battery of an alternator fitted car or remove the alternator from the engine, without disconnecting the battery earth lead.

2 Don't disconnect any charging circuit lead, including battery leads, when the alternator is running.

3 Don't run the alternator with any of its leads disconnected.

4 Never check any car circuit connections by flashing a bare lead to earth.

5 Always ensure that a battery is reconnected with the

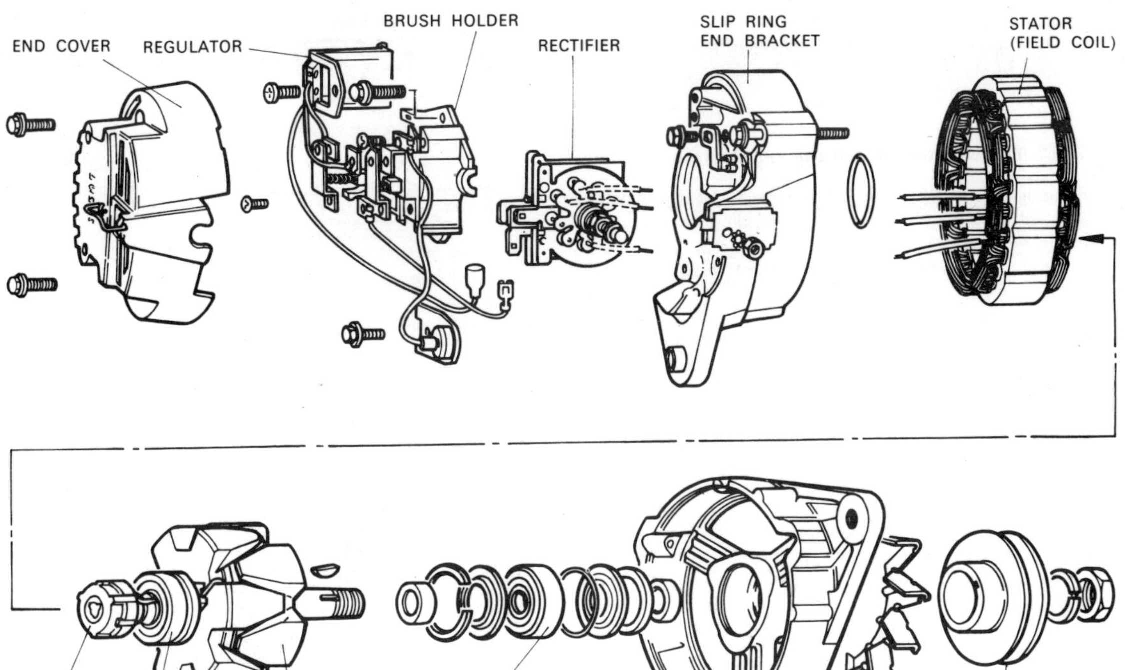

FIG 3:20 Exploded diagram of a Lucas 16 ACR alternator

right polarity – even momentary reversal of the battery connections will overheat and irreparably damage the diode rectifier pack. For this reason never attempt to change the polarity of an alternator fitted car.

6 There is a considerable variety of alternators and associated electrical units – ensure that replacement parts are for a system of the car's polarity and that the new unit is identical in connections, shape, size and coding to the discarded part.

Failure to observe any of these rules will almost certainly result in the need for a new alternator.

3:14 Alternator charging circuit maintenance

Every 3000 miles the tension of the fan belt should be checked in the same way as for a dynamo charging circuit (**Section 3:5**). Apart from ensuring that the alternator connections are firmly made and clean and that there is no build up of grease and dirt obstructing the cooling slots in the end cap no further maintenance of the alternator circuit is possible.

3:15 Removing and dismantling an alternator

There are a number of types of alternator which will vary in detail from the description given below. The procedure refers to the Lucas ACR range (see **FIG 3:20**). However, individual variations should not prevent basic stripping of the unit to replace regulator, diode rectifier or brushes.

Disconnect the battery before attempting any work on the alternator.

Withdraw the terminal connector block at the rear of the alternator. Loosen the clamp bolt and two upper mounting bolts. Slip the fan belt off the pulley. Undo all three bolts and the unit can be removed from the engine compartment. Clean off any surface grease and dirt before transferring the unit to a clean work-bench.

Remove the two screws or small hexagon headed bolts and take off the end cap. Detach the short lead with Lucar connector from the rectifier pack. The brush assembly can be released by undoing four screws. Three more screws have to be undone to separate the regulator and brush holder. Before freeing the regulator from the brush holder note down the connections to be made in reassembly.

To remove the diode pack it is necessary to unsolder the stator leads from the diodes. Grip each diode lead with long-nosed pliers to act as a heat sink while unsoldering. This process should be completed as quickly as possible to prevent heat damage to the diodes. Undo the rectifier pack nut noting the order of washers and withdraw the unit.

At this stage it is possible to carry out tests on the stator and rotor, inspect and service the slip rings, replace the brushes, test the diodes and replace the regulator (see **Section 3:16**). Do not proceed with further dismantling unless bearing wear is indicated by rough running of the rotor (clamp the unit in a vice and spin the pulley listening for bearing noise or a catch in the rotation), there is undue end float or the rotor can be rocked from side to side in its bearings.

Three retaining bolts hold the two casing halves clamped over the stator. Mark both halves and the stator ring before removing the bolts to assist correct reassembly. With the bolts withdrawn, the unit can be levered apart and the stator ring removed from around the rotor.

To replace the rear end bearing the slip ring has to be unsoldered and pulled off the shaft. The bearing is also pulled from the shaft. Fortunately this bearing takes very little strain and rarely wears out. For resoldering the slip ring a special grade of solder called Frys HT3 has to be used – ensure the connections are well tinned before making the joints.

To replace the front bearing undo the pulley nut almost to the end of the rotor shaft and gripping the pulley in one hand give the nut a sharp tap to free the pulley. Pulley and fan can then be withdrawn. Remove the Woodruff key and the rotor shaft can be gently tapped out of the bearing.

The bearing is retained with a circlip. Withdraw the circlip and distance piece and note the order of cover plate, bearing, O-ring and felt washer. When fitting new bearings pack them with Shell Alvania RA grease.

When reassembling the front bearing remember to tap home the casing over the motor shaft using a tube drift which bears on the inner race only.

Reassembly of the alternator is the reverse of the stripping procedure. Use M grade solder (45-55 tin-lead) for connecting the stator to the rectifier pack. Complete the soldering as quickly as possible using heat sink pliers in the same way as during dismantling.

The slip ring should be cleaned with fine glass paper before refitting the brush holder. The outer ring brush wears faster than the inner brush – but both may need replacing. Brushes must protrude a minimum of 0.2 inch (5 mm) from the brush holder and if a spring tension tester is available a check should be made to see that the pressure required to bring the brush face level with the brush holder is 9-13 oz.

Remember to tension the fan belt correctly when refitting the alternator to the engine.

3:16 Testing the alternator circuit and components

With the alternator stripped down:

1 Check field winding insulation with a circuit tester in series with a 12 volt battery connected between one slip ring and (if it can be reached) a lobe of the rotor or the pulley. The bulb should not light. The recommended test procedure is to use a 110 volt ac source and a 15 watt test lamp but very few home electricians will have the requisite transformer. **Do not** attempt to use the mains electricity supply for testing.

2 Check the field winding continuity by connecting an ammeter in series with a 12 volt battery across the two slip rings. The current reading should be 3 amps which is equal to a field winding resistance of about 4 ohms. No reading at all indicates a break in the winding – a higher reading indicates an internal breakdown of insulation.

3 Check each diode in the rectifier pack in turn by connecting a circuit tester in series with a 12 volt battery across the diode lead and the heat sink plate to which it is connected. Repeat the test on each diode in both current flow directions. The test light should only light in one current direction. A diode can fail conducting in both ways or not conducting at all. Failure of a single diode requires replacement of the whole rectifier pack.

4 Check stator windings insulation using a test lamp in series with a battery connected across each stator lead in turn and the stator core. The lamp should not light. (Once again a 110V ac source is the recommended test).

5 Check stator windings continuity with a test lamp and 12 volt battery connected across one pair of stator leads at a time. The lamp should light on each occasion.

Testing the voltage regulator is beyond the scope of the book. However, it will fail in one of two ways. Either it will prevent current flow from the alternator altogether or it will allow a much higher voltage than normal to flow. The latter fault will result in overcharging of the battery which can be spotted by frequent need for battery topping up, gassing or overheating of the battery and often an acid smell from the battery. Another clue is that lights will glow brighter, and motors like the windscreen wiper motor will run a lot faster due to the higher voltage. Suspect voltage regulators should be taken to an expert vehicle electrician for testing.

3:17 Emergency measures to get you home

Flat battery:

Dynamo fitted cars with manual gear boxes can be push started. Alternator fitted cars and those with automatic gear boxes can be started using jump leads from the battery of another vehicle. The procedures are described in **Chapter 4, Section 4:8**. Remember that reversing battery polarity will damage alternators.

Broken fan belt:

This is one of the most common motoring mishaps. The best solution is to fit a new fan belt – always carry a spare of the right type. If no fan belt is available it is feasible to tie a thin rope or a lady's stocking or tights round the crankshaft pulley, dynamo/alternator pulley and water pump pulley. Engine speeds should be kept low to avoid straining the emergency belt. Provided the battery is in good condition the emergency belt can be tied round the crankshaft and water pump pulleys only. This avoids the strain that rotation of the dynamo or alternator would impose. Limited running with the dynamo or alternator stationary is possible provided that all possible power consuming accessories are switched off. It is not possible at night because the lights would drain the battery too quickly.

Faulty dynamo control box:

If the dynamo control box develops a fault it is possible to isolate the box and the dynamo by placing a thin strip of card, for example, from a cigarette carton, between cut-out points. However, control box faults usually develop as a result of circuit problems elsewhere in the car's system. Do not proceed on battery power unless the original fault, perhaps a short circuit, has been found and cured.

CHAPTER 4

The starter motor system

4:1 Starter motors

To stir the engine into life, turning the crankshaft against the compression of the pistons, and churning part of the transmission in cold, thick oil, a very powerful electric motor is required. The starter motor is designed to cope with these loads and on most modern cars it is able to turn a cold engine at over 50 rev/min, the minimum necessary to get it started.

During the starter motor's short bursts of activity it has a very high current demand – up to 360 amps during the momentary surge when it is first switched on falling to around 100 amps as it reaches full rotating speed.

Because of these high current demands the starter motor has its own electrical circuit divorced from the rest of the car's system.

A thick lead capable of carrying the high current runs direct from the battery to one terminal of the starter solenoid (this same terminal is often used as the main supply point for the rest of the car's system). The solenoid is a heavy duty switch operated electro-magnetically by a low current circuit switched by the start position on the ignition switch (see **Chapter 1**).

The starter solenoid's other main terminal is connected by a thick lead to the connecting bolt on the motor. The earth return of the circuit is provided inside the motor housing which is usually made of a strong but light alloy. To ensure proper earth connection via the engine block to which the starter motor is bolted, it is usual to have a braided earth strap between the engine and the car's body. This strap is often fixed to the engine block by one of the starter motor bolts.

The starter motor itself is a relatively simple direct current motor with its field windings connected in series with the armature windings so an equal current flows through each. Most starters have four field poles with low resistance windings of high current carrying copper or aluminium strip.

The motor has multiple armature windings connected to a commutator which changes the dc supply current to ac in the rotating coils. Four brushes are mounted in spring loaded sockets on the motor end plate. Two brushes are earthed to the motor housing – the other two are connected to the field windings (see **FIG 4:2**).

Two types of brush and commutator assembly are in use in starter motors today. The more recent design has a flat circular face commutator with radial copper segments on the end of the armature (**FIG 4:3**). The brushes are pressed against the commutator by coil springs. The older type of motor has a drum commutator of copper segments about an inch long; the brushes are arranged radially around it and kept in contact by flat coiled springs (**FIG 4:4**).

The design of the starter motor is admirably suited to its application. With series windings a very high current can flow immediately the starter motor circuit is switched on – and the result is an enormous turning force, or torque. But as the load of the engine begins to turn and the motor is able to speed up, the torque requirement is reduced – thus less current is required. In fact the motor itself regulates the current simply because a series wound motor is capable of operating as a generator – the rotating motor coils are cutting the magnetic lines of force created by the field coils and a current is generated within them. This current attempts to flow in the opposite direction to the motor circuit current – it is called the back electromotive force (emf). As the back emf opposes the motor driving current more as the motor speeds up, the overall current flow is automatically reduced as the car's engine revolutions build up.

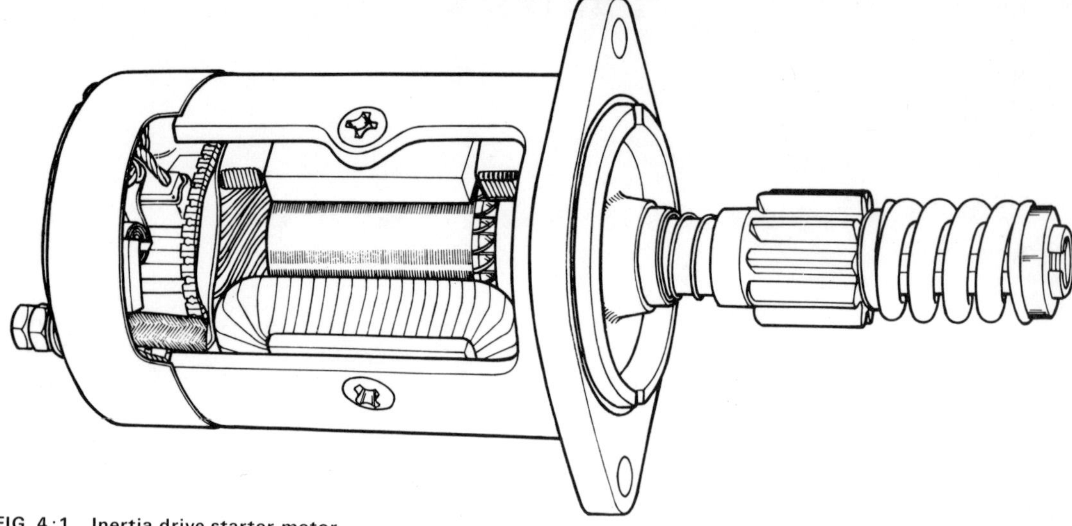

FIG 4:1 Inertia drive starter motor

4:2 Starter motor solenoids

To handle the high current loads in the starter motor circuit a special switch has been developed, the starter motor solenoid. This is a device by which a small switching current applied to the solenoid coil via the start position on the ignition switch (or a separate switch on older cars) activates a plunger which closes heavy current carrying contacts in the main motor circuit (see **FIG 4:5**).

There are two types of starter solenoid in use on today's cars. The older type is a simple solenoid switch, with or without a push button for manual operation. Mounted separately from the motor, often on the adjacent engine compartment bulkhead, the unit can be distinguished by the heavy battery and motor leads bolted to its large terminals – the terminal bolts are concealed under easily removed heavy rubber or plastics insulating caps. The solenoid also has a small Lucar spade or tag terminal and this is the connection for the supply wire from the ignition switch. It is usual for an earth return from the solenoid windings to be provided via the mounting plate bolted to the engine or car body.

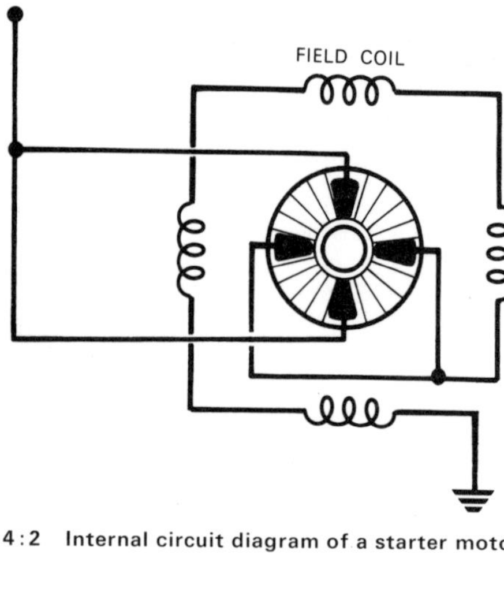

FIG 4:2 Internal circuit diagram of a starter motor

The second type of solenoid being used increasingly on higher priced cars is the pre-engaged type which has two functions. First of all it acts as the motor circuit switch in the same way as a separate solenoid, but the plunger's action also serves to engage the starter motor gear or pinion with the engine's flywheel gear ring. This type of solenoid is mounted on the starter motor body and its switching action and connections are exactly the same as the simple solenoid.

4:3 Starter motor engagement

Two ways of engaging the starter motor pinion with the flywheel ring and disengaging them once the engine has ignited have been developed.

Inertia or Bendix drive starter motor:

A common solution to starter motor engagement is the use of the inertia or Bendix drive. In this type of motor the drive shaft terminates in a coarse screw over which is threaded the pinion.

The action of the Bendix drive is to throw the pinion along the thread into engagement with the flywheel gear ring as soon as the starter motor begins turning. While the motor is under load turning the engine, the pinion remains in engagement. However as soon as the engine starts turning of its own accord the flywheel drives the pinion faster than the motor drive shaft is turning and so it screws itself back along the drive shaft out of engagement. Since this action is quite violent a buffer spring is retained on the drive shaft to arrest the pinion's movement (see **FIG 4:7**).

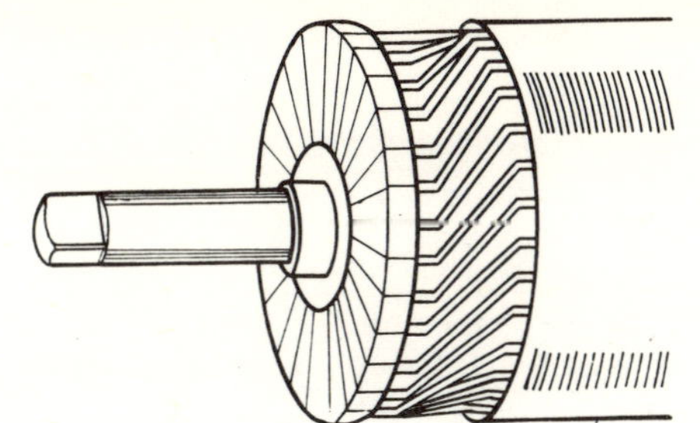
FIG 4:3 Face type commutator

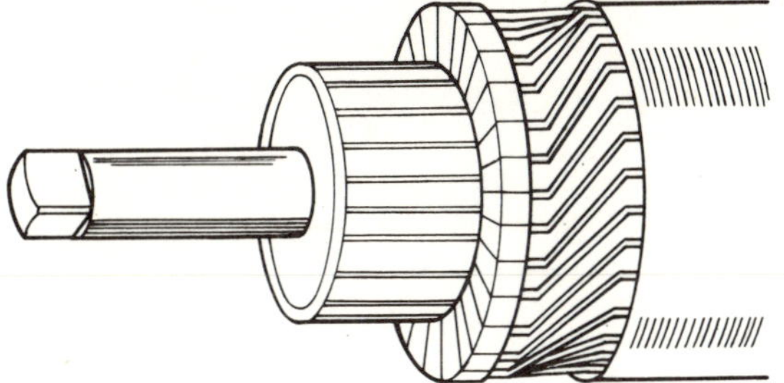
FIG 4:4 Drum type commutator

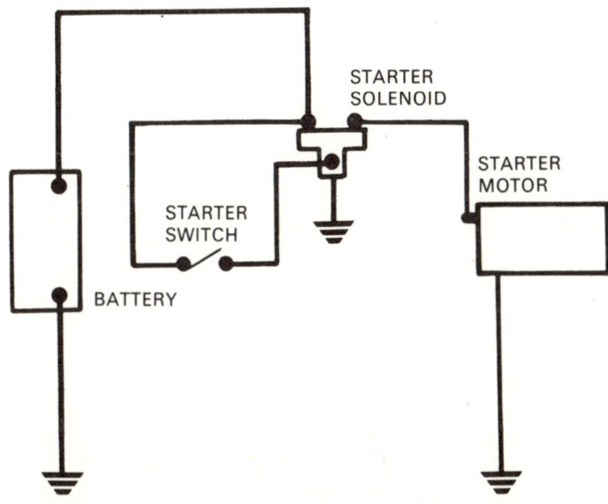

FIG 4:5 Starter system circuit diagram

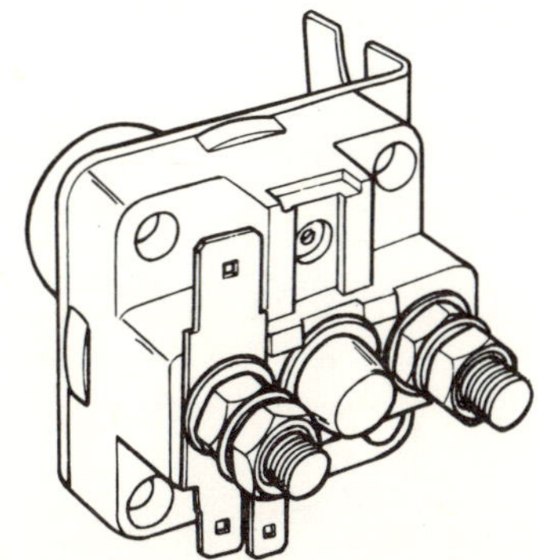
FIG 4:6 Starter solenoid with push button

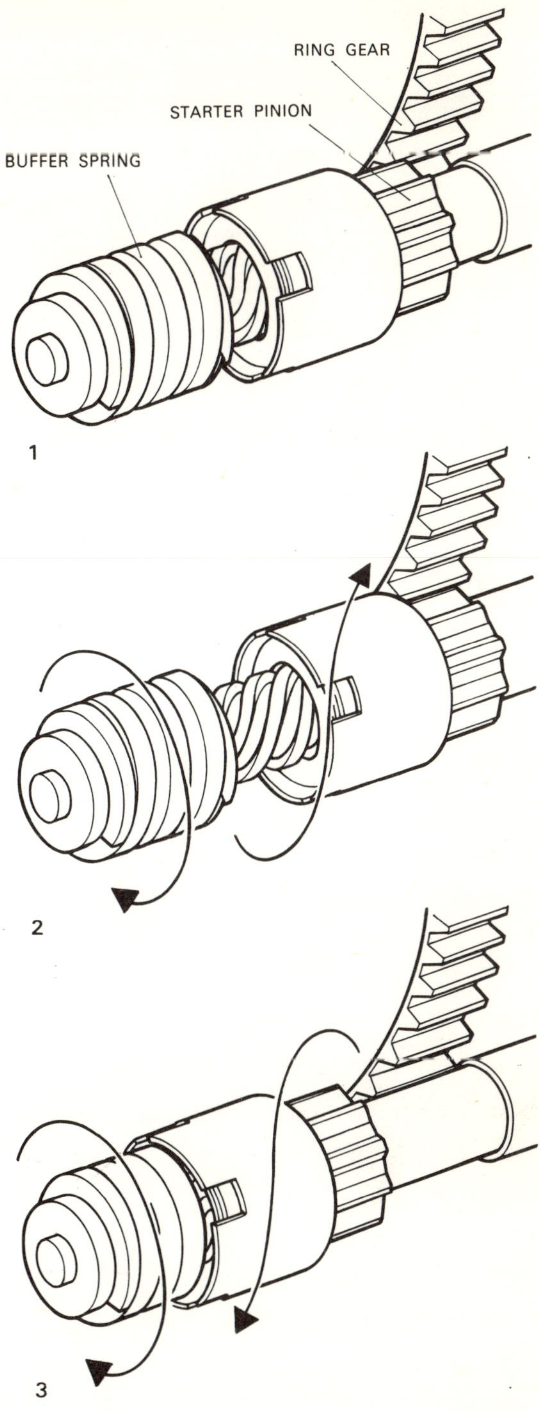

FIG 4:7 Operation of the inertia drive mechanism

Key to Fig 4:7 1 At rest the pinion is not engaged with the flywheel ring gear 2 As the starter begins to turn the pinion screws along the shaft into engagement 3 When the engine starts it turns the pinion faster than the starter, so the pinion is screwed back out of engagement

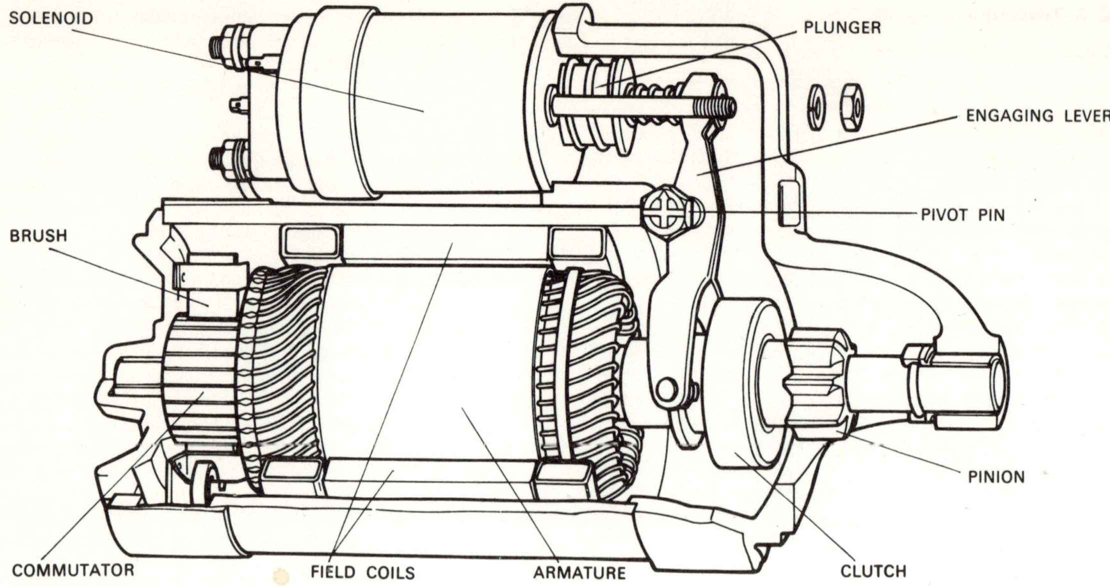

FIG 4:8 Pre-engaged starter motor

Pre-engaged drive:

The movement of the starter solenoid's plunger can also be harnessed to move the starter motor pinion into engagement with the flywheel gear ring. The solenoid is mounted on the motor body. One end of the plunger activates the electrical contacts but the other end acts on a lever pivoted over the drive shaft (see **FIG 4:8**). Movement of the lever by the plunger pushes the pinion along a splined section of the drive shaft into engagement with the flywheel gear an instant before the motor begins to turn. The pinion continues in engagement with the gear ring while the solenoid is actuated.

The pinion itself is mounted on a small over-run clutch so that when the engine fires and the pinion begins to be driven by the flywheel the motion is not transmitted to the motor drive shaft. Switching off the solenoid allows the plunger return spring to push the lever and disengage the pinion. Again buffer spring protection is provided to protect the pinion and clutch assembly from the violence of disengagement.

4:4 Starter motor circuit maintenance

The most important maintenance requirement of the starter motor circuit is to ensure that the connections in the main supply lead remain tight, clean and free from corrosion. Because such high currents flow in this circuit an obscure intermittent fault may develop at any one of the connections – overheating and oxidation resulting in greatly increased circuit resistance.

The most common place for this to happen is at the battery post itself and it is essential to ensure a tight clean connection here – the terminal may carry the lower current demand of the rest of the car's electrical systems but fail to conduct a high starter motor current. Check also that the earth strap to the engine or the motor from the body of the car is making a good connection.

4:5 Starter motor circuit fault-finding

Preliminary checks:

1 Ensure all circuit connections are tight.
2 Check battery condition with hydrometer and voltmeter and by ensuring headlamps operate at normal light output.
3 Test solenoid operation by listening to it clicking when the starter switch is operated.

Checking other faults:

Symptom	Fault
Motor fails to turn and headlamps remain bright	If solenoid operates correctly the starter motor is defective (on automatic cars ensure gear selector is in correct position).
Motor fails to turn and headlamps dim considerably	Discharged battery, jammed starter motor pinion or engine seizure.
Motor turns but fails to engage	Bendix drive type: pinion jammed on shaft. Pre-engaged type: solenoid not acting on engagement lever or over-run clutch failed.
Motor operates, starts engine but fails to disengage (to the accompaniment of a great deal of noise)	Bendix drive type: jammed pinion. Pre-engaged type: jammed pinion or engaging lever
Ringing or crashing sound on pinion disengagement	Cracked or otherwise damaged pinion buffer spring or drive shaft.

4:6 Testing a solenoid

Separate solenoid type:

With a voltmeter or circuit tester ensure that current reaches the low current terminal of the solenoid when the starter switch is operated. Another clue to correct solenoid operation is whether or not the click of its action can be heard.

The following checks can be made with a voltmeter connected across the two main current terminals of the solenoid:

1 With the solenoid inactivated the reading should be about 12 volts (battery voltage).

2 The instant the solenoid is activated the meter reading should fall to zero (a higher reading indicates a resistance in the switching contacts).

These checks are sufficient to indicate if the solenoid is operable. Separate solenoids are not repairable items – the only electrical repairs that can be made are to the terminal connections. As they are generally very reliable units it is often a good idea to replace a defective solenoid with a used unit from a scrapyard or vehicle dismantler. Make sure it is operable before purchasing.

If the solenoid is faulty the car may be started using the manual facility built into most units. There is either a large rubber push button at the opposite end of the unit to the main terminals or a small black or red plastics or rubber button placed between the two main terminals. Very firm pressure on the button will operate the starter motor.

If the solenoid fault lies in the switching terminals it is still possible to start the motor by removing the insulating caps from the main terminals and, using a stout metal blade or rod such as a screwdriver, shorting across the two terminals.

Pre-engaged type:

The same voltmeter or other circuit tests can be made on a pre-engaged type solenoid as on the separate type. In addition shorting out the main terminals of the unit to operate the motor will tell whether or not it is the solenoid that is at fault. However there is no manual operation facility on this type of solenoid and even if the motor can be made to run the pinion will not be thrown into engagement. Thus the engine cannot be started.

It is not wise to replace a pre-engaged type of solenoid with a scrap part. A new unit must be purchased.

4:7 Starter motor faults and repairs

The starter motor is rugged and generally reliable – if only because on a properly maintained car it operates for a tiny fraction of the car's running time.

There are five main ways in which the starter motor can fail:

1 Circuit connections (dealt with in **Section 4:4**).

2 Wear of brushes or commutator scoring and burning due to high current arcing.

3 Bad workmanship on the main motor supply connection – tightening the terminal nut and lock nut without care can damage internal connections.

4 Mechanical damage caused by misuse (e.g. rapid repeated use) or by loose mounting bolts which results in broken pinion teeth, worn Bendix drive, broken buffer spring or tooth damage on the flywheel gear ring.

5 A build up of dirt, grease and corrosion in the area of the engagement mechanism can render the unit inoperable or contribute to mechanical damage.

A starter motor can be removed from the engine very easily by undoing the two or three mounting bolts that secure it to the clutch and flywheel housing flange on the block. Disconnect the battery and the main battery lead to the motor before beginning, however. Take care when undoing the motor's main lead as turning the connecting bolt can damage the motor's field windings.

Examine the pinion and engagement mechanism for signs of damage and wear. Pinion teeth may be chipped, worn or burred. The pinion should be perfectly free to slide up and down the drive shaft. If it isn't brush petrol or methylated spirits onto the mechanism to get rid of dirt and work the unit by hand until it is free. Do not use oil or grease on the unit or allow solvent to enter the motor.

It is possible to replace the pinion on Bendix drive types. With some motors it is necessary to use a spring compressor to tension the buffer spring while removing the circlip which retains the mechanism. On others the removal of a split pin allows unscrewing (usually a left hand thread) of the castellated retaining nut. Before reassembly ensure that the splines of the drive shaft are free from burrs. A carborundum stone can be used to smooth off the edges of the splines. Use no oil or grease in reassembly.

Further dismantling of Bendix type with drum commutator:

For simple inspection of drum commutator and brush gear remove the clamped ring dust cover. Brushes should be at least $\frac{3}{8}$ inch long and the commutator should be free from burns, scoring and, as far as possible, wear of the copper segments.

To gain access to the brush gear carefully undo the fixing nut on the main supply terminal and remove washers and spacer noting their order for reassembly. Undo the two long bolts, withdrawing them carefully to avoid damage to field windings. The end plate can then be levered off. **FIG 4:9** illustrates this type of motor.

Clean the commutator using a strip of glasspaper while taking care to ensure that grit does not enter the motor body. A worn or damaged commutator means replacing the whole motor with an exchange unit.

If new brushes are required they have to be soldered into place. A set of four starter motor brushes has two with insulated leads and two with uninsulated leads. The two insulated leads are connected to the field windings (note carefully that one is longer than the other). Since the field windings are usually aluminium and a special process is used to connect the leads to them it is necessary to cut the old brushes away leaving enough copper lead by which to solder on the new brushes.

The two uninsulated brushes are connected to the end plate (thus earthed) and it is best to solder the new leads to a loop made in a short remaining portion of the old leads after cutting off the worn brushes.

Refit the brushes into the holders on the end plate but, for the time being, lodge the clock springs which tension the brushes onto the edge of the holder. This makes it much simpler to slide the end plate onto the commutator. The end plate locates on a notch in the lip of the main motor body so it is not possible to reassemble the part incorrectly.

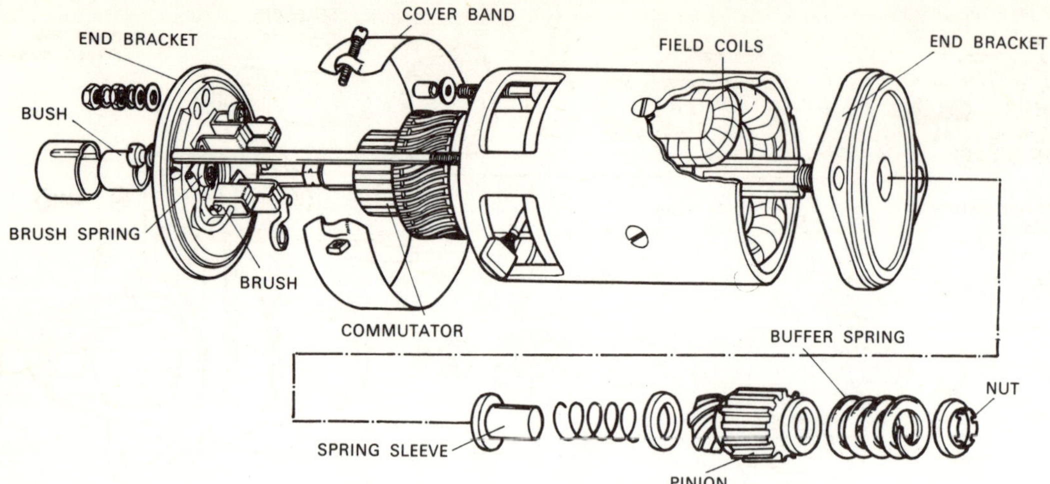

FIG 4:9 Exploded diagram of a Lucas starter with inertia drive and drum commutator

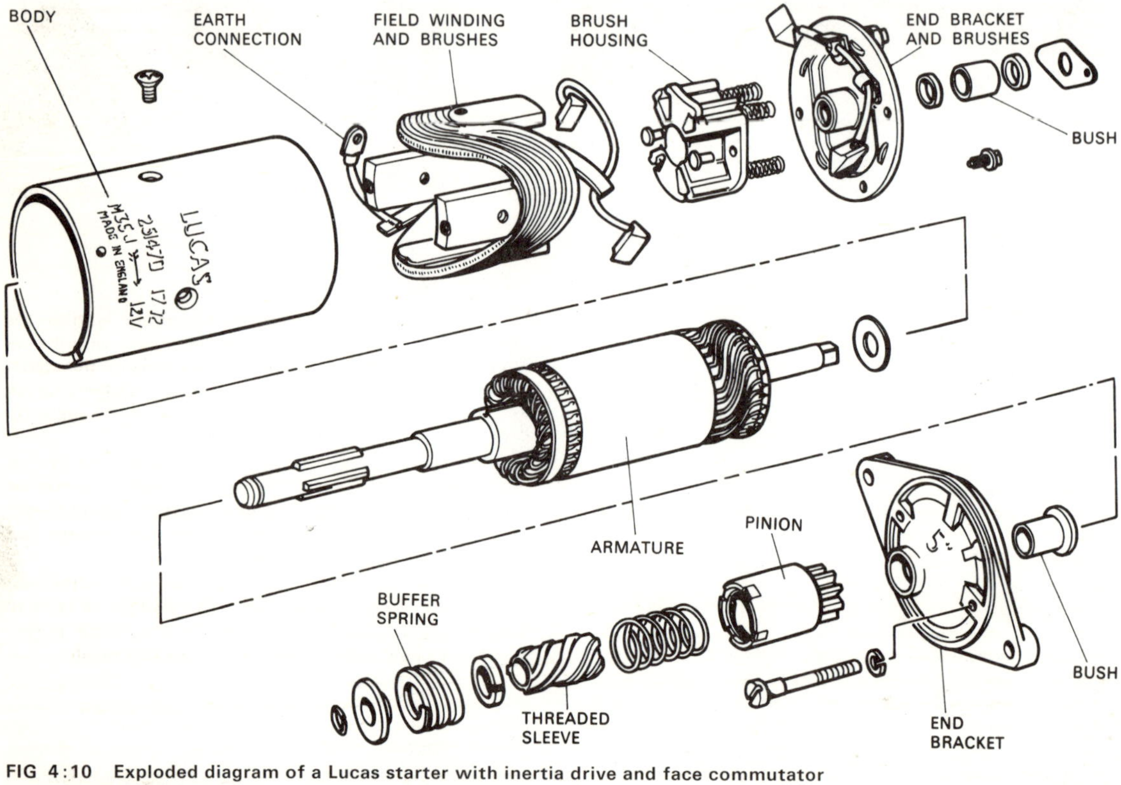

FIG 4:10 Exploded diagram of a Lucas starter with inertia drive and face commutator

Care is necessary when re-inserting the long bolts as they can damage the windings. Do not overtighten them on reassembly. Also ensure that the main supply terminal fixing nut is tightened down with the nylon insulating spacer in the correct position. Any looseness of this nut may allow the terminal bolt to turn and damage its internal connection.

Once the end plate is in place a thin probe or small screwdriver can be used to lift the clock springs into position on the brushes so that they are correctly tensioned.

In replacing the motor on the engine tighten the mounting bolts a little at a time in sequence. Reconnect the main supply lead using a second spanner on the terminal fixing nut to ensure it does not turn as the cable retaining nut is tightened.

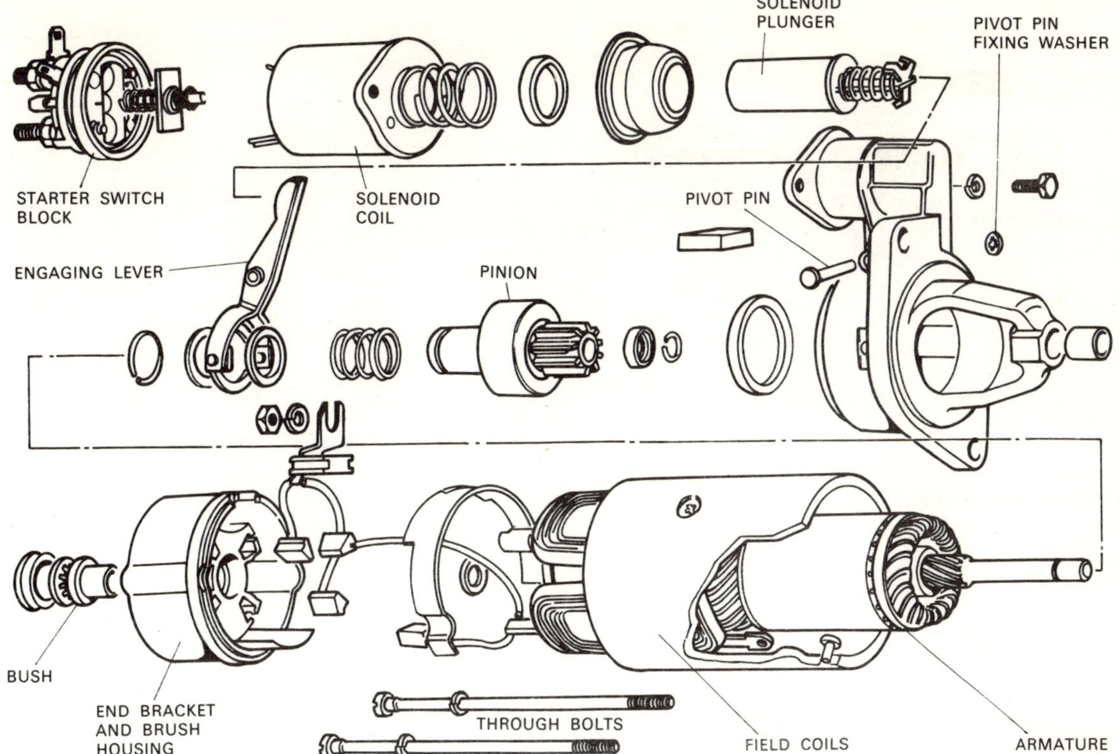

FIG 4:11 Exploded diagram of a Lucas pre-engaged starter

Further dismantling of pre-engaged type with face commutator:

The steps are similar to the stripping of the Bendix drive type. In addition, however, it is necessary to remove the solenoid from the body of the motor before examining the engagement mechanism. This is achieved by undoing two retaining nuts on the solenoid and pinion housing and withdrawing the solenoid unit which has to be lifted slightly to free it from the pivoting engagement lever. On some units it may also be necessary to remove the motor end cap to free the solenoid from the main supply terminal connection. **FIG 4:11** shows a typical pre-engaged motor.

Withdrawal of the pivot pin and unscrewing the two long bolts enables removal of the end cap and the engagement mechanism housing.

It is not wise to attempt any other repair than cleaning of the pre-engaged mechanism – damage here requires a replacement motor unit.

Face type commutators should not be cleaned using any abrasive paper. Methylated spirit is the best solvent.

The brushes for the face type commutator are retained in slots in a plastic holder. Ordinary coil springs in the holder provide brush tension. Two brushes have to be soldered to the leads from the field windings in the same way as for the repair of drum commutator types. The other two brushes are usually simply slotted into the holder.

Reassembly of this type of motor is straightforward reversal of stripping.

WARNING:

1 Always disconnect the battery before working on the starter motor. Never operate the starter motor with the car in gear – with automatic transmissions tests on the starter motor may override the built in protection and enable the car to start when in Drive. See gear lever is in neutral (or Park on automatics).

2 If parts like gear teeth are missing from the pinion, flywheel gear ring or engagement mechanism it may be necessary to remove the engine or gearbox to find them – they could migrate into parts of the transmission and cause further extensive damage.

3 It is unwise to remove the armature from within the body of the motor or to remove both endplates at once so the armature is without location in the motor body – damage to field and armature windings can result.

4:8 Emergency measures to get you home

If the solenoid is faulty:

Short out the two main terminals on the solenoid with a screwdriver or use a battery jump lead from the non-earth terminal of the battery to the main terminal on the motor side of the solenoid.

If the starter motor won't stop running:

Disconnect the low current lead from the spade terminal on the solenoid and if necessary give the solenoid unit a sharp tap.

If the starter fails to turn and the headlamps dim to a dull glow:

Turn the square end of the armature (it may be under a rubber or plastic dust cover) about $1\frac{1}{2}$ turns with a spanner – but first ensure that no one operates the starter while the spanner is being used. This measure can free a jammed pinion or allow brushes to contact an unburnt portion of the commutator. On starters with no square end to the shaft (usually pre-engaged type with face commutator) a sharp tap on the motor body with a hammer or wheel wrench will often work.

If the starter motor turns but fails to engage the flywheel gear:

Rock the car while in gear to present a new set of gear ring teeth to the starter. Try the starter again with the gear lever in neutral. This method may also be used to free a pinion which is stuck in engagement.

If the motor still fails to turn:

Push start the car by obtaining help to push the car up to a fast walking speed, engaging third gear and declutching when the engine fires.

If the battery is flat or the car has automatic gears:

An automatic car cannot be push-started and, as in the case of a flat battery, the best solution is to use high current carrying battery jump leads to obtain a current supply from a second vehicle with a well-charged battery. When connecting the jump leads ensure that the correct polarity is observed – connect negative terminal to negative terminal and positive terminal to positive terminal.

Attach the leads to the fully charged battery first, then to the flat battery. This order avoids any danger of sparks igniting gas from the charged battery. The car can then be started in the normal way.

CHAPTER 5

The ignition system

5:1 Conventional ignition systems

The ignition system of a car is designed to produce a fat electric spark across the spark plug gap at exactly the right time in the engine's combustion cycle. The right moment for a spark varies from engine to engine and also changes with the loads under which the engine operates and its speed of revolution. The ignition system takes all these factors into account and yet it is robust, simple to maintain and its parts are relatively cheap. Perhaps this is why it is one of the most neglected systems of the car and one that is very likely to cause a roadside breakdown.

The major units of the ignition system are the distributor, spark plugs and ignition coil. This last unit transforms the car's system voltage (12 volts) up to about 30,000 volts – a high enough electrical pressure for the electron flow to jump the air gap between the tip of the spark plug and earth on the engine. The ignition coil is a compact unit fitted inside a uniform sized aluminium can. The can contains two coils – the primary and secondary windings packaged in an iron jacket and a heat transfer and high voltage insulating material (sometimes a special oil is used).

The two windings – there are a few hundred turns in the primary winding and several thousand in the secondary winding – are formed concentrically (primary outermost) round a laminated core (see **FIG 5:2**).

Current is provided to the primary windings via the ignition switch and the earth return is through the contact breaker points in the distributor. Parting the contact breaker points switches off the current to the primary winding causing a collapse of the magnetic field created in the core. The lines of force in the field collapse inwards intersecting the secondary winding and generating a high voltage current. The voltage produced depends on the ratio of primary to secondary windings, the speed of field collapse and the strength of the magnetic field. Coil output is in the region of 30,000 volts because although only about 12-14,000 volts are necessary to produce a spark, resistance in the high tension circuit considerably reduces the voltage available at the plug gap.

The switching action of the contact breaker points takes place in the distributor (see **FIG 5:4**). This important unit has two tasks. It switches off the primary winding current to cause a high tension impulse at the right time in the engine's combustion cycle. Simultaneously it distributes the high tension impulse to the correct spark plug.

The rotary motion necessary for this dual switching role is provided by the distributor drive shaft, which is usually driven by a skew gear off the engine's camshaft or crankshaft. Most distributor shafts rotate at half engine speed however many cylinders there are.

In all distributors, switching of the high tension current to the spark plug is performed within the insulating cap of the unit. A thickly insulated lead from the ignition coil conducts the high tension impulses to a carbon brush in the centre of the cap. The brush bears on the centre of the rotor arm which is fixed to the top of the rotating distributor shaft. Leads to each of the spark plugs emanate from terminals fitted round the inner circumference of the cap. There is no contact between the rotor arm shoe and the terminal – the high tension impulse jumps the short gap between the two as the shoe rotates in close proximity to each terminal. This gap is beneficial to the performance of the high tension circuit – it aids rapid build-up of the secondary winding voltage.

The vital contact breaker action takes place below the rotor arm. Distributors vary in the position of the base plate on which the contact breakers are mounted. Most

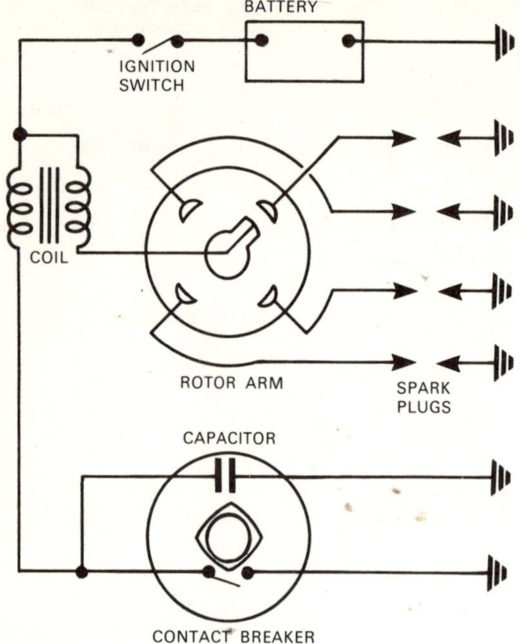

FIG 5:1 Ignition system circuit diagram

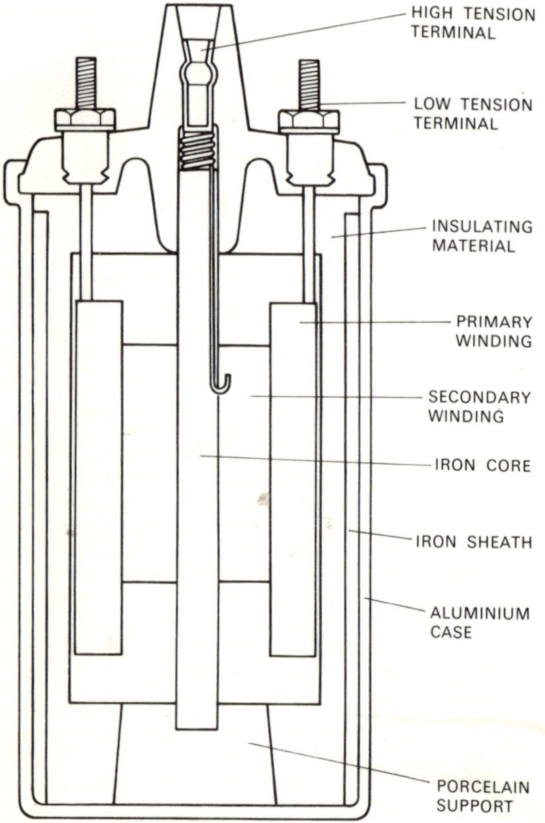

FIG 5:2 Cross-section of ignition coil

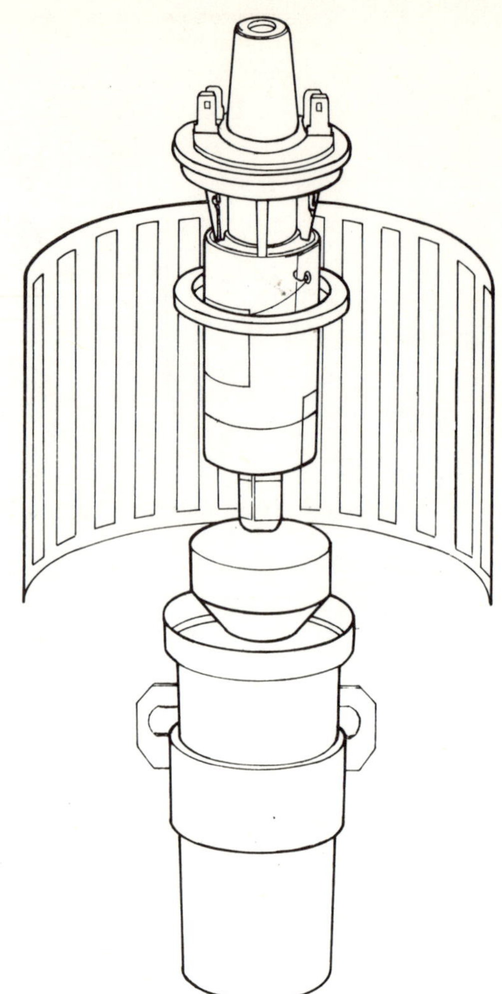
FIG 5:3 Components of a typical coil

distributors have the base plate above the centrifugal advance weights (see later) – some AC Delco (Vauxhall) and Marelli (Italian cars) distributors have a base plate mounted below the weights.

The contact breaker points themselves are small pads of an especially hard tungsten alloy. One is fixed to a steel mount adjustably positioned by a screw fixing to the base plate. The other contact is on a short length of spring steel and moves with a hard plastic heel which bears on a cam driven by the distributor shaft. The cam has a number of lobes, one for each cylinder of the engine, equally spaced around it. The action of the cam lobe is to push the two contacts apart, thus switching off the primary winding current and generating the high tension impulse.

The gap created between the two contacts when the cam moves the heel is a vital parameter of engine performance. It contributes to efficient contact breaking operation and affects the build-up of a high magnetic field in the coil. The gap is adjustable (see later).

The width of the gap determines a factor called the

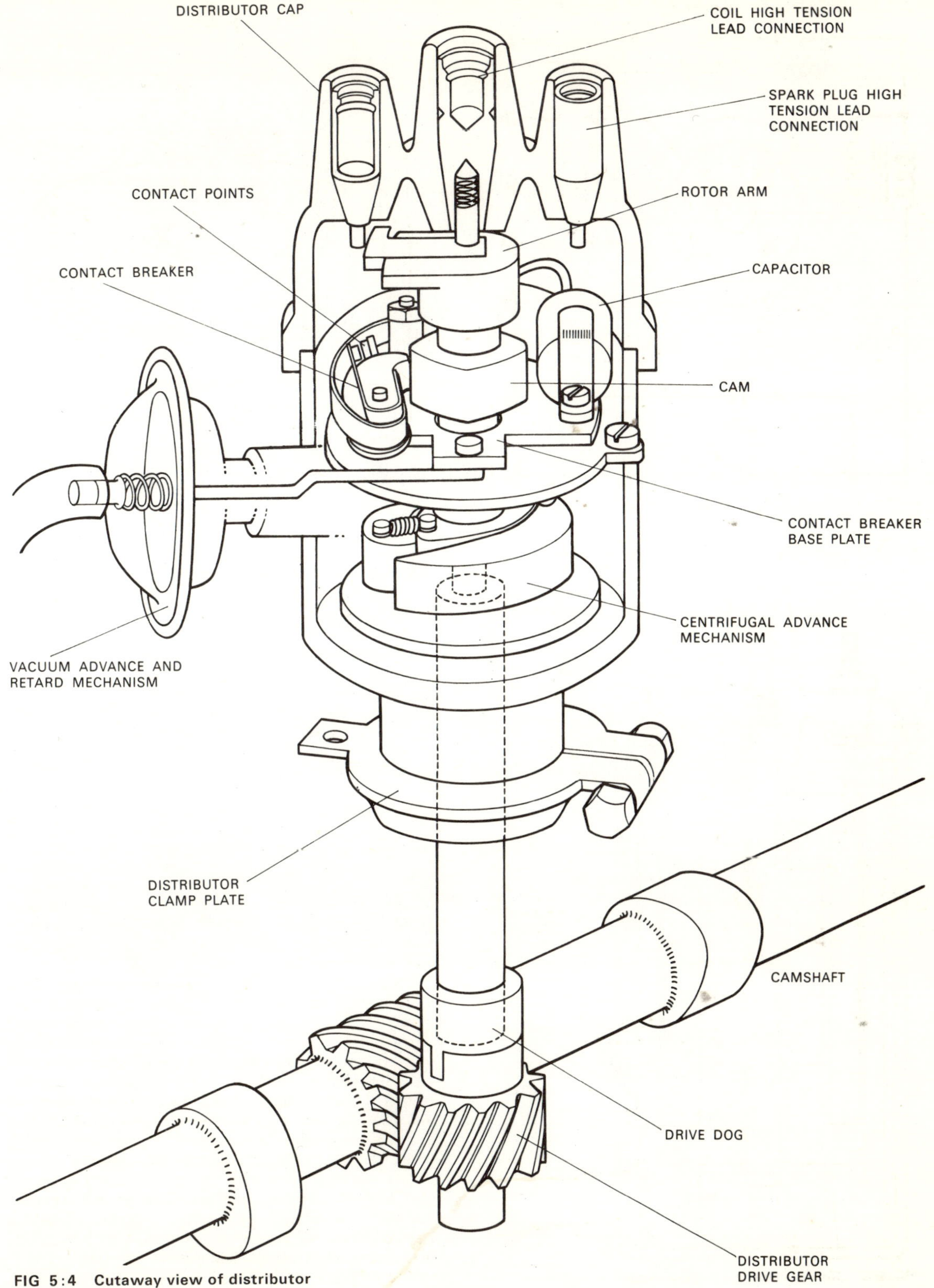

FIG 5:4 Cutaway view of distributor

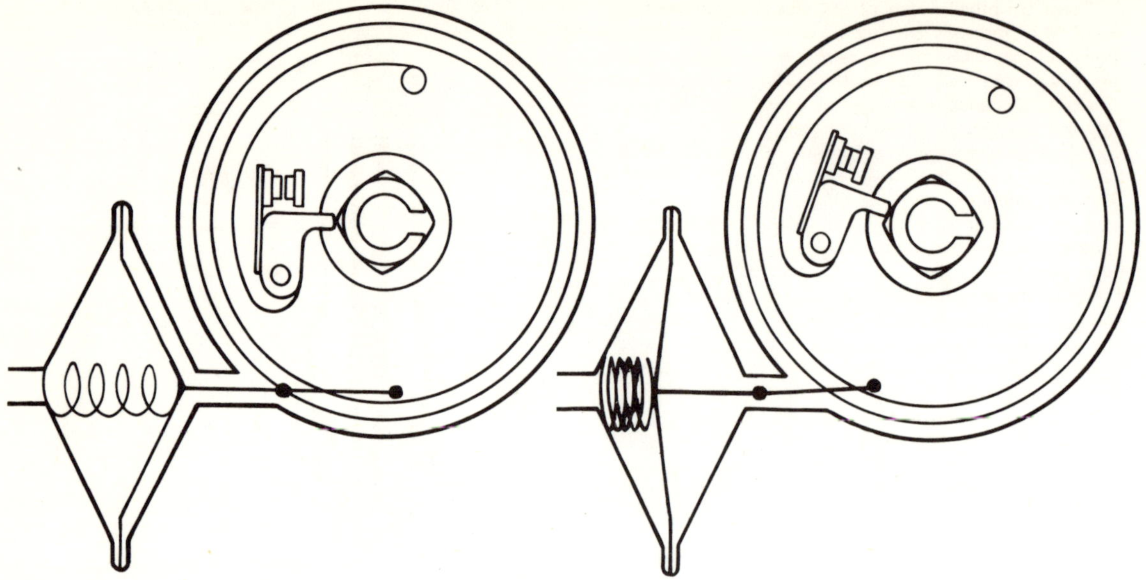

FIG 5:5 Operation of vacuum timing control

dwell angle. Simply, this is the number of degrees of cam rotation that occur during the time the contact breakers are closed. The wider the gap the longer the time they take to close and the smaller the dwell angle. Smaller dwell angles mean the coil has less time to develop its full magnetic field – especially at high engine speeds. The distributors of some high performance engines have no conventional contact breaker gap adjustment. An external adjustment screw is fitted and this is tuned using an instrument called a dwell angle meter.

The base plate is usually in two parts and designed in such a way that the points have a small degree of freedom to rotate around the cam. This movement is controlled by a vacuum diaphragm acting against a return spring. The diaphragm operates from the vacuum created in the engine's induction manifold to which it is connected by a thin bore plastic or metal pipe. Rotation of the base plate mounted points in this manner, in sympathy with the induction state of the engine, switches the primary winding current (and thus the spark) earlier (advanced ignition) or later (retarded ignition) in the combustion cycle.

There is also provision for the cam to rotate a few degrees about the drive shaft. The movement is controlled by the centrifugal advance weights – as engine speed increases the weights part against the retaining spring tension rotating the cam in the opposite direction to shaft rotation. The result is to advance the ignition.

On most cars the distributor has both types of automatic advance and retard adjustment, vacuum and centrifugal. A few cars have centrifugal control only, a smaller number vacuum control only. A few recent models have a second vacuum diaphragm acting in opposition to the first and coupled to a different point in the inlet tract.

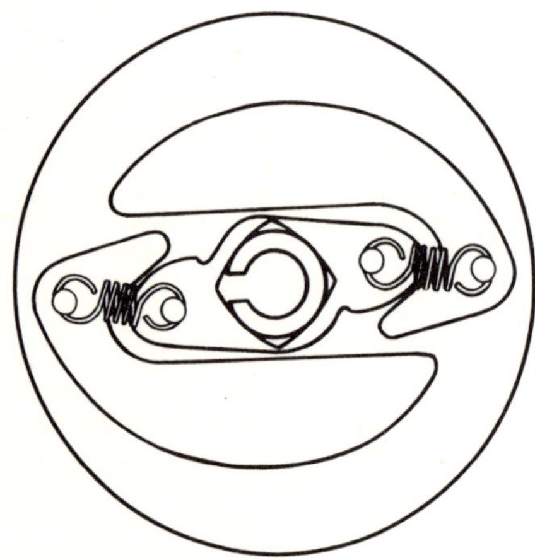

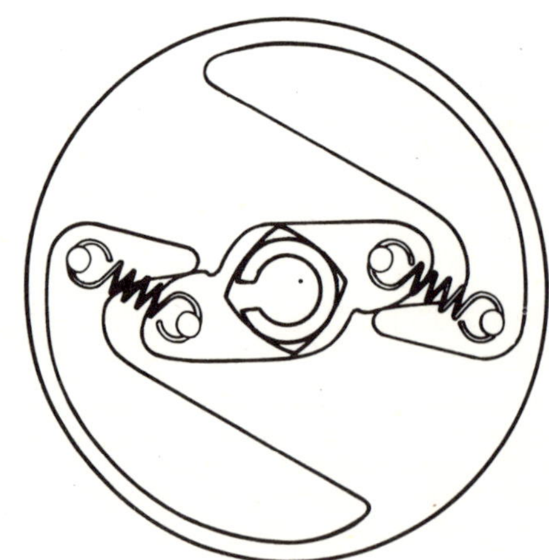

FIG 5:6 Operation of centrifugal timing control

There are other means of advance and retard adjustment. The crudest is the rotation of the whole distributor body in the clamp which secures it to the engine. This is only used for coarse adjustment during tuning. Manual fine tuning is usually provided by a thumb wheel Vernier adjuster which acts on the base plate.

One more very important component is usually housed within the distributor body – the capacitor or condenser. This is connected with its single lead to the moving contact breaker terminal. Its second connection is provided via the metal capacitor can's fixing to the base plate (earth). The capacitor performs two functions.

When the magnetic field collapses in the ignition coil the lines of force intersect the primary winding as well as the secondary winding. The result is an induced current of up to 300 volts in the primary winding – it is a back emf because it flows in the opposite direction to the primary winding supply current. This pulse attempts to arc across the contact breaker points as they are opening but is intercepted by the capacitor which soaks it up or supresses it. Without the capacitor the arcing would rapidly burn and pit the contacts causing misfiring of the engine.

The capacitor momentarily stores the energy from the back emf before it feeds back into the primary winding and aids the collapse of the magnetic field. This reinforces the high tension impulse from the secondary winding.

The spark plug itself appears to be a very simple item but in fact it is a highly developed component designed to withstand electrical pressures of up to 30,000 volts while operating with the tip at up to 900 deg. C in the combustion chamber when the outer end may be below freezing point.

The spark plug (**FIG 5:7**) consists of a metal shell with a threaded shank that screws into the engine's cylinder head. A ceramic insulator is fixed inside the shell with a special cement which also seals the spark plug to prevent gas leakage from the cylinder. Ribs on the insulator are intended to prevent flashover of the high tension current along the spark plug body. Running from the nose of the plug to the terminal top is the centre electrode and conducting rod. The spark plug gap is formed between the electrode tip and the earth electrode, a special alloy spur welded on the metal shell.

The polarity of the high tension pulse should always be negative at the spark plug terminal. If the polarity is wrong the voltage required to fire the plug will be increased. This can shorten plug life and cause engine misfiring. On a positive earth system the lead from the coil's + terminal must go to the contact breaker. Some coils have terminals marked 'CB' and 'SW' – the connections indicated apply to a system of specific polarity. In other cars the terminals have numbers corresponding with those to be found in the car's wiring diagram.

5:2 Maintenance of the ignition system

Ignition coil:

The ignition coil is a sealed unit and no maintenance of its connections is possible. Regularly check to see that the supply and contact breaker terminals (usually Lucar connections) are clean and tight. There are two types of high tension connection to the coil – a screw cap that traps the end of the high tension lead or a push fit protected by a plastic or rubber shroud. Ensure this connection is tight. Wipe away all grease, dirt and moisture from the terminal end of the coil and the coil body.

Coil life will be extended by keeping the ignition switched off when the engine is stationary. This is because the engine normally stops in the contacts-closed position so current is supplied to the primary winding. This generates heat which cannot be dissipated efficiently without a cooling flow of air from the engine fan or front grille.

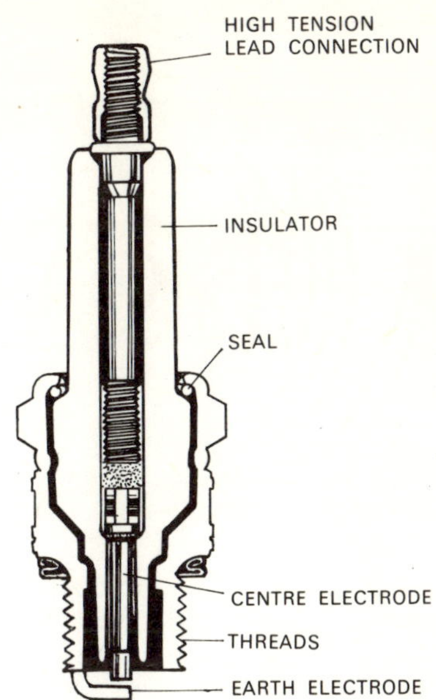

FIG 5:7 Cross-section of sparking plug

High tension leads:

Leads in the high tension system are of two main types (see **Chapter 2, Section 2:1**). Maintenance consists of monthly examination of the surface of the lead insulation for cracks, minute blisters or crazing. Surface imperfections may house moisture which will allow the high tension current to leak along the insulation (tracking). Replace leads affected in this way with a new length of lead of the same type. Dirt will harbour moisture and can provide a conductive path – clean the leads with methylated spirit soaked rag. Check that shrouds and spark plug terminal caps are not cracked or split.

During the winter spray ignition coil, leads and the distributor cap with a proprietary brand of water repellent sealer at monthly intervals. Make sure all dirt and grease is cleaned off components before spraying.

Spark plugs:

Under normal engine conditions (correct ignition timing and correct carburetter mixture setting) spark plugs need only be serviced at 5000 mile intervals. At 5000 miles the plugs should be removed, their condition should be examined for clues about engine performance (see checking section later) and they must be cleaned and gapped.

To remove spark plugs use a special box spanner of the correct size or a plug socket. Undo the plug for a few turns and with a clean, soft brush, clear away any rust or dust particles around the spark plug gasket (a compressed air line will do this job much better especially if the plug is recessed in the cylinder head). Take particular care with this operation – it is important to prevent abrasive particles entering the cylinders. The plugs can now be fully removed. If extensive engine servicing is being carried out, block the plug holes with clean rag or tissue paper.

Take care when removing or replacing plugs in an aluminium alloy cylinder head – stripping of the threads is a common mistake. Stripped threads can be repaired using a specially designed helical steel coil; it is a job best carried out by a garage.

Examine the plug's porcelain insulator – discard if there are any signs of cracking as it renders the insulation ineffective. If the plugs are of a modern emission control design known as the air-surface gap plug – there are three earth electrodes at the tip instead of one – do not attempt to clean them or reset the gaps.

Conventional plugs are best cleaned by a compressed air grit blasting process – most garages have a special machine to do this. Second best method is to clean the threads, plug tip and earth electrode with a fine wire brush.

After cleaning use a spark plug tool (combined feeler gauges, gapping lever and contact file) to bend the earth electrode away from the tip enough to insert the contact file. Use the file to square off the plug tip and the earth electrode surface adjacent to the tip.

Reset the plug gap to the dimension stated in the car handbook (between 0.023 inch and 0.030 inch) taking care not to strain the earth electrode during bending.

Plugs have a special metal gasket to ensure that the joint with the cylinder head is gastight. Before replacing the plug make sure that this is not completely flattened or broken. (Some plugs have a tapered seat – ensure this is not damaged). Plugs should be replaced finger tight (a smear of graphite grease on the threads eases tightening, especially on alloy heads, but do not use any other kind of lubricant) and then tightened up about a quarter turn further with the plug spanner.

Clean the plug's ceramic insulator with a methylated spirits soaked rag.

When reconnecting the plugs **ensure that the right order of leads is observed**. Many cars having the order printed on the ignition leads – it is a wise precaution to paint unmarked leads with the cylinder number before plug removal.

Ideally plugs should be replaced at 8000 to 10,000 mile intervals but conscientious cleaning and gapping of plugs will extend their life to around 16,000 miles provided there are no other factors causing plug damage (see checking section).

The distributor:

Maintenance of distributors should be carried out at 6000 mile intervals. The sequences described here refer to Lucas units – individual differences between these and other types are summarised in the next section.

1 Distributor cap and rotor arm. The distributor cap is removed by levering off the two steel clips hinged to the side of the unit. Remove the cap with plug leads. Examine the cap for signs of tracking (jagged streaks of dirt between the contacts inside the cap usually reveal this high voltage short circuit) and hairline cracks – renew the cap if either fault is found. If the cap is sound clean out the inside with a dry cloth.

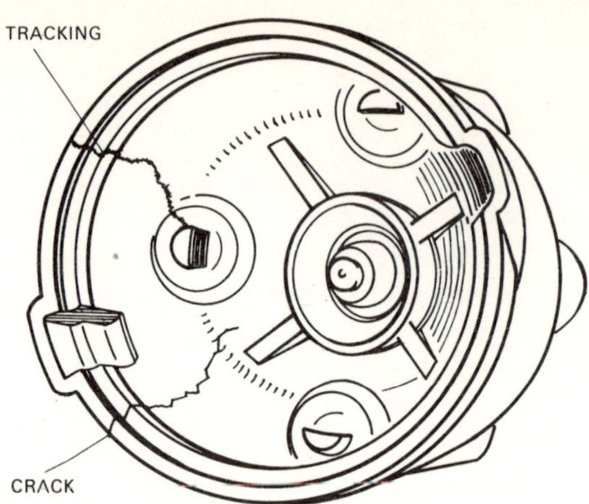

FIG 5:8 Distributor cap defects

Examine the condition of the carbon brush in the centre of the cap. A fixed brush worn flush with its mounting means renewing the entire cap – spring loaded brushes that are worn, or have corroded springs can simply be replaced.

Carbon deposits on the cap electrodes can be cleaned off with methylated spirits (do not use abrasive as the rotor arm gap will be widened) but pitted and burnt electrodes mean cap renewal.

Pull or carefully lever the rotor arm off the end of the distributor shaft. Examine it for cracks or tracking, renewing it if necessary. Clean away any dirt deposits with methylated spirits; renew the arm if it is pitted or burnt.

2 Contact breaker points. Open the contact breaker points by rotating the engine until the cam lobe lifts the contact breaker heel (use a spanner on the engine crankshaft pulley nut, pull the fan belt or rock the car to and fro in top gear). Inspect the contact faces for pitting, burning or other damage – renew the contact breaker if any fault is found. Dirty points can be cleaned with a cloth.

Contact breakers should be replaced at a maximum of 12,000 miles but, better, every 6000 miles. Remove the old set, carefully noting the order of screws, washers and tag connectors, by undoing the nut securing the moving contact spring, extracting the plastic 'top hat' insulator, pulling aside the low tension leads and taking the moving contact off its pivot. Take the insulating washer off the pivot and undo the fixed contact securing screw – the fixed contact can then be removed. Clean the base plate with a cloth.

The new contact breaker set should be of the correct type for the particular distributor. Two types of set are available – one-piece or two-piece. For many Lucas distributor applications they are interchangeable (see **FIGS 5:9** and **5:10**).

To refit a two-piece set locate the fixed contact on the main pivot pin and replace the securing screw but do not

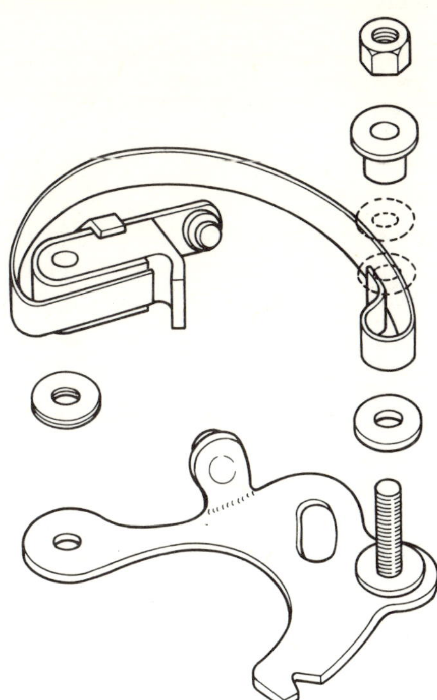

FIG 5:9 Lucas two-piece contact set

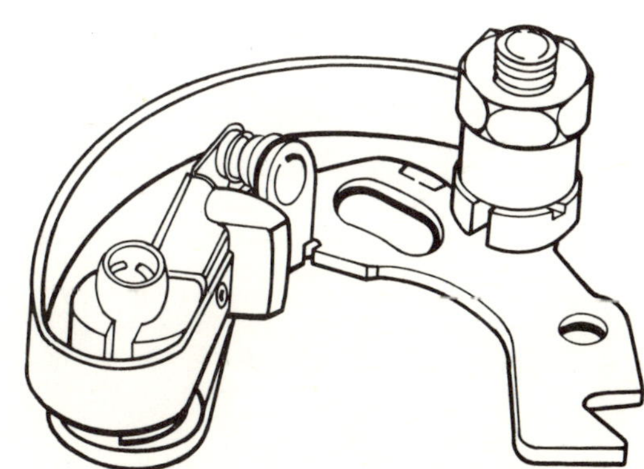

FIG 5:10 Lucas one-piece Quikafit contact set

fully tighten it until the gap has been adjusted. Put the insulating washer on the spring pivot, followed by the moving contact spring. Reposition the leads and insert the 'top hat' insulator through them and over the pivot. Tighten the nut down on the insulator.

A one-piece set is simply located on the main pivot pin and secured by the fixing screw. The leads are secured to the contact by a plastic nut which must not be over-tightened.

3 Contact breaker gap adjustment. Check that the moving contact heel is on the highest point of the cam so the points are fully open. If the points have not been renewed, loosen the fixed contact securing screw. Place the blade of a screwdriver in the adjustment slot and twist the screwdriver to fully open the contact points. Insert a feeler gauge (0.015 inch) between the points and, turning the screwdriver, carefully move the fixed contact plate to close the points on to the feeler gauge. The feeler should just be pinched by the points with almost no tension placed on the moving contact. Tighten the fixed contact screw, move the cam through one revolution and recheck the gap, adjusting if necessary. Lucas allow an adjustment range of 0.014 inch-0.016 inch for all applications of their distributors.

Some point sets are protected when new by a waxy film over the contacts. This must be removed by wiping with a petrol soaked rag. Ensure that on reassembly the low tension leads are positioned away from the distributor's moving parts.

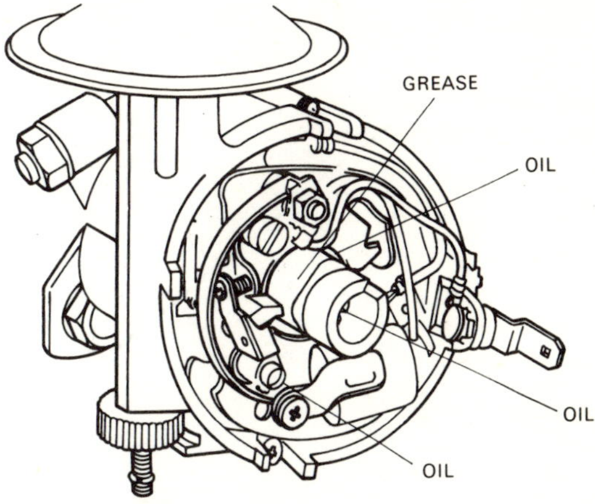

FIG 5:11 Lubricating the distributor

4 Cam and contact breaker lubrication. Inspect the cam faces for scoring and corrosion patches – renew cam if there is evidence of either. The cam faces should be lightly smeared with high melting point grease. Two drops of oil should be applied to the cam screw under the rotor arm and another two drops should be trickled into the gap between the base plate and cam. A drop of oil on the pivot of the moving contact breaker is sufficient – use a tiny smear of grease on the pivot of a one-piece set. Carry out lubrication carefully and clean off any excess grease or oil.

5 Checking vacuum advance. The vacuum advance diaphragm unit is located on the side of the distributor body – a plastic or metal pipe connects it to the induction manifold on or near the carburetter flange. Check the operation of the vacuum diaphragm by undoing the push fit connection at the carburetter and sucking hard on the end of the pipe maintaining the vacuum by placing the tongue over the end of the tube. The base plate should move and maintain its position until the vacuum is released.

If the base plate does not move, first check that it is free to move and that the vacuum tube is obstruction free (remove it completely and blow through it). If the tube is open the fault lies in the diaphragm unit – it is either pierced or jammed. A slow return of the base plate while maintaining vacuum also means a pierced diaphragm.

Faulty diaphragm units can be removed by unhitching

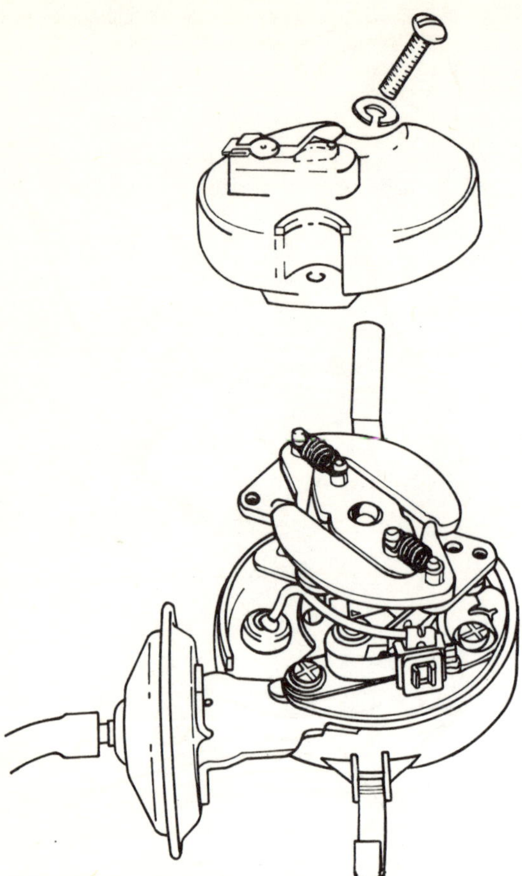

FIG 5:12 AC Delco distributor

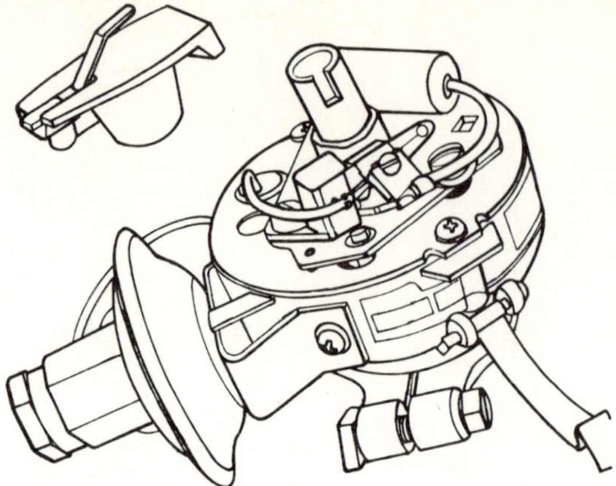

FIG 5:13 Motorcraft/Autolite distributor

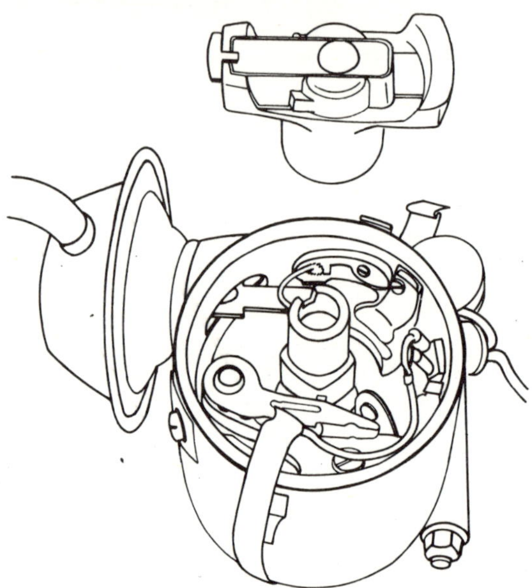

FIG 5:14 Bosch distributor

the operating spring from the base plate, removing the spring clip and fine tuning nut (do not lose its retaining spring), and withdrawing the unit. Retune the engine by static or stroboscopic means (see later) after fitting a new diaphragm unit.

6 Checking centrifugal advance mechanism. The weights of the centrifugal advance mechanism should be free to move outwards against the tension of the restraining springs. To check this movement replace the rotor arm on the distributor shaft, and determine the normal direction of rotation (it is often marked by an arrow on the rotor arm). Grip the rotor arm firmly and rotate the cam in the direction of rotation. On releasing the rotor arm it should spring back if the weights are free to move.

If they are not operating correctly, remove the distributor base plate (two or three screws locate it on the distributor body) to gain access to the weights. Note their mounting position before removing and cleaning them, paying particular attention to the pivot points. Replace the weights and fit new restraining springs.

7 Other maintenance checks. Ensure the capacitor earth connection to the base plate is tight and that the capacitor lead to the moving contact is routed away from moving parts. Inspect wiring of coil lead terminal (a Lucar spade fixed in a plastic insulator slotted into the distributor) for security and clean away dirt from around internal and external connections. Try side to side movement of the cam to check play between distributor shaft and cam and between the shaft and its plain bush bearing. If play is visible it is best to fit an exchange unit.

5:3 Variations in distributor design

AC Delco (Vauxhalls):

The centrifugal advance weights on some AC Delco units are mounted above the base plate and contact breaker points. The rotor arm is a circular plastic cap secured by two screws to the weight retaining plate. The rotor arm's centre contact is a sprung leaf which must be bent up the correct distance to ensure it contacts the fixed brush in the distributor cap (see **FIG 5:12**).

The contact set is similar to Lucas except that the low tension leads are secured by a plastics clip. The gap for most AC Delco points is 0.019 inch-0.021 inch.

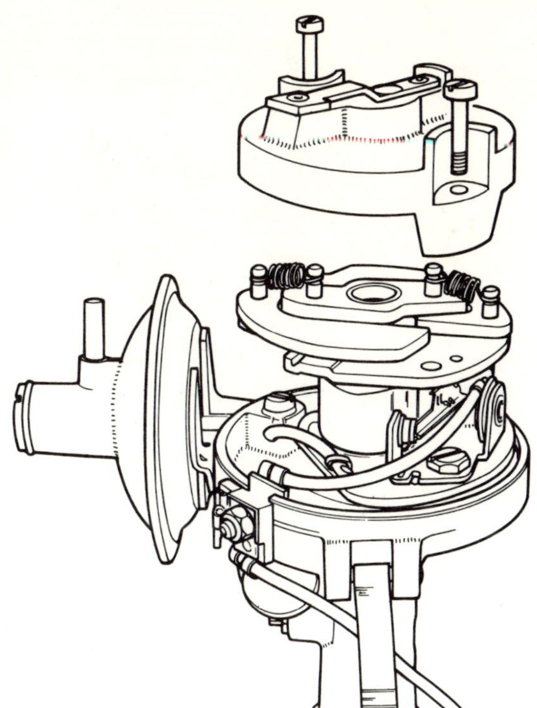

FIG 5:15 **Marelli distributor**

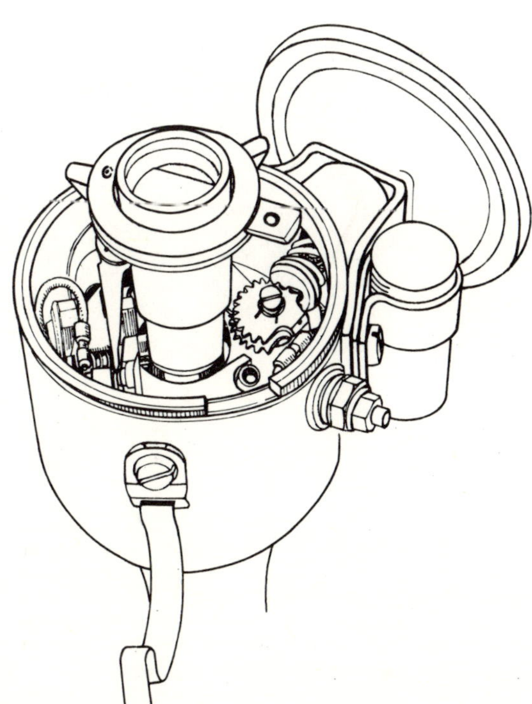

FIG 5:16 **Ducellier distributor**

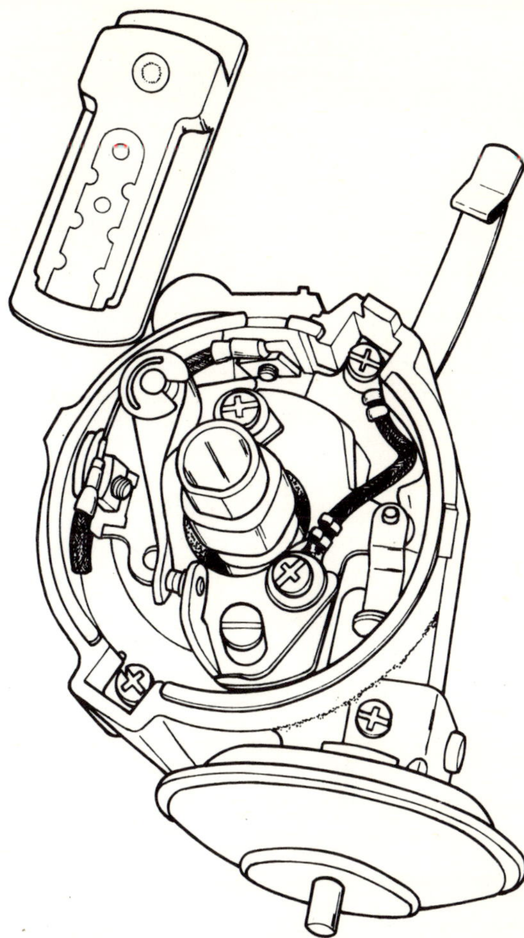

FIG 5:17 **Hitachi distributor**

Motorcraft/Autolite (Fords):

The rotor arm has a sprung centre electrode contacting a fixed brush in the cap. A compact one-piece contact set is used and the low tension leads are secured by a terminal screw (see **FIG 5:13**). Vacuum advance is best checked by revving the engine and watching for movement of the external connecting link between the diaphragm unit and the distributor body.

Bosch (some German, Swedish and Italian cars):

The only major difference between Bosch units (see **FIG 5:14**) and Lucas is that a circular condensation shield is often fitted on the distributor shaft under the rotor arm. The moving contact is retained on its pivot by a small spring clip – take care not to lose it in the distributor body during removal. Points gap for most Bosch applications is 0.015 inch-0.017 inch.

Marelli (some Italian cars):

Two screws retain a circular rotor arm on the centrifugal

advance weight mounting which is above the contact breaker and base plate (see **FIG 5:15**). Some older Marelli units have an external wick for lubrication of the shaft. Points gap is between 0.018 inch and 0.020 inch.

Ducellier (some French cars):

Two-piece contact set retained to the base plate by screw and spring clip – a special tool is recommended for points setting (0.017 inch to 0.020 inch), but the job can be done with a screwdriver. Felt pad at centre of cam for shaft lubrication (see **FIG 5:16**).

Hitachi (Datsun):

Conventional distributor with one-piece contact set, weights fitted beneath base plate, and capacitor mounted on outside of some units. Points gap between 0.018 inch and 0.020 inch for most applications (see **FIG 5:17**).

5:4 Removing and refitting a distributor

Car manufacturers do not always site distributors in the most convenient position for service and maintenance on the vehicle so it may be necessary to remove the unit. A simple procedure makes it easier to line up the distributor for refitting in the correct position to minimise timing difficulties.

1 Turn the car engine so that it is on the No. 1 cylinder compression stroke, remove the distributor cap and the rotor arm should be approaching No. 1 cylinder contact.

2 Disconnect the low tension lead and vacuum advance pipe.

3 Score the distributor clamp and body, and the engine block with a line to ensure correct repositioning – also mark the rotor arm position on the distributor body.

4 If retiming is inevitable undo the clamp bolt and remove the distributor – however it is possible to avoid retiming if the clamp mounting bolts are undone instead of the clamp itself.

5 Withdraw the distributor taking care not to damage any O-ring oil seal that may be present under the clamp – if the unit has an integral skew gear drive it will have to be rotated through a small angle. To aid repositioning make a note of the angle turned.

Refitting the distributor is the reverse of removal – ensure that all the marks on the distributor body and engine line up. It is a good idea to renew any oil control O-ring on the distributor drive shaft – it may have been minutely damaged during removal.

5:5 Static ignition timing

Once set, the ignition timing (simply, the point in the combustion cycle at which the distributor delivers the spark impulse to the plug) should not vary provided that the base plate is secure inside the distributor and the distributor is firmly clamped onto the engine. However well the marks have been lined up during distributor refitting it is wise to retime the ignition – the procedure is also necessary when a new distributor is fitted and advisable when new contact breakers are fitted.

There are two ways of setting the ignition timing, the static and stroboscopic methods. A few modern cars, notably Audis, some VWs, Datsun and Volvo should only be timed with a stroboscope although the static timing procedure can be used during engine assembly to achieve an approximate distributor position.

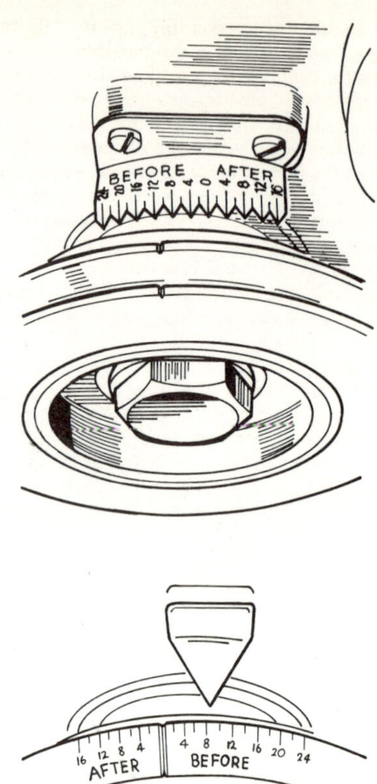

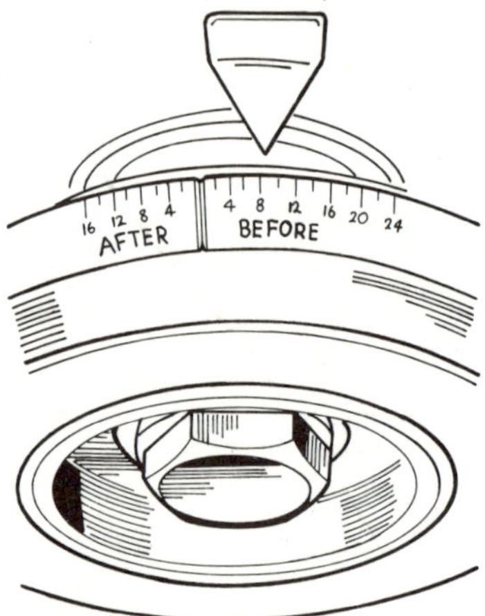

FIG 5:18 Typical timing marks

All engines have timing marks – one or more marks on the crankshaft pulley, or, in many transverse engined cars, on the flywheel, which align with a fixed mark or marks on the cylinder block or flywheel housing. When the marks are on the flywheel there is an inspection hole in the flywheel/clutch housing covered by a small plate. Very often the only way to see the marks through the hole is to use a mirror and a torch. Keep the mirror in position by sticking it to the flywheel housing with a lump of putty or Plasticene.

In most cases there is a pair of marks which align when the piston in the timing cylinder – usually No. 1 cylinder, sometimes No. 4 or 6 (refer to the car handbook) – is at the top of its stroke, a position referred to as top dead centre or tdc.

For most engines the correct timing point is a certain time, measured in degrees of crankshaft rotation, before top dead centre, btdc – possibly up to 15 deg, the precise figure being given in the handbook or servicing instructions for each model. With the advent of emission control regulations some models for some markets are timed at or even after top dead centre (atdc).

Often a timing scale is provided in addition to the tdc marks so that the correct timing point can easily be found. With a pulley turning clockwise (most engines) fixed marks for points btdc will be anticlockwise of the tdc mark, marks on the pulley for points btdc will be clockwise of the tdc mark (see **FIG 5:18**).

A few exceptions, like the later VWs already mentioned, have only a single pair of marks indicating not tdc but the actual timing point.

If a precise timing mark is not provided cut a circle of card the same diameter as the crankshaft pulley. Draw a line on the card from the centre to the edge. Using a protractor draw a second line from the centre to the edge the correct number of degrees btdc (or atdc) from the first line (see **FIG 5:19**). Place the card over the pulley with the first line on the pulley's tdc mark. Using paint or a punch or scriber, make a timing mark on the pulley at the point indicated by the second line.

Use the following procedure for static timing.

1 Ensure the timing cylinder is near top dead centre on its compression stroke; this may be achieved by rotating the engine using a spanner on the crankshaft pulley nut until a finger or thumb held tight on the plug hole of the timing cylinder is forced off by the pressure. Remove the distributor cap and check the rotor arm is adjacent to the electrode for the timing cylinder.

2 As accurately as possible, line up the timing marks at the correct number of degrees btdc (or atdc).

3 With the ignition on, connect a test lamp between the low tension contact on the side of the distributor and a good earth.

4 Slacken the distributor clamp bolt until the body of the distributor can be turned freely.

5 Ensuring that the rotor arm remains in the correct position to fire the timing cylinder, rotate the distributor body until the test lamp lights up, indicating that the points have opened. Try this adjustment a few times until the exact point at which the light comes on can be determined. Tighten the distributor clamp bolt without disturbing the position of the distributor.

6 Check the accuracy of adjustment by slowly rotating the engine for a few turns. The lamp must light at the point when the timing mark lines up with the reference point. On some distributors fine adjustment can be made using the Vernier screw. Repeat the procedure if any inaccuracy is found in the test.

An alternative method sometimes recommended involves connecting the test lamp across the two low tension contacts on the ignition coil. In this case the lamp will go out as the points open, so the distributor must be set at the exact point at which the light is extinguished. To avoid confusion decide which method is easier to use on your car and stick to it.

5:6 Stroboscopic ignition timing

A stroboscopic timing light (strobe) is used for this timing method which is performed while the engine is running. For really accurate results it is also necessary to have a reliable tachometer (rev-counter). When the

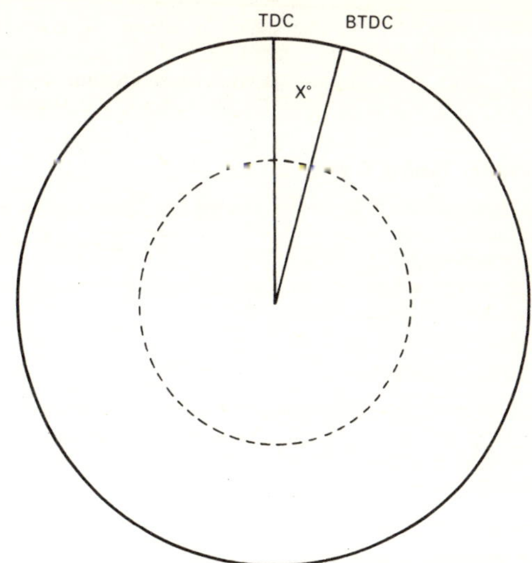

FIG 5:19 Timing card

specified revolutions for stroboscopic timing (see car handbook) are in the region of 600-750 rev/min reasonably accurate results can be obtained by setting the carburetter idle adjustment to a slow, smooth idle.

There are two types of strobe used for timing – the cheapest and simplest is connected in series with the plug lead of the timing cylinder. A more expensive type, often with an adjuster and dial to set the number of degrees required, has a sensor which is fitted in series with the timing cylinder plug lead and low tension leads which are clipped to a live battery supply point (such as the live side of the starter solenoid) and earth (the car body).

Use the following procedure for stroboscopic timing.

1 Check that the engine's timing marks are clearly visible – it is useful to pick them out in white paint or chalk.

2 If the handbook indicates the timing should be carried out with the vacuum advance mechanism disconnected remove the vacuum pipe at the carburetter end. Plug the carburetter vacuum connection – a short length of rubber or plastic pipe with a small lightly greased bolt stuck in the end is a simple solution to this.

3 Connect up the timing light and start the engine. Adjust the carburetter idle screw so the engine runs at the required speed. (A few cars are timed at quite high revolutions – up to 3000 rev/min – and for these it may be necessary to have a helper to operate the accelerator).

4 Point the light at the timing marks. Adjust the fine tuning Vernier of the distributor until the correct degree timing mark appears stationary in line with the reference mark. If there is no Vernier adjustment or the timing is so far out of true that the fine adjuster cannot bring it into line get a helper to loosen the distributor clamp bolt and turn the distributor until the marks come into line. Extreme care must be taken during this procedure to ensure that the distributor remains stationary while the bolt is retightened.

The strobe light can also be used to check the operation of the centrifugal advance weights and the vacuum advance mechanism. With the vacuum disconnected, blip the throttle to raise engine revs and the timing marks

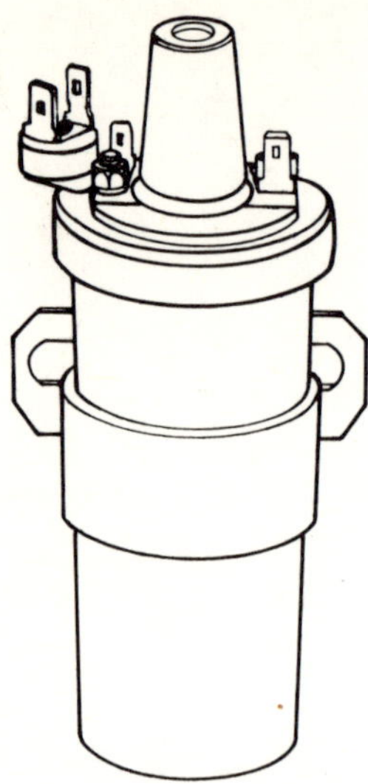

FIG 5:20 Coil with ballast resistor

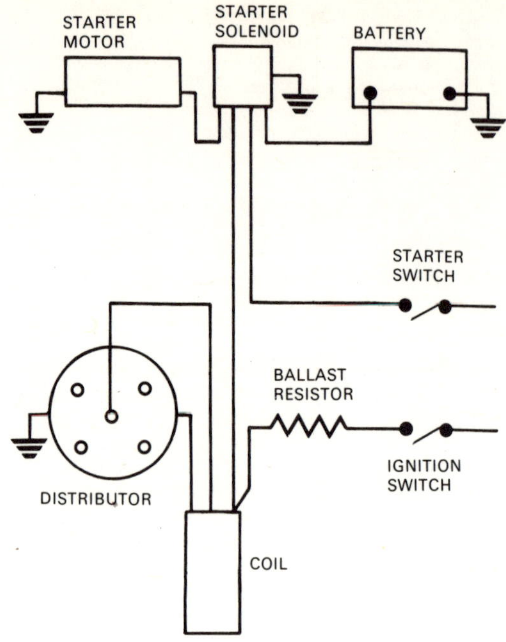

FIG 5:21 Ballast resistor system circuit

should appear to move steadily backwards, returning to the correct timing when the engine slows. This procedure shows the centrifugal advance is working. Reconnect the vacuum pipe, rev the engine to a steady 2000 rev/min and disconnect the pipe. The timing marks will appear to move steadily forward on disconnection of the pipe and on reconnection the marks will appear to move backward. If this effect is not observed fit a new vacuum advance unit.

5:7 Modern ignition systems

The conventional ignition system described above has a number of weaknesses which may not show up in the day to day use of a well-maintained family saloon but do become problems on high performance engines and those with more than six cylinders. The requirements of these engines and more stringent laws on exhaust emissions have led to the development of more sophisticated solutions to spark distribution and timing. Some more advanced systems for ignition are available to the enthusiast and family motorist alike in kit form; others will become commonplace on the lower priced saloons of tomorrow.

What are the disadvantages of the conventional ignition system? The coil's weakness is that when the battery voltage becomes lowered by starter use (especially in cold weather) or its performance is deteriorating the primary winding voltage may not be sufficient to produce a fat ignition spark. The result is difficulties in cold-starting. Ballast resistor coils overcome some starting problems.

But by far the weakest link in the ignition system is the contact breaker set. The points wear and need frequent gapping and replacement. They carry a current of up to 5 amps causing arcing and metal transference from one point to the other. Even if the points are properly gapped it is possible that uneven metal build up on one spot on a point will narrow the effective contact area and reduce the voltage available to the primary winding. At high engine speeds the heel may bounce from peak to peak on

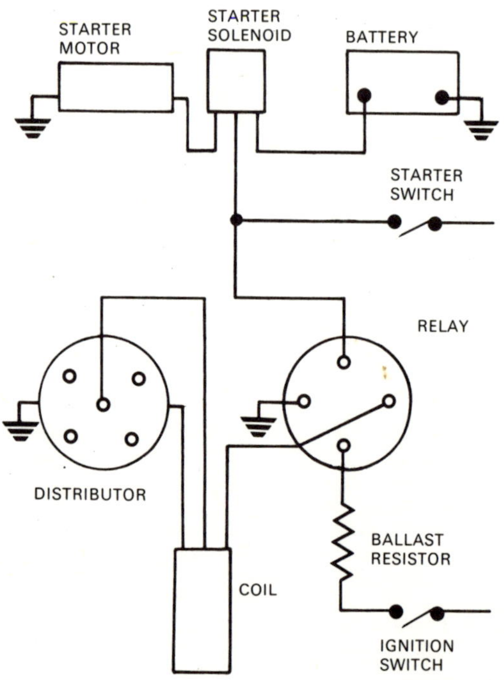

FIG 5:22 Ballast resistor system with relay

the cam keeping the contacts open longer and reducing the amount of time the coil has to build a strong magnetic field. The result is erratic timing of the spark or reduced secondary winding output. Several systems which completely eliminate contact breakers are currently on

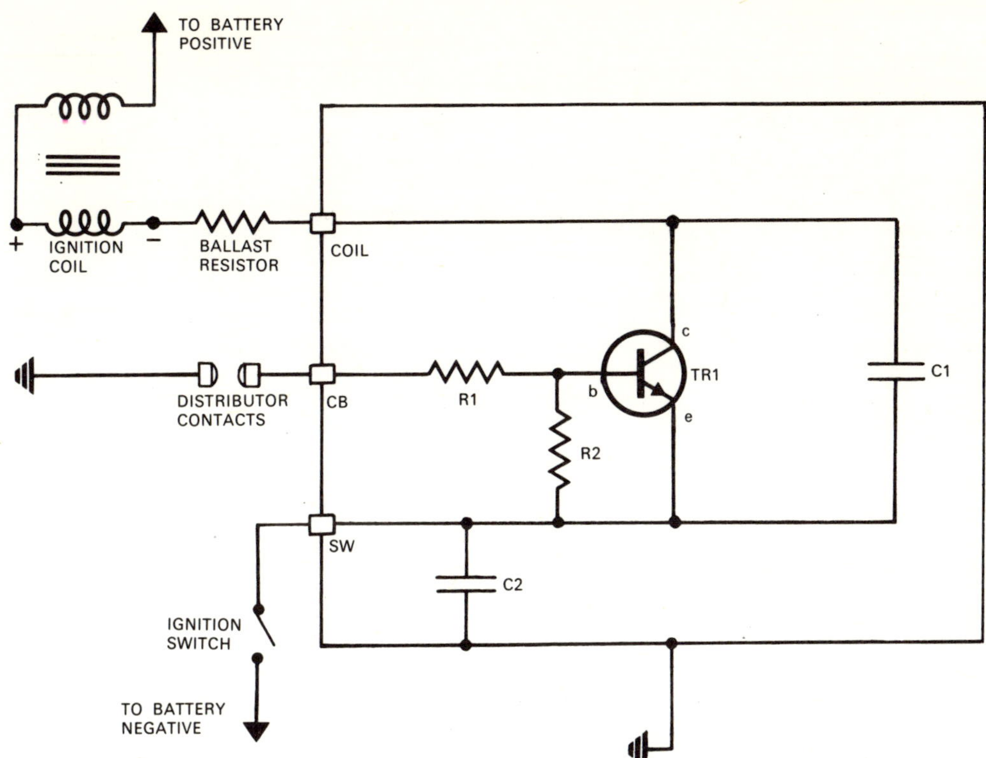

FIG 5:23 Positive earth TAC circuit

the market. In addition, there are many systems which decrease the current load on the points, reducing metal transfer and wear. Ballast resistor ignition systems for reducing cold start problems and five methods to eliminate or reduce wear on contact breaker points are described in the sections which follow.

5:8 Ballast resistor ignition systems

Many modern cars are fitted with a ballast resistor ignition system because use of the starter motor can reduce battery voltage at the primary winding of a conventional system to as little as 7 volts, insufficient to generate a good spark. The ballast resistor coil is designed to operate efficiently at 6-8 volts.

Normal battery voltage of 12 volts is dropped to about $7\frac{1}{2}$ volts by a 2 ohm ballast resistor placed in series between the ignition switch and the low tension terminal on the coil (see **FIG 5:21**). (Some early systems, for example on Saabs, used a resistor between the coil and the contact breaker). The resistor may be in the form of a resistance wire bound into the car's loom, or a small unit fixed on or near the coil.

To give an extra boost to the coil's performance during starting a lead by-passing the resistor is connected from the starter motor terminal of the solenoid to the coil. This has the effect of applying full battery voltage to the coil while the starter motor is operated. Even if the starter motor reduces the battery voltage to about 7 volts the coil will still give a high tension impulse equivalent to its normal output. The battery voltage may not fall as low as 7 volts but the coil is designed to cope with momentary overloads of up to 12 volts.

Delco-Remy Cold-Start systems have an additional unit in the circuit – a relay, switched by the starter position on the ignition switch, supplies by-pass current to the coil (see **FIG 5:22**).

Never use a cold-start, ballast resistor coil in a conventional circuit – the coil will quickly be damaged without the protection of the ballast resistor. Conversely a conventional coil will not operate in series with a ballast resistor.

The resistor normally runs hot and it is advisable to prevent radiator or screen washer water splashing on to it.

5:9 Transistor assisted ignition

Some of the problems associated with use of mechanical contact breaker points can be overcome by performing the switching of the low tension current to the primary winding with a power transistor. In a transistor assisted ignition (sometimes called TAC – Transistor Assisted Contacts) system the contacts are relegated to switching the transistor control current of about 100 milliamps (instead of up to 5 amps) so there is no arcing across the gap and points wear is greatly reduced. The transistor has a very clean switching action, a definite break of the circuit, so the back emf from the coil cannot possibly maintain the primary current and certainly can't arc. So a capacitor is no longer needed. On positive earth systems one transistor can fulfil the ignition switching function but problems of polarity necessitate the use of two transistors for negative earth systems.

Operation of positive earth system:

When the contacts are closed current flows in the transistor's base circuit and the transistor is conductive across the collector and emitter leads, thus the primary winding is energised (see **FIG 5:23**). When the contacts open the transistor becomes non-conductive and the coil's field collapses to produce the high tension impulse. Resistors R1 and R2 reduce the current flowing through the contact breaker points. Capacitor C1 protects the transistor from high voltage surges and capacitor C2 is a radio interference suppressor.

Operation of negative earth system:

Transistor TR2 in **FIG 5:24** is introduced into the circuit to control the switching action of TR1. With the contact breakers closed the base of TR2 is shorted to earth so no current can flow in its collector-emitter circuit. But current can flow via R1 to the base of TR1 which allows the primary current to energise the coil. When the points open TR2 becomes conductive making an easier current path than to the base of TR1 - so TR1 becomes non-conductive and the primary current is switched off.

The major advantage offered by TAC ignition is reduced contact maintenance. A points set will run for up to 25,000 miles without adjustment or replacement. As there is no variation between switching performance in hot or cold engine conditions a constant high voltage spark is obtainable from the coil. There is some truth in the claim that a system of this kind saves petrol - simply because it is possible to neglect distributor maintenance, as so many people do, without deterioration of ignition performance. It is not, however, a panacea for all ignition ills - TAC just maintains peak ignition conditions for longer.

5:10 Capacitor discharge ignition systems

There are several kits on the market offering a form of ignition based on capacitor discharge - two well-known examples are the Mobelec and CD systems (see **FIG 5:25**).

Capacitor discharge ignition systems combine the advantages of a transistor assisted circuit which relieves the contact breaker points of carrying the full primary winding current with a means of stepping up the voltage supplied to the coil primary. Inside the finned heat sink black box, the heart of a typical system, the battery voltage is transformed up to about 400 volts dc while the contacts are closed. The transformed current is stored in a capacitor until the contact breakers open - it is then discharged through the primary winding.

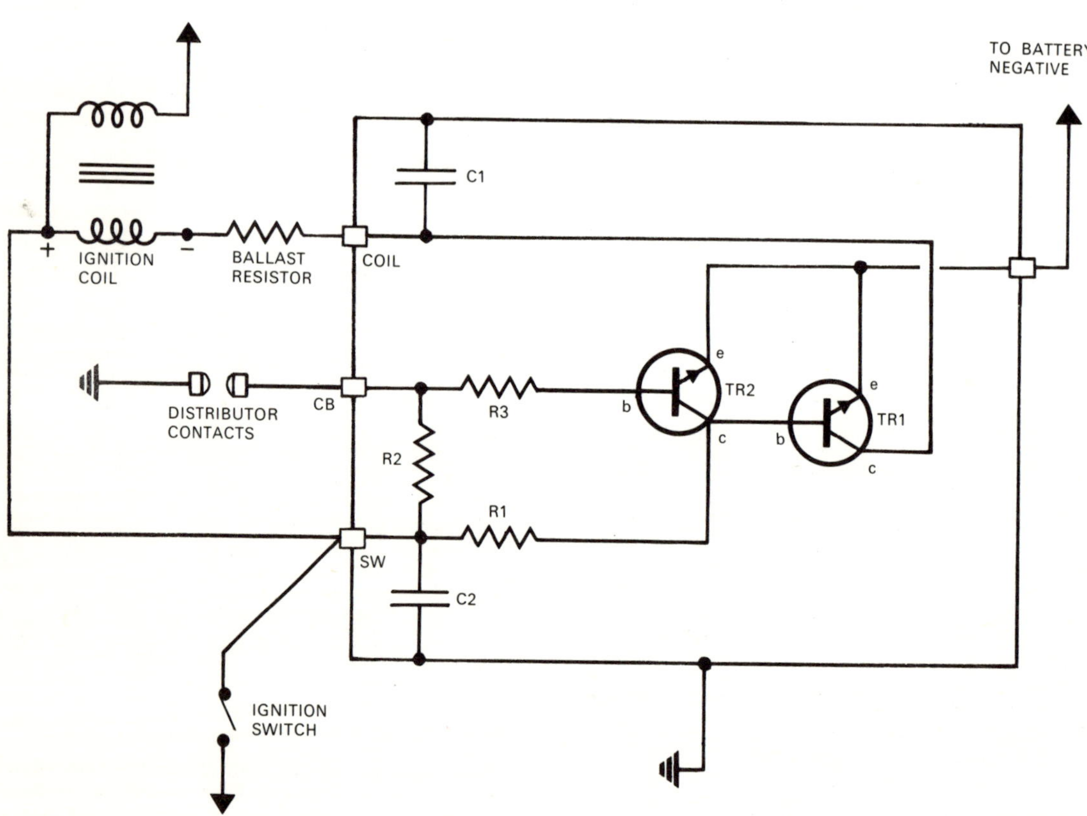

FIG 5:24 Negative earth TAC circuit

The advantages claimed for the capacitor discharge system are an even, high voltage output from the coil secondary winding assisting cold-start conditions with the addition of electronic control of the dwell angle, eliminating the effects of points bounce.

These systems can also be combined with a method of eliminating the contact points altogether, similar in operation to the Lucas Opus system described in the next section.

Capacitor discharge systems can be used with conventional ignition system coils but not with those fitted in ballast resistor systems.

5:11 Contactless ignition systems

Most of the problems associated with conventional ignition systems can be eliminated by a combination of ballast resistor ignition and replacement of the contact breakers by a transistorised (solid state) switching device. Kits offering this advanced principle are available – the best known are the Piranha and Lumenition types.

The Lumenition system shown in **FIG 5:27** fitted as standard to some high performance cars (for example, Jensen) has a simple and elegant method for contact breaker replacement. The distributor cam is replaced by a segmented metal disc (actually clipped over the now defunct cam in a conventional Lucas or Autolite distributor). Fixed to the base plate in place of the contact breaker set is a trigger unit consisting of a semi-conductor light source (gallium arsenide) with a lensed face arranged opposite a photo-transistor (a device that senses light). The main transistorised control unit provides current to the coil primary winding when the light beam from source to sensor is unbroken. But when a segment of the disc rotating on the distributor shaft passes between the light source and photo-transistor a signal passes to the control unit. The unit switches off the current to the coil primary winding causing a spark impulse in the conventional manner.

The advantage of this system is that once the position of the trigger unit is set on the base plate little attention needs to be given to the distributor apart from periodic lubrication and maintenance of the high tension circuit. The ballast resistor coil used with this system gives the normal advantages of good cold-starting performance.

The dwell angle is automatically fixed by the width of the disc's segments – the narrower the segments the shorter time the light beam is broken and the greater the dwell angle. This disc is manufactured to very close tolerances.

The Piranha system varies only in detail from the Lumenition unit. It has a similar light source and photo-transistor trigger unit but in this system the control unit switches off the primary winding current when a slot in the rotating disc allows the light beam to pass from lamp to sensor.

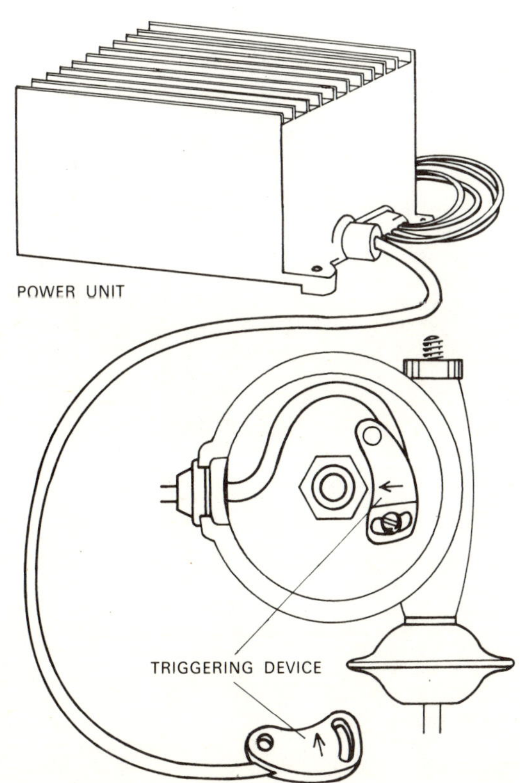

FIG 5:25 Mobelec ignition system

Lucas Opus ignition system:

Jaguar/Daimler V12 engined cars have an ignition system that is specially designed to cope with the problem of high tension distribution arising from the large number of cylinders (also to satisfy emission requirements in export markets). It is a development of the Lucas Opus system, once promised by Lucas as a kit conversion for conventional ignition systems but now exclusively used on these high performance cars. More export models and, possibly, some lower priced UK saloons may shortly be fitted with this system.

The Opus system consists of a special distributor, transistorised amplifier unit, ballast resistor and special Opus coil. The distributor has no contact breakers – switching of the amplifier unit is performed by small ferrite rod magnets mounted round the edge of a nylon disc rotating on the distributor shaft (see **FIG 5:26**). The magnets, one per cylinder spaced at regular angular intervals pass very close to a tiny magnetic pick-up mounted on the base plate.

The pick-up is a transformer – as the magnets pass by a small current is induced in its primary winding, which in turn induces a current in the secondary winding. The current is a signal for the amplifier unit to switch off the coil primary current, triggering the spark impulse in the conventional manner. The distributor also performs its normal function of passing high tension impulses on to the correct cylinder.

British Leyland all-electronic ignition system:

The ultimate ignition system which obviates the need for a distributor is now undergoing development by British Leyland and may be fitted to higher priced saloons fairly soon – although probably on export models only.

It has been widely recognised that emission problems caused by the mechanical aspects of conventional ignition systems (contact breaker maintenance requirements, wear and back-lash in the distributor drive, and so on) can only be overcome by total electronic control of ignition. British Leyland propose a system in which the timing impulses are generated by a light interrupting blade on the clutch or flywheel (in direct contact with the crankshaft) passing between a lamp and sensor mounted on the clutch/flywheel housing. A small integrated circuit computer, with up to 6000 transistor junctions, balances inputs from a vacuum transducer and the light sensor to advance and retard timing according to engine requirements. Coil generation of the high tension impulse is retained but an additional circuit controlled by a transducer on the engine camshaft arranges the distribution sequence probably via relays in the high tension circuit.

5:12 Checking and fault-finding

Ignition system failures are usually very easy to spot. The chart below gives some of the engine symptoms which can be checked by further investigation procedures (detailed later).

Symptom	Probable fault
Engine misfires and is difficult to start	Contact breakers out of adjustment Coil connected with wrong polarity Faulty capacitor Faulty spark plug, high tension connections or plug lead Tracking on one or more high tension leads
Engine cuts out or fails to start	High tension leads and distributor are water soaked Failure of supply to coil or faulty coil Tracking on rotor arm or distributor cap Worn or jammed distributor cap brush
Engine misfires at speed only	Failure of centrifugal advance mechanism Points bounce caused by weakened moving contact breaker spring
Misfire on engine overrun only	Faulty vacuum advance mechanism
Engine 'pinks'	Timing too far advanced

Checking the ignition coil:

1 Ensure that there is a current supply to the ignition coil when the ignition switch is on by a circuit tester connected between coil SW (or + on negative earth cars, − on positive earth cars) terminal and earth.

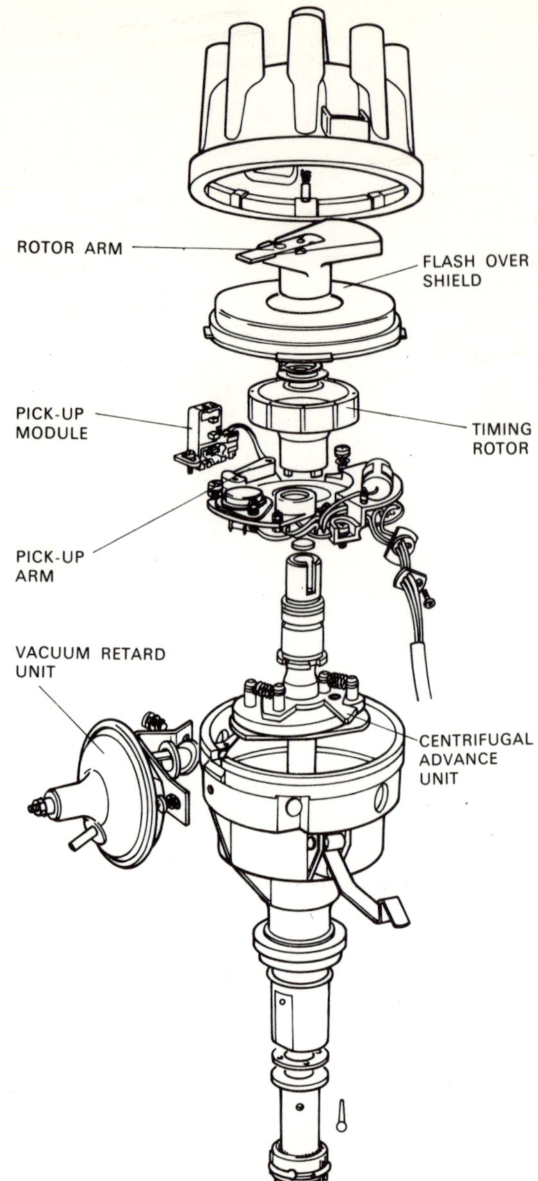

FIG 5:26 Exploded view of Lucas Opus distributor

2 Ensure contact breaker points are conducting current and check continuity of lead to contact breaker by connecting circuit tester in series between CB terminal (+ on positive earth cars, − on negative earth cars) and lead connector. The bulb should light with contact breaker closed.

3 Check high tension output of coil by removing coil to distributor high tension lead at distributor cap and holding bare end of lead near to bare metal of engine block. When the engine is turned (ignition on) by the starter motor

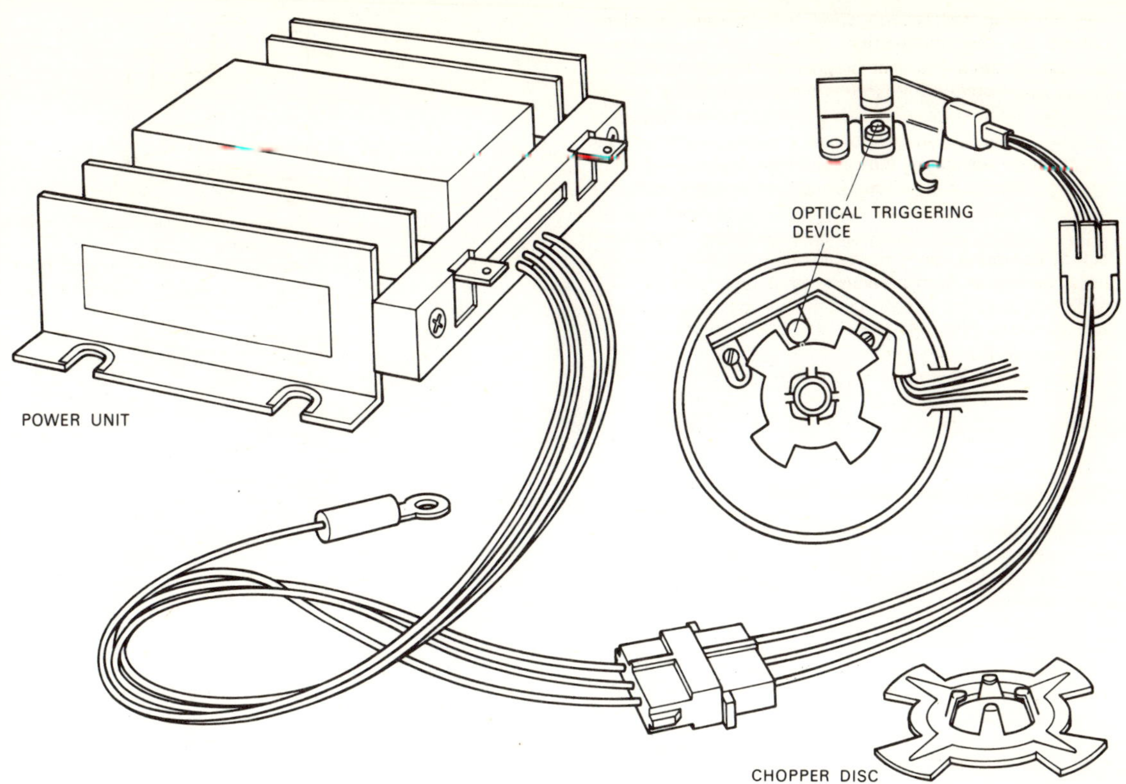

FIG 5:27 Lumenition ignition system

(operate solenoid by hand or have a helper to switch on starter) a fat spark should jump a gap of about $\frac{1}{4}$ inch. A weak spark which will not jump this kind of gap (it may look orange rather than blue in colour) may mean the coil needs replacement, or that there is a fault in the coil-distributor lead. If the low tension circuit of the coil appears to be in order (tests **1** and **2**), substitute a new length of high tension lead from the coil and repeat test **3**.

Checking the high tension circuit:

1 Remove each spark plug in turn and, with lead attached, rest the shell of the plug on a bare patch of metal on the engine. Rotate the engine with the starter and observe if a spark passes. Failure to spark on one plug means a defective plug lead, faulty connection at the plug or distributor cap, or faulty spark plug. Tighten all connections and try a known good plug and lead. Failure to spark on all plugs means tracking on rotor arm, failure of distributor cap brush (it may have jammed in its socket) or tracking in distributor cap caused by dirt, moisture or a crack. Inspect the cap inside and out for cracks, clean and dry it and repeat test.

2 If the fault is not found in the distributor cap check the rotor arm by holding the bare end of the high tension lead from the coil to the cap about $\frac{1}{4}$ inch from the rotor arm and either flicking the contact breakers open or turning the engine on the starter. If a spark is observed the rotor arm is faulty – replace it.

Checking the capacitor:

The best way to ensure the capacitor is operating correctly is to substitute a new capacitor for the suspected unit. The usual clues to a faulty capacitor are pitted and burnt contact breaker points and misfiring of the engine. Capacitors can also fail by short-circuiting the primary coil current to earth – if the contact breakers have no effect on the continuity of current to the coil the fault may lie in the capacitor or its connections.

Reading the condition of spark plugs:

The condition and appearance of the spark plug tip provide important clues to electrical faults, engine condition and carburetter tuning.

Light tan or grey deposits with electrode wear of up to 0.001 inch per 1000 miles indicate good condition.

Dry sooty black deposits on all plugs indicate either weak ignition, retarded timing, low compression or, most usually a rich mixture. If only one or two plugs are in this condition a faulty high tension lead or tracking on the distributor cap can be suspected.

Overheated plugs with white tip deposits and accelerated electrode wear point to over-advanced timing, worn distributor or weak mixture (possibly caused by manifold air leaks).

Short plug life and a characteristic pattern of wear on the earth electrode, which appears dished, indicate reversed polarity of the ignition coil.

One or two plugs with burnt or melted electrodes indicate pre-ignition in the cylinder due to glowing cylinder or piston deposits but can also mean distributor cam or bearing wear.

Oily black deposits on the plugs result from oil getting into the combustion chamber either past the piston rings or down the valve stems. This indicates wear of the components concerned. Some engines have rubber oil seals round the top of each valve stem, and deterioration of these will allow oil to pass down the stem.

5:13 Emergency measures to get you home

The most common on-the-road faults to occur with ignition systems are: water soaked cap or high tension leads; tracking due to deteriorating insulation of the rotor arm, cap or leads; capacitor failure; and loose connections in the high or low tension circuit. An important part of the touring spares kit are the following ignition system items: rotor arm, spark plugs, contact breaker set, capacitor, length of high tension lead. When touring abroad it is also a good idea to carry a spare distributor cap.

In the absence of the appropriate spares the following measures can be taken to make temporary repairs to the ignition system:

1 Tracking in the distributor cap, on the rotor arm or along the outside of high tension leads or plug shrouds can be stopped by cleaning all affected components thoroughly and spraying with a proprietary ignition sealer or hair lacquer. Pay particular attention to cracked components ensuring a thin layer of lacquer covers the split.

2 Wet systems must be thoroughly dried using a clean cloth or paper tissues – final drying might be aided by suspending components over the hot exhaust manifold or the radiator if the engine has been running.

3 Pitted or burnt contact breaker points can, in an emergency, be filed square and regapped – but investigation of the cause of the damage should not be delayed long.

4 A faulty capacitor (the usual value of the capacitor is 0.3 microfarads) can temporarily be replaced by any handy capacitor of near value – such as a 1 microfarad radio suppression capacitor.

5 A faulty high tension lead can be temporarily replaced by a length of low tension lead (with as heavy a current carrying rating as possible) provided it is wrapped thickly with extra insulation for its entire length. A useful insulator is a plastic bag or polythene sheet wrapped tightly around the wire and bound with insulating tape or sellotape. Make sure the temporary lead is kept as far away as possible from earth points.

CHAPTER 6

The lighting system

6:1 Lighting units

Since the motor car was invented one of its systems has attracted more legislation than any other – the lights. They are a foremost safety system of some complexity that affects the driver's ability to perform his task without endangering himself or other road users and, when badly maintained, can dazzle or lure other motorists into accident situations.

The day is long past when the standard lamp consisting of a glass lens protecting a metallised reflector of about 7 inches diameter with separate bulbs for main and dipped beam was universally used. The designers of today's cars can go to a lamp manufacturer and obtain almost any shape or kind of light they require to fit the styling of a new car. Improvements in glass and lamp manufacture and in the technology of bulbs have made this variety of lights possible. Today's motorist is presented with new opportunities to uprate his lighting system from among a bewildering range of accessories and replacement units. In this growth of lamp types the car's lighting circuitry has become more complex and so too have the laws that govern vehicle lighting.

Headlamps:

There are three main methods of lighting used for car headlamps; the double filament bulb (with or without dipper shield), the quartz-iodine (QI) bulb and the sealed beam unit.

Double filament bulb:

Most modern headlamp systems using the old fashioned double filament bulb are pre-focussed. Simply this means that the bulb, conventional twin tungsten filaments inside a glass envelope filled with inert gas, is mounted on a metal flange with a cutaway that ensures exact positioning of the bulb within the reflector. **FIG 6:1** shows a typical bulb.

The main beam filament is located at the focus point of the reflector so that its light is reflected straight out of the lamp in a parallel beam. The dipped beam filament is offset from the reflector centre and slightly above the main beam filament so that its light is thrown down and to the left or right of the road depending on the dipped beam requirements in the country of use. A tiny metal shield, welded to the filament supports, is sometimes used to provide an efficient cut-off of the dipped light beam.

Connections to a pre-focus headlamp bulb may be made by a conventional socket with sprung contacts (older cars) or two or three Lucar type spade connectors. Two connections are for the supply leads to each filament and the third terminal or the metal lamp mounting provides the earth connection.

Main beam power is usually 60 watts and dipped beam power 45 watts – a combination expressed as 60/45w for the purposes of bulb identification. Lower powered bulbs exist – a common light rating on older cars was the 50/40w bulb, and the highest powered bulb in common use is the 75/50w.

Quartz-iodine bulbs:

Quartz-iodine (QI), tungsten-halogen, quartz-halogen: all three names describe a relatively new type of light bulb which consists of conventional filaments mounted in a quartz envelope filled with a halogen gas such as iodine vapour. QI bulbs run at a higher filament temperature than conventional bulbs, and so are brighter,

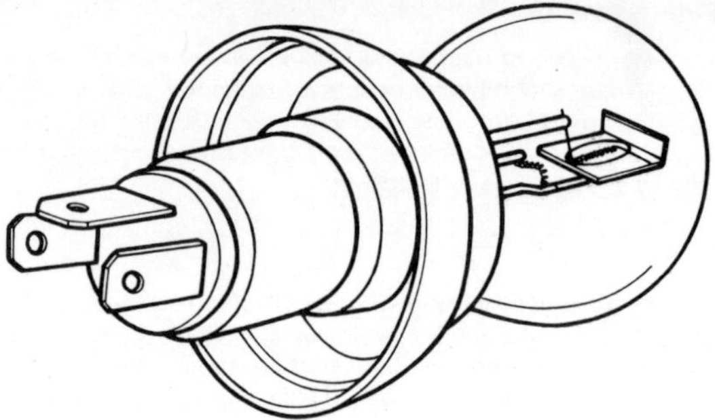

FIG 6:1 Double filament headlamp bulb with shield

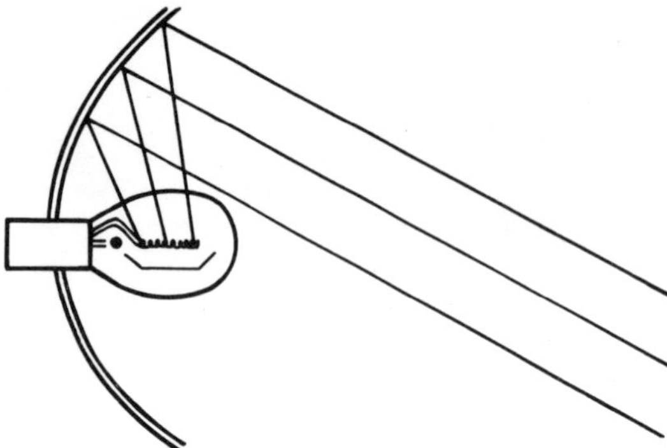

FIG 6:2 Dipped beam light path, shielded bulb

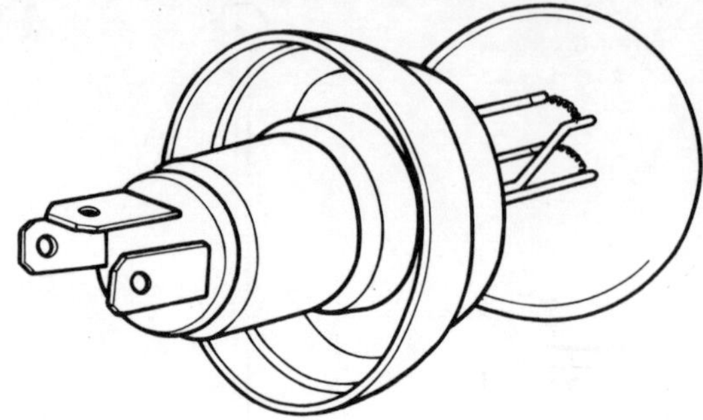

FIG 6:3 Headlamp bulb with offset dipped filament

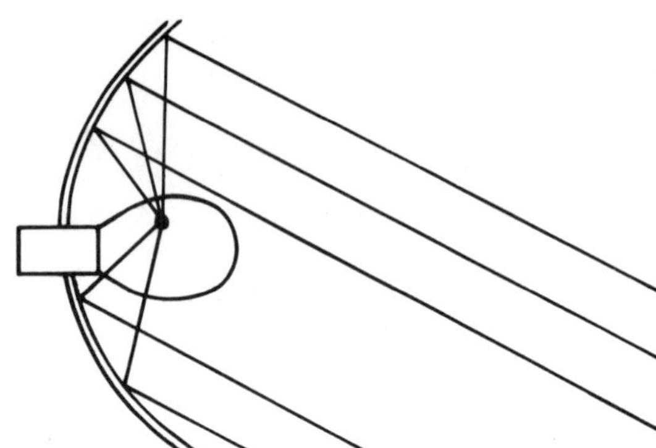

FIG 6:4 Dipped beam light path, offset filament

although the envelope is smaller than a normal glass enclosure. The filaments are prevented from burning out too rapidly by chemical interaction with the gas which also has the effect of increasing the brilliance of the light output and preventing blackening of the envelope.

QI bulbs are pre-focussed, mounted and connected in the same way as conventional bulbs (see **FIG 6:5**).

In replacing or otherwise handling QI bulbs avoid skin contact with the quartz glass envelope. Sweat on the hand can damage the material – handle them by the metal mounting only, or use a clean cloth.

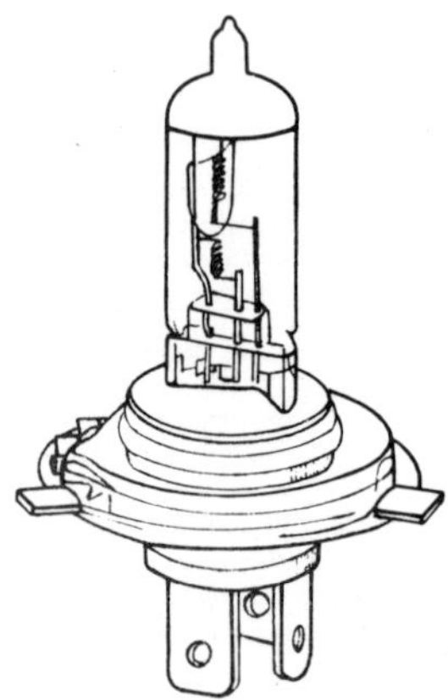

FIG 6:5 Quartz-iodine headlamp bulb

Sealed beam units:

A sealed beam unit is in effect a very large light bulb. It is a complete lamp unit consisting of the lens fused to a metallised glass reflector and containing the two filaments (see **FIG 6:7**). The filaments are not enclosed in a separate bulb. In some units a circle of the glass envelope is left unsilvered to enable a sidelight bulb to shine through.

The advantage of a sealed beam unit is that the blackening of the bulb with age and the almost unavoidable tarnishing and corrosion of the reflector, due to

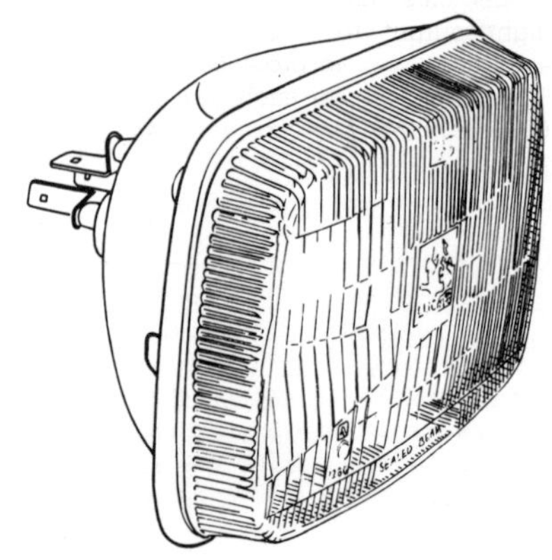

FIG 6:6 Sealed beam headlamp unit

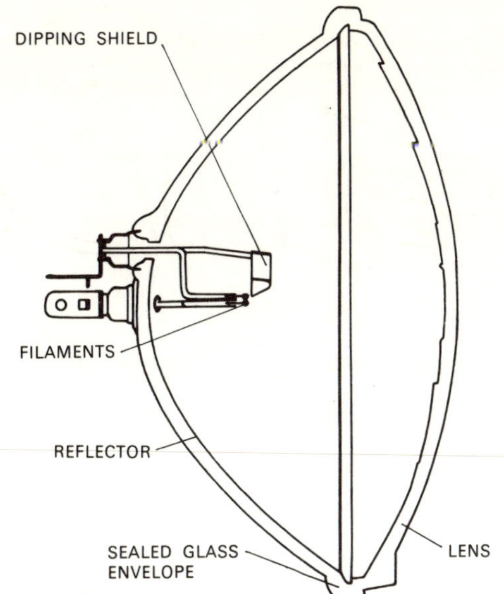

FIG 6:7 Cross-section of sealed-beam unit

ingress of moisture and dirt, cannot occur. A sealed beam unit maintains a high level of light output for far longer than a bulb and reflector combination.

Connections to the sealed beam unit are made in the same way as those to a bulb. The connector block may have a small bayonet or screw socket for a sidelight bulb attached to it.

In instances where a bulb/reflector type headlamp has been superseded by a sealed beam unit on a later model of the car it is very often possible to convert the older headlamps to sealed beam operation.

Like conventional bulbs the commonest sealed beam unit power rating is 60/45w. Sealed beam units are available in many shapes and sizes and a recent development has been to use a QI lamp inside a sealed beam package.

Two and four headlamp systems:

Most cheaper cars have a two headlamp system but greater light output for more expensive and higher performance cars is often provided by a four headlamp system. The outer lamp of each pair gives conventional double-filament dipped beam and main beam output. The inner lamp of each pair is a single high-power filament sealed beam or QI unit designed as a long range driving lamp. This lamp is only switched on when the dip-switch is at the main beam position.

The importance of the lens:

All headlamp units have glass lenses designed and formed to give prismatic correction of the shape of the light beam produced. Simply, the lens prevents scatter of the light, directing the main beam into a narrowly divergent ray and assisting in creating an even spread of light in both main beam and dipped beam conditions. So the lens is important to the efficiency of the lamp.

Sidelights, stoplights and indicators:

Smaller power, conventional single and double filament bulbs with either bayonet or screw fixings are used for the sidelights, stoplights and indicators. The double filament type is used to combine rear lights with stoplights behind a single red reflector unit.

Foglights:

Standard or accessory foglights have a single filament high power bulb, sealed beam or QI unit mounted in a reflector and lens combination that produces a wide beam that is sharply cut-off at the top. This prevents light scatter in fog at the driver's eye level. Some foglights have coloured lens units (often yellow) – there is no convincing proof that this enables better vision in fog. Choice of colour is very much a matter of individual preference.

Spotlights:

Standard or accessory spotlights have a single filament high power bulb, sealed beam or QI unit with a reflector and lens that is designed to throw a pencil beam of light for a long distance with very little divergence.

6:2 Flashing indicators

Modern cars are equipped with flashing direction indicators connected in a circuit that may also include small repeater lights on the door pillar or side of the front wing as well as a single or double facia warning light to show that the system is operating.

The flashing action is performed by a small sealed unit – either a round three connection type or a square type with two connections (see **FIG 6:8**). This flasher unit is usually found on the engine compartment bulkhead or under the facia.

The three-terminal type operates in a slightly different manner to the two-terminal model. In the former, operation of the indicator switch allows a current flow to the right or left indicator lights via a taut resistance wire (see **FIG 6:9**). At this stage the lights do not receive enough current to light because of the wire's resistance. But the current is enough to heat the wire and allow it to slacken. The wire is attached to a contact and the slackening enables this contact to close bypassing the current around the resistance wire. The higher current flow possible when the contacts close lights the indicators and, as the supply also passes through a relay winding, closes a second contact which supplies current to the facia warning light.

But the resistance wire is deprived of current, so it cools, tightens and pulls the contacts apart. This reduces the current to the lamps, which extinguish, and opens the warning light contacts. The switching cycle is repeated at 60 to 120 times a minute until the indicator switch is cancelled.

Two-terminal units normally have the contacts closed so the indicators come on immediately the indicator switch is operated (see **FIG 6:10**). The facia warning light is connected across the right and left hand output terminals of the indicator switch. Its earth return is via the unlit side of the indicator circuit but such a small current flows that the lamps do not operate. Two- or three-terminal flasher units are not interchangeable.

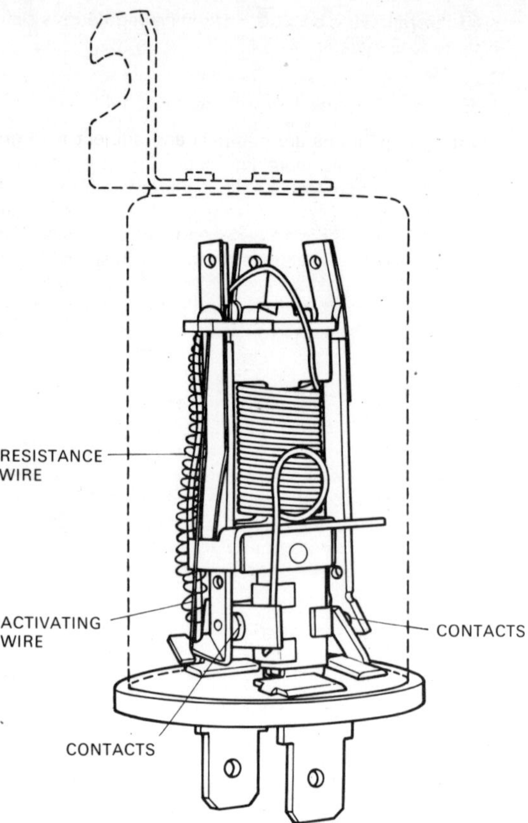

FIG 6:8 Direction indicator flasher unit

Flasher units are only designed to operate for a fixed circuit load. If the power of lamps in the circuit is changed or additional loads are placed in the circuit (perhaps when towing equipment is fitted) a heavy duty flasher unit must be fitted, in place of the normal type.

6:3 Courtesy, boot and bonnet lights

Small wattage lamps of the festoon type, or bayonet or screw capped lamps are used for courtesy, boot and bonnet lights. In most cars the lights are provided with a permanent live supply from the fuse box and are switched on the earth side of the circuit by special contact switches. The switches consist of the earthed mounting, a sprung collar which is a push-fit into the door-pillar, boot lip or bonnet surround, and a moving contact isolated from earth by a plastics collar (see **FIG 6:11**). When the door, boot or bonnet lid is closed a small plunger separates the contacts and the lamp circuit is switched off. When the door or lid is opened a spring pushes the two contacts together and the light comes on. In the case of a courtesy light which doubles as an interior light (most cars) the door switches are bypassed by a switch inside the lamp housing.

Faults in the courtesy light circuit can often be traced to the door pillar switches. They become loose in their socket and make bad earth contact. The loose fit may also allow the plunger to become displaced and bent by the door's closing action – a bent plunger keeps the contacts closed and the lights stay on. A boot light may be arranged to take power from the number plate light supply (in parallel) so that it is only lit at night.

6:4 Uprating a car's lighting

Most lower priced and basic model saloons have minimum power headlamp systems with 60/45w bulbs

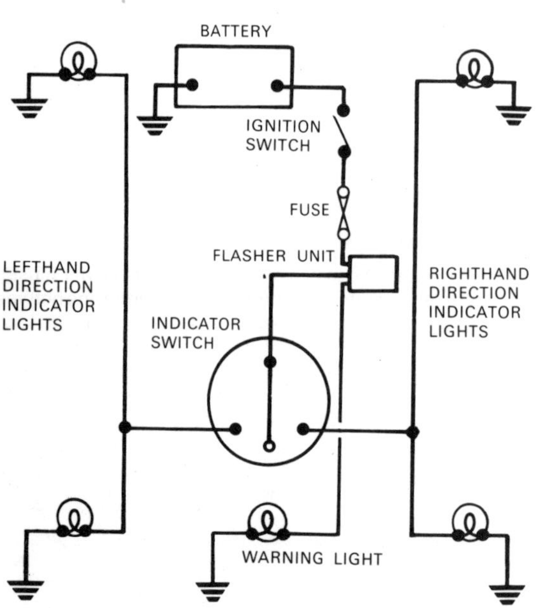

FIG 6:9 Circuit with three-terminal flasher unit

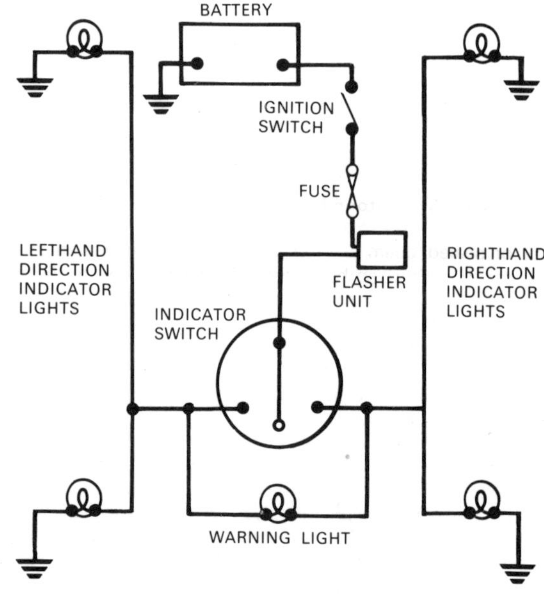

FIG 6:10 Circuit with two-terminal flasher unit

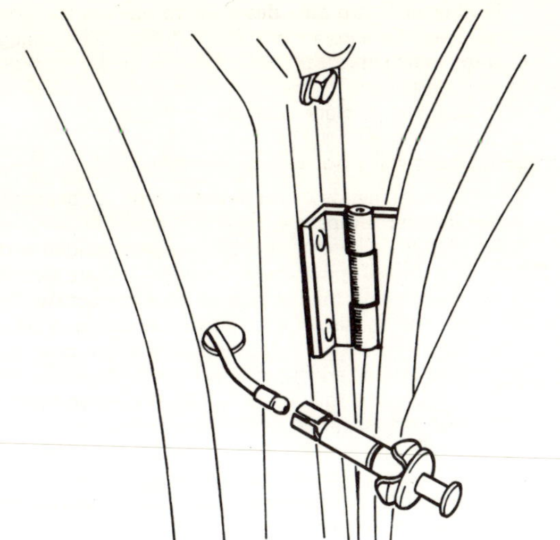

FIG 6:11 Courtesy light switch

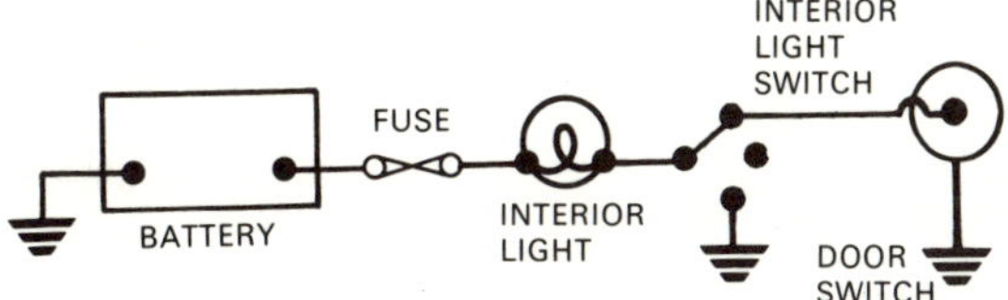

FIG 6:12 Courtesy light circuit

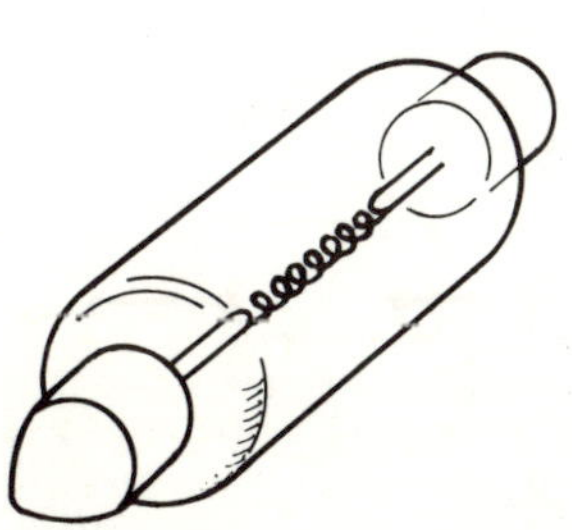

FIG 6:13 Festoon bulb

or sealed beam units. Considerable improvements in a car's lighting can be made by replacing these with more powerful bulbs or sealed beams. For instance most British Leyland cars are fitted with standard 7 inch round headlamps – 60/45w 7 inch units can be replaced by the 70/55w units fitted to the more expensive cars produced by BLMC, such as Jaguars. Most lighting manufacturers and several accessory firms are now marketing quartz halogen bulbs and sealed beam units that are interchangeable with the standard bulbs or beam units on a wide variety of cars. These units are straight replacements for the car's standard fittings – no extra wiring is usually required.

Most keen motorists want to uprate their lighting systems by fitting spotlamps or foglights. The proper way to do this is described in **Chapter 9** but it is essential to read the following section on lighting regulations before fitting auxiliary lamps.

6:5 Legal lighting requirements

Lighting regulations are complex and subject to a great deal of change as more and more European laws are adopted in Britain. In the simple guide which follows the current position is given for vehicles first used on or after 1 January 1974. Vintage cars and other cars used before this date may be exempt from some of these provisions – check with the legal advisers of a motoring organisation, the police or an advice bureau if you are contemplating making changes to a car's lights.

Front lamps:

The law requires every vehicle to have two front lamps. They must be mounted at the same height and if over 7 watts in power the maximum height allowed is 3 ft 6 inch. The centre of each light must not be more than 12 inch in from the vehicle's widest point.

These provisions particularly relate to combined headlamp and sidelight units on modern cars.

Headlamps:

As headlamps are over 7 watts in power the above rule of 3 ft 6 inch maximum height applies with the addition that they must not have centres lower than 2 ft from the ground. The dipped beam must not dazzle at a height of 3 ft 6 inch and a distance of 25 ft. There is no legal obligation to have a left dipping beam provided it does not infringe this dazzle requirement. As well as complying with the requirements for front lamps, headlamps must also be more than 600 mm apart and symetrically placed about the car's centre line to within 25 mm. The outer edge of the headlamps must not be more than 400 mm in from the vehicle's widest point.

The headlamps must be a matched pair in shape, size and colour of light – only white or yellow light is permitted. It is not permissible to have the light at each side under the control of separate switches. At least one filament in each lamp must be over 30 watts. On four headlamp systems the outer pair must give the dipped beam and on dipped beam the inner lights must be extinguished.

Obligatory rear lights:

Two identical red lamps of at least 5 watts power must be mounted symmetrically about the car's centre line between a maximum height of 3 ft 6 inch and a minimum height of 15 inch. They must not be more than 16 inch in from the vehicle's widest point. Two red reflectors must be fitted within the same height dimensions as the rear lamps.

Direction indicators:

The only significant parts of the direction indicator legislation relevant to the car electrician are that the lights must be amber front and rear, each lamp must have a power of between 15 and 36 watts, and the rate of flashing must be between 60 and 120 times per minute.

Direction indicators must at all times be maintained in a clean condition and in efficient working order.

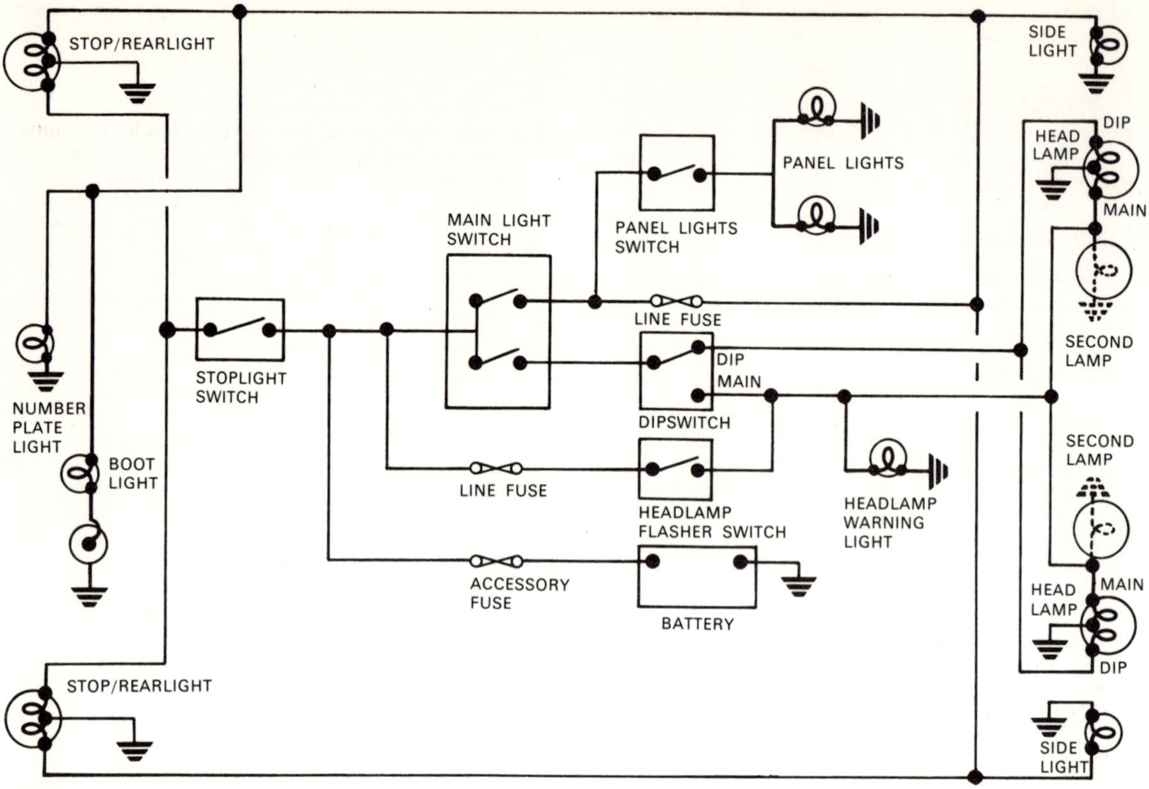

FIG 6:14 Lighting system circuit diagram

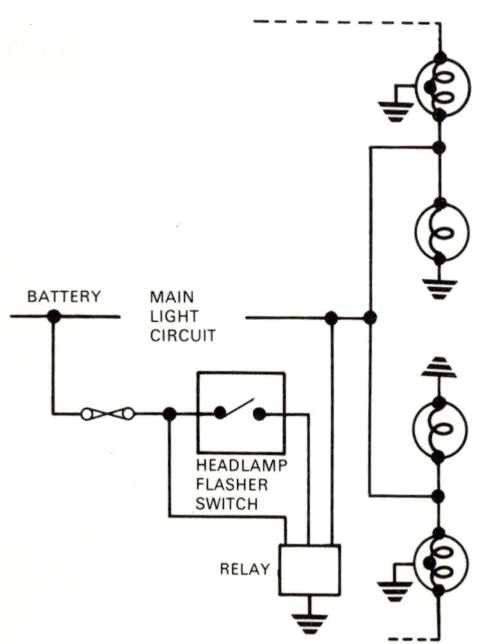

FIG 6:15 Headlamp flashing circuit with relay

The use of hazard warning flashers is permitted only when the vehicle is stationary as a result of a breakdown, accident or other emergency.

Stop lamps:

Two red stop lamps of a power between 15 and 36 watts must be fitted a minimum of 600 mm apart, not lower than 400 mm from the ground and not higher than 1500 mm at the rear of the vehicle.

Foglights and spotlights:

Auxiliary lamps fitted below 2 ft from the ground can only be used in fog or falling snow. They can only be used in place of headlights if they comply with the headlight regulations. Maximum height above ground for auxiliary lights is 3 ft 6 inch. There is no necessity to fit auxiliary lamps in matched pairs. However, single lamps can only be used in conjunction with the car's headlights.

Reversing lights:

No more than two reversing lights are allowed, of maximum power 24 watts each. The lights must be operated by a gearbox switch or panel switch (in which case a facia warning light must be used to warn when the reverse light is on). Lights must not dazzle an observer at 3 ft 6 inch height and 25 ft distance. The lights must only be used for reversing the vehicle.

Registration plate light:

A light capable of illuminating the rear number plate (maximum power 7 watts) must be fitted in such a way that the light itself is not visible from the rear.

6:6 The lighting circuit

On most cars the main lighting system is fed by a direct supply from the battery/generator usually taken from the live side of the starter solenoid, fuse box, or control box (see **FIG 6:14**). Headlamp circuits are not normally fused – the safety advantages of circuit protection are outweighed by the necessity to prevent extinguishing of the lights. If a fuse is fitted it is usually of the thermostatic interrupter type (see **Chapter 1, Section 1:7**) used on some Vauxhalls – it does not fail altogether but gives adequate warning of a fault and allows a reduced current flow to maintain flickering lights. There may be a line fuse provided to protect the sidelight circuit.

Stoplight, indicator lights and courtesy light current supplies are taken from the car's main fusebox. Stoplights and indicators are supplied from the ignition switched fuse (accessory fuse) while courtesy lights are connected to the non-switched fuse.

Switching in the main light circuit is in two stages. The main light switch usually has two positions for sidelights only and for headlamps. On most modern cars the dip-switch and headlamp flasher is combined into a single stalk switch mounted on the steering column. (Older cars may have separate switches – many cars used to have a floor mounted dipswitch). The stalk switch may also control the direction indicators.

Wires connected to the switch are combined into a multiple spade connector under the facia or in the plastics housing on the steering column itself. The switch is complex with many contacts and if it is faulty it is not usually repairable – an expensive replacement is the only answer. Self-cancelling for the indicators is normally provided by means of an adjustable height spur on the steering column which engages with a sprung arm on the direction indicator portion of the switch. Rotation of the spur past the sprung arm in the return direction of the steering wheel after a corner is taken flips the indicator switch into the off position.

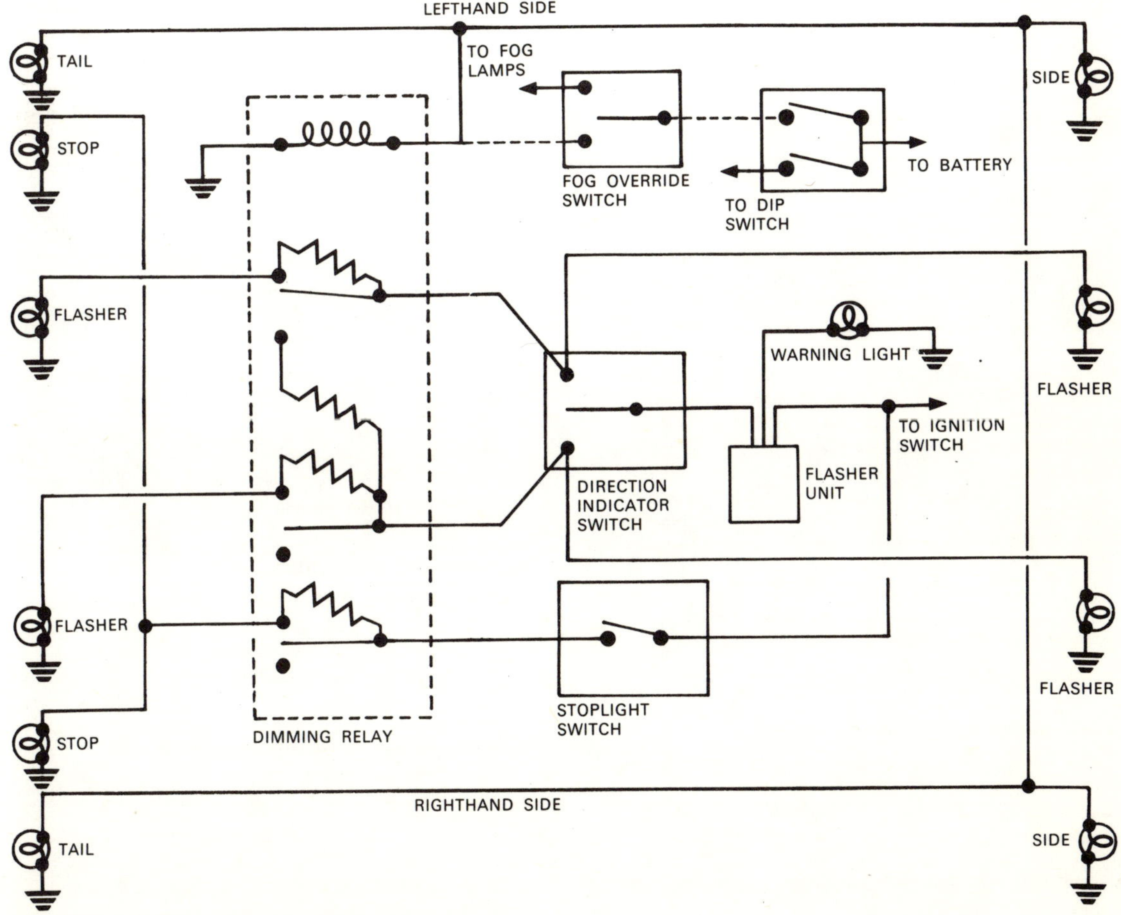

FIG 6:16 Two level signalling system circuit

Two types of headlamp flashing circuit are in use on today's cars. In one a pull-up or push-down of the stalk switch connects the main beam of the headlamps directly with a battery live supply point thus bypassing the action of the main light switch. But on four headlamp systems the current demand of four main beam filaments is very high – a minimum of 20 amps. This current could damage switch contacts so the headlamp flashing circuit is protected by a relay.

Some two headlamp systems also employ this means of protecting the headlamp flashing switch.

The stoplights are operated by a switch linked in some way to the braking system. At one time the switch was commonly connected by a spring to the brake pedal linkage; such a switch would be inside the car under the facia, in the engine compartment or even under the floor where it was exposed to the elements and prone to corrosion and jamming.

A few makers – Toyota for one – fit a push button switch under the brake pedal. But more often the switch is mounted above the arm of the brake pedal and operates rather like a courtesy light switch: depressing the pedal releases the switch plunger which moves under spring pressure to make contact. This type of switch can often be adjusted so that it is actuated by the lightest touch on the pedal.

The other common type of brake light switch is a unit installed in the hydraulic brake line which is sensitive to the system pressure. It can usually be found low down on the engine compartment bulkhead on the master cylinder below the brake fluid reservoir or at the junction where the brake lines to the front and rear separate. These hydraulic switches are usually very reliable.

Some cars are now being fitted with a two level signalling system, the aim of which is to reduce unnecessary dazzle at night. During the daytime the direction indicators and brake lights operate at full intensity in the usual way. When the side or headlamps are switched on for night driving, current is also fed through the winding of a multiple contact relay. This switches the supply to the direction indicators and brake lights so that they are fed through small resistors and operate at lower intensity (see **FIG 6:16**). In some cases there is also a manual fog override switch so that the driver can select full signal brightness while the headlamps are in use in conditions of bad visibility.

Circuit connections throughout the lighting system are of the bullet type – often four-way bullet connectors are used for the junctions between lighting cables. Some of the connectors at the front of the car behind the radiator grille are exposed to road dirt and moisture. When checking circuit connections (see **Section 6:8**) it is advisable to start by examining these connectors.

6:7 Lighting system maintenance

Check that all the car's lights are operating before setting out on a journey, at rest halts on long journeys and, in any case, at least weekly. Checking brake lights and indicators on one's own is tedious – save time by looking for the lights' reflections on a wall or the garage door. (During the journey check these lights by their reflection on a following car).

Clean the surface of lenses and reflectors front and rear regularly especially in winter when road dirt can cut down their efficiency by over 60 per cent. Stubborn grease and tar deposits on a headlamp lens can be removed with a petrol soaked rag.

Headlamp cleaning equipment to wipe or wash road dirt off lenses is already mandatory in Sweden and may become so throughout Europe in a few years time. There are several accessory kits on the market consisting of a rotating brush or wiper blade fixed to the headlamp lens and driven by a small motor. Washer jets mounted on the bumper or front apron are supplied from the screen wash bottle or a separate reservoir by a screen wash pump. The kits are a useful addition to the car's safety equipment.

Headlamps must be maintained in adjustment especially if the loaded condition of the car raises or lowers the headlamp height. Most garages have an instrument like the Lucas Beamsetter to assist accurate setting of the lamps at regular service intervals – a beam test is also a part of the annual DOE test procedure. Lamps are best set using this instrument – home beam setting using the procedure below should only be undertaken when it is impossible to reach a garage with the proper equipment.

Carry out beam setting before any long heavily loaded journey (especially holiday trips or when towing a caravan). Try to get the car loaded as nearly as possible to the condition for the journey before setting the beams even if it means a trial loading of the car and a trip down to the garage for the whole family.

Home beam setting procedure for emergency use only:

1 Run the car as close as possible up to a plain wall on level ground.

2 Mark the wall with points corresponding to the centre of the headlamps.

3 Draw two large crosses through the centre marks on the wall.

4 Reverse the car 25 ft away from the wall in a straight line.

5 Remove the headlamp trim – one screw usually holds the surround on round lamps but some round and square lamps require removal of the whole front grille for access to adjusters.

6 Switch on the headlamps to main beam and cover up one lamp while making adjustments to the other.

7 There are two or three adjuster screws round the circumference of each light. On three screw adjusters only two, at the top and one side, should be used. Turn the

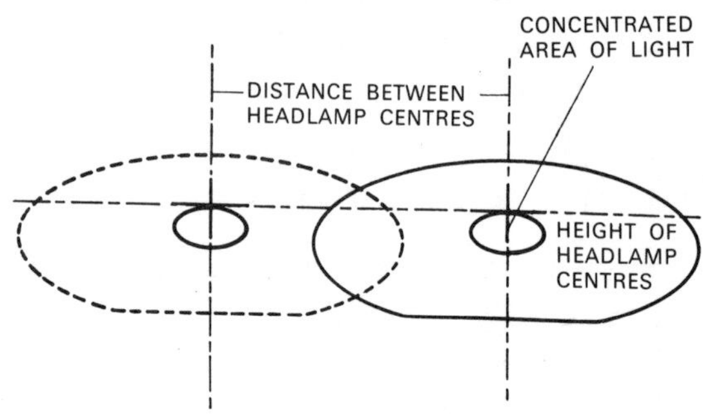

FIG 6:17 Wall marks for emergency beam setting

screws slowly to bring the brightest patch of the light on the wall just below the horizontal line of the cross. The bright patch must be centred on the vertical line (see **FIG 6:17**).

8 Repeat the procedure on the second lamp. Replace the headlamp surrounds ensuring that they do not foul the lamp and alter the adjustment. Once the main beam is set the lamp design ensures that the dipped beam is cast down and to the left.

Modern rectangular lamps tend to have a more evenly diffused beam than round lamps so it is very difficult to pick out the brightest spot in the beam. These lamps are best set at a garage which will use the sharp cut-off of the dipped beam to set the lights very accurately indeed. Four headlamp systems must be set using the beam-setting instrument.

Some European cars (Renault, Citroen, Wartburg) have dashboard, front grille or under-bonnet headlamp adjustment levers. For the purposes of complying with the law it is wise to use them only when it is strictly necessary to adjust the beam for an unusual load condition.

Continental motoring:

Plain or yellow coloured plastics lens units can be obtained to change the British left hand dipping pattern to European right hand dipping. The lenses clip over the front of the lamp under the trim surround. Most modern tungsten filament sealed beam units have a peg moulded into the lens front on which the dipping lens can be located. The plastic lenses should only be used for lamps of the symmetrical type.

Some modern tungsten lamps and most quartz-halogen units are of the asymmetrical type – the dipped beam rises at the left hand side to show more of the road edge or pavement. Plastics dipping lenses should not be used with these lamps – a special adhesive film can be obtained to obscure the raised part of the beam to prevent dazzling oncoming left hand traffic.

Both these methods of modifying the dipped beam are not really satisfactory for long periods abroad – the lenses cut down light transmission and the adhesive reduces dipped and main beam efficiency. Dealers for the specific model of car should be able to supply right hand dipping bulbs or sealed beam units to replace the British lamp – bulbs are obviously a cheaper solution than sealed beam units.

On some Continental cars – Renault, for example – the lamps can be changed from left to right dipping and vice versa simply by repositioning each bulb slightly in its holder; a movable locating peg is provided for the purpose.

6:8 Lighting system fault-finding

Headlamps:

Headlamp failure is usually a result of filament breakage. Bulbs can be removed for inspection of the filament – blackening of the bulb is often a sign that a filament has burnt out but it is normally possible to see the break. It is not so easy to see filament breakage in a sealed beam unit – use a low wattage test lamp in series with a battery connected across the earth and each terminal in turn to determine if there is a break in the dipped or main beam filament.

If the headlamp fails completely (usually only one filament will blow) and the bulb or sealed beam unit appears serviceable check the connections to that lamp from the terminals of the lamp (spring contact type lamp connections may have an insulated washer that has failed in which case the short circuit will be revealed by dimming of all lights) back to the bullet connector on the main lighting loom.

Dimness of both headlamps can signify a poor earth connection in one of the lamps – the current destined for one filament is leaking back through the common connection of the other three filaments and reaching earth through the opposite lamp. This effect frequently occurs when the bulb mounting of one lamp becomes corroded.

Total headlamp failure (uncommon) indicates a fault in the supply lead to the main light switch or between this and the dipswitch – it may be a blown fuse if one is fitted. Try a new fuse of the correct rating – if this blows there is a short circuit or the circuit is overloaded (perhaps by fitting accessory lamps or higher rated bulbs).

The combined stalk lamp and dipswitch can be removed from the car and each of its switching functions tested separately using a test bulb in series with a battery connected across the input and output leads.

Sidelights, rearlights and stop lights:

Again bulb failure, usually betrayed by blackening of the glass, is a common fault with the sidelight, rearlight and stop light circuit. Bad earth connections are found in the same way as with headlamps – the other lights in each circuit may glow dimly. Total failure can mean a blown fuse – fuses can blow because of old age but the usual cause is a short circuit to earth. Likely shorting places are inside the bayonet light socket (note that twin filament rear/stop lights can only be replaced in the correct position because the bayonet pins are staggered on the bulb mounting), and inside the boot where abrasion and damage to sockets and loom due to bad loading is common. Corrosion of contacts or connectors is the other likely trouble.

Check the stoplight switch by shorting out its terminals with a screwdriver blade or a short loop of wire. If it is a faulty hydraulic switch carry out a full flushing and brake bleeding procedure after fitting a new unit. Stop light switch leads occasionally short and/or get tangled and damaged by brake pedal linkages.

Indicator lights:

Flasher units are not very reliable components and should be the first item in the circuit to be checked if the light bulbs prove to be serviceable. Slow flashing, fast flashing or a single short glow from the warning lamp when the indicator switch is operated are indications of bulb failure. Check the flasher unit by shorting together its B and L connections – the indicator lights should then come on when the indicator switch is operated.

Failure of the indicator switch to cancel may be a fault in the switch itself. Remove it and investigate – a common reason is that the spur on the steering column has become loose or out of adjustment. When replacing or readjusting it, make sure the lock nut is done tightly. Occasionally a loose spur will also cause damage by breaking off one of the spring cancelling arms on the switch – switch replacement is the only cure. It is illegal to carry on flashing after turning a corner, although a cancelling mechanism is not mandatory.

Courtesy, boot and bonnet lights:

After checking the bulbs the most suspect component in the courtesy, boot and bonnet light circuit is the frequently flimsy interior light switch itself or the door and lid switches which may fail completely or operate intermittently. Total failure to operate may indicate that a line fuse has blown somewhere in the circuit – line fuses in this circuit, like those in the side/rear light circuit tend to be tucked away in the most obscure places. The holder may be behind the facia but it has also been known to be fitted behind the roof lining and occasionally inside the windscreen pillar trim.

Checking fuses and circuit connections:

It is often difficult to find the fault which is causing a fuse to blow. The simplest method, which can be performed at the cost of one or two fuse cartridges, is to disconnect all the outgoing wires connected to the faulty fuse, fit a new fuse and with all the car's systems turned on refit each wire to the fuse in turn. Note the wire replaced when the fuse goes and find out, either from its colour code or the failure of some accessories, what its purpose is. Confine further checking to this circuit.

Failures in circuit connectors are equally frustrating – there are often so many bullets in the lighting circuit. However, by careful reference to the faulty component and the wiring colour code it is possible to identify the bullet connectors associated with a particular circuit. Switch on the faulty circuit and use a sharp probed circuit tester to check the input and output on each connector in turn. The circuit tester should be connected between earth and the wire entering the connector. The probe must be pushed into the wire insulation to make good contact – contacting the connector itself is not a sufficiently definitive test.

Panel light failures:

Panel lights are normally reliable low wattage bulbs connected in parallel with the sidelight circuit. However, because of their location on the instrument module they are often inaccessible to the home electrician. Replacement can require removal of the printed circuit card which forms the instrument wiring on modern cars. This is a skilled job often best left to a garage. However, if it appears possible to gain access to the lamp socket, the usual way of fixing the bulbs into the back of an instrument is by a small cap with a bayonet-type fastening. A pushing and turning action will free the bulb. It is sometimes necessary to uncouple the speedometer cable and the oil-pressure gauge thin bore pipe to gain access to the instrument module.

6:9 Emergency measures

Strictly speaking it is illegal to drive a car without its full complement of obligatory lights in working order – however, it is a reasonable defence to be aware that the light is defective and to prove that some action is being taken to rectify the fault. The only good insurance against the possibility of lighting system failures is to carry a spare set of bulbs – one of each type on the car. Spare fuses, bullet connectors and a length of wire capable of carrying full headlamp current (up to 25 amps) are essential for emergency repairs to the car's lighting circuit. Here are a few first-aid measures:

1 After a minor accident. If the lens units on stop light and indicator lights are broken but the bulbs are serviceable cover the lights with paper or cellophane of the appropriate colour – mainly to prevent dazzle to following drivers.

2 After a major accident. It is important to switch off the lights as well as the ignition after a major accident because damaged bulbs or leads – especially at the rear of the car – may short on the bodywork and cause sparks which could set light to petrol vapour.

3 If the outer sealed beam unit, headlight or rearlight fails and no spare is immediately available, swap the defective unit for the good unit from the other side of the car – it is always best to show lights on the offside of the car.

4 If a fuse blows and the fault is not apparent – track down the circuit causing the problem by the procedure suggested above and isolate that circuit by disconnecting the wire from the fuse box, taping it to one side and also disconnecting the lamp or other consumer unit from the other end of the lead.

CHAPTER 7

Auxiliary equipment

There are many electrical devices in the car that do not constitute separate electrical systems – they are auxiliary units and present individual problems of maintenance, repair and fault-finding. In this chapter the main auxiliary equipment units are described and where it is possible to carry out any repairs they are described. Unfortunately many of these units are sealed or the individual components are not available on the market for the home electrician.

7:1 Horns

Most cars are fitted with a simple unrepairable horn (or a pair of horns). The operation of a horn is similar to that of the solenoid.

A typical horn consists of an iron plunger centrally mounted on a spring steel diaphragm. The plunger is free to move inside a coil fed with current via a pair of contacts. One is a fixed contact and the other is sprung so it is moved by the diaphragm or plunger. When the coil is activated by pressing the horn push (often spring contacts inside the steering wheel or a part of the combined headlamp dipswitch or indicator switch) the plunger is attracted into the coil and the contacts part. This deactivates the coil and the plunger returns with the spring reaction of the diaphragm. The cycle is repeated at a speed dependent on the resonant frequency of the diaphragm, a factor determined by the diaphragm size and the way in which it is mounted. It may be several thousand times a second.

There are many variations in horn circuitry. On the majority of cars the horn button provides a return to earth. But to work efficiently the horn requires a fairly high current and this can cause arcing at the horn push contacts. Some manufacturers overcome this by connecting the horn via a relay.

Horn relays can be of two types having three or four terminals. In the three terminal type the low current magnetic winding is supplied via an internal connection to the battery supply terminal with a return to earth via the horn push. British relays have terminals labelled C2 (battery), W1 (horn push) and C1 (horn). On four terminal types the W1 terminal is to the relay winding supplied via the ignition switch and a W2 terminal provides the return to earth via the horn push. The C2 terminal is supplied separately from the battery auxiliary fuse and the C1 terminal connects to the horn. Refer to the car's circuit diagram for the connections on other cars.

There are also considerable variations in the design of the horn itself. The cheapest kind simply has a diaphragm bolted or riveted to the cylindrical horn body. A type known as the wind-tone horn has an additional trumpet to refine the clarity of the note produced by the vibrating diaphragm. Both types may have a screw which can be used to alter the travel of the plunger and hence the volume and frequency of the sound emitted.

Air horns – often fitted as an accessory – have an air pump unit connected by plastics tubing to a number of horns. The horns consist of a vibrating diaphragm mounted across the orifice of a trumpet. The size of the diaphragm and the trumpet control the volume and frequency of the sound emitted.

Legal aspects of horns:

It is a legal requirement for a car to have an audible warning of its approach and location. The electric horn is the most practical way of fulfilling this requirement.

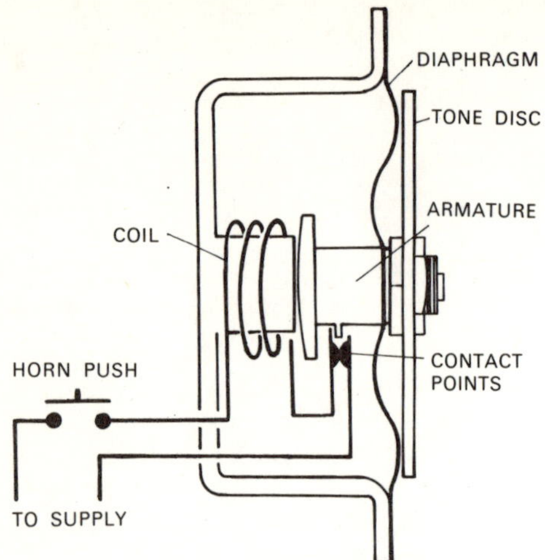

FIG 7:1 Cross-section of a typical horn

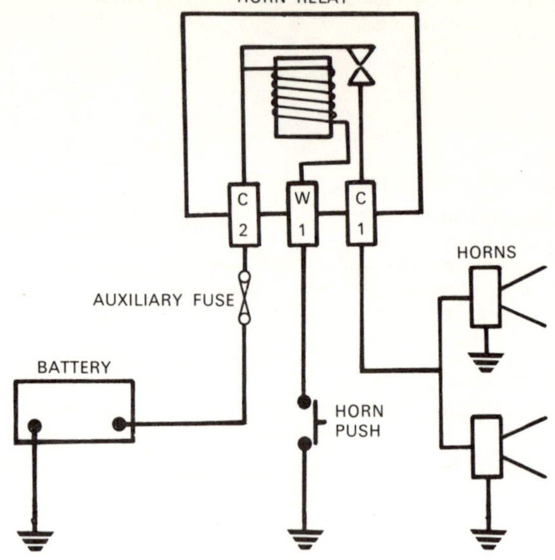

FIG 7:2 Horn circuit with three-terminal relay

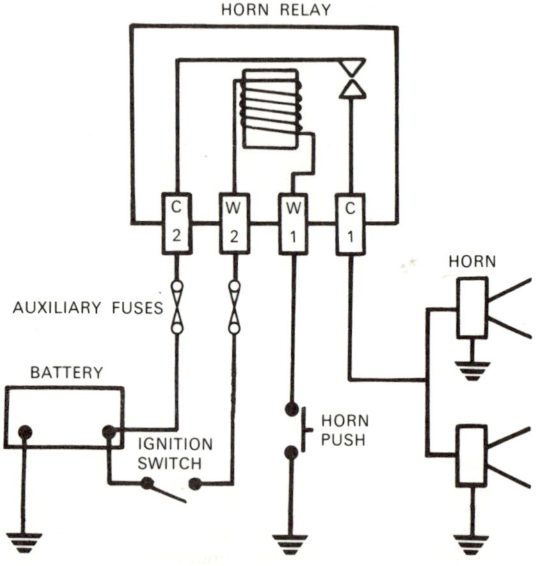

FIG 7:3 Horn circuit with four-terminal relay

The horn's sound must be continuous – that is, the use of horns (particularly air horns) emitting two or more tones is restricted to the simultaneous emission of the two sounds – horns that play tunes are forbidden.

The audible warning on a car must not sound like the gongs, bells, sirens and two tone horns allowed for police and other emergency vehicles.

The use of horns is banned from 23.00 hrs at night until 07.00 hrs in the morning and when the vehicle is stationary (this restriction does not apply when the horn is used as part of an anti-theft system – see **Chapter 9**).

A curious legal necessity is that the horn must not be strident – although how a horn is able to fulfil its warning function without being strident has yet to be defined in the courts.

Fault-finding in the horn circuit:

The horn is generally a very reliable unit despite the fact that it is usually mounted at the front of the car and often exposed to the elements. The commonest fault that occurs is corrosion of the horn terminals.

Check, clean and remake all the circuit connections and if the fault still persists use a circuit tester to investigate the continuity of the horn supply. Remember that to check the operation of a relay it will be necessary to have a helper to operate the horn button.

If it is the horn itself that is faulty it is much cheaper to replace it with a unit from a scrapyard provided that the part is tested before purchase. A horn relay is sealed and, if faulty, must be replaced by a new unit.

7:2 Windscreen wipers

There are numerous types of windscreen wiper motor – some have permanent magnets, others electromagnetic field windings and a few have a combination of both types. Add to this the two main methods of producing two speed operation, two types of wiper drive and several basic parking switch types and it can be seen that opening up a wiper motor is like taking the lid off Pandora's box – it is difficult to guess beforehand what will be found. The service and stripping procedures described below refer to Lucas motors. On cars in which it is possible to strip wiper motors – many sealed units are used on modern vehicles – the designs will not vary greatly from those described.

Wiper drive:

Two methods of wiper drive are used to transmit movement from the motor to the wiper arms. One type is the spring rack, a stiffly coiled but flexible spring moving to and fro in a guide tube, acting on gears fixed on the wiper arm spindles. A worn gear or rack can be cured by:

1 moving the rack so that the gear bears on an unworn part, or **2** turning the wiper arm spindle so unworn gear teeth mesh with the rack.

The other type of drive employed is a rigid arm linkage moved by a crank on the motor drive shaft. Rigid arm types are usually unrepairable.

Wiper motor types:

Permanent magnet. Most recent windscreen wiper motors are of the permanent magnet type. That is, two permanent field magnets are mounted inside the motor's circular casing. The motor's armature is supplied with current by two brushes fed from the ignition switched fuse via the wiper switch.

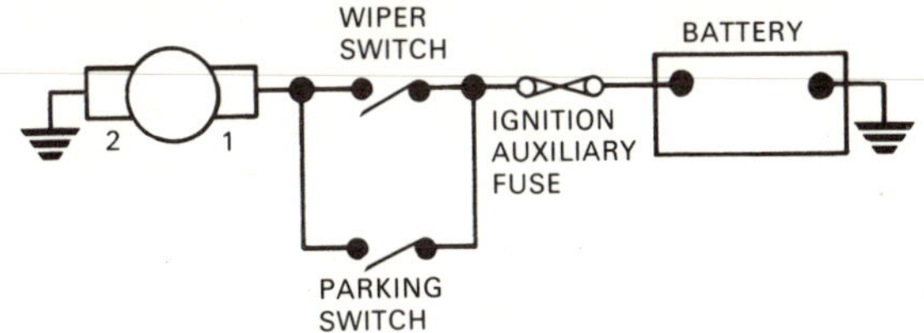

FIG 7:4 Circuit for two-brush wiper motor

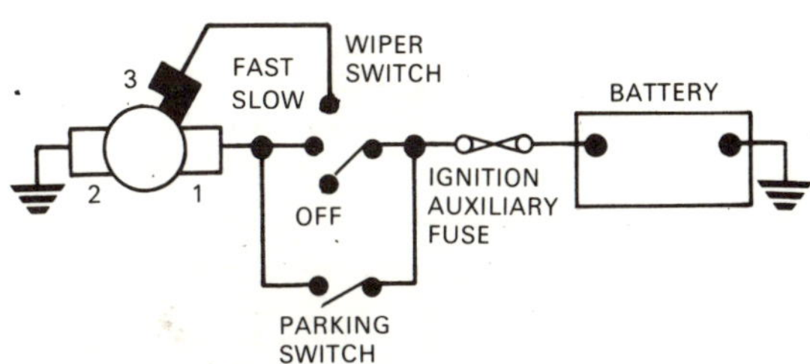

FIG 7:5 Circuit for three-brush wiper motor

On single-speed, two-brush types the brushes are arranged facing each other on each side of the commutator. In two-speed, three-brush types the additional brush is set at a small angle to one of the other brushes. To get a higher motor speed current is switched to this third brush from an additional position on the wiper switch. The high speed brush may be distinguished by the fact that it has a narrower tip than the other two brushes.

Shunt field type. On some modern and many older types of wiper motor the field magnets are electromagnets connected in parallel with the current supply to the armature.

A two-speed motor of this type has a resistor which is connected in series with the field winding by an additional position on the wiper switch.

Parking or self-cancelling switches:

Most modern wipers are provided with a parking facility. There are many types of parking switch – all perform the same function of maintaining current supply to the wiper motor after the main wiper switch has been switched off but only until the wipers reach the park position. The small parking switch may be operated from the action of the

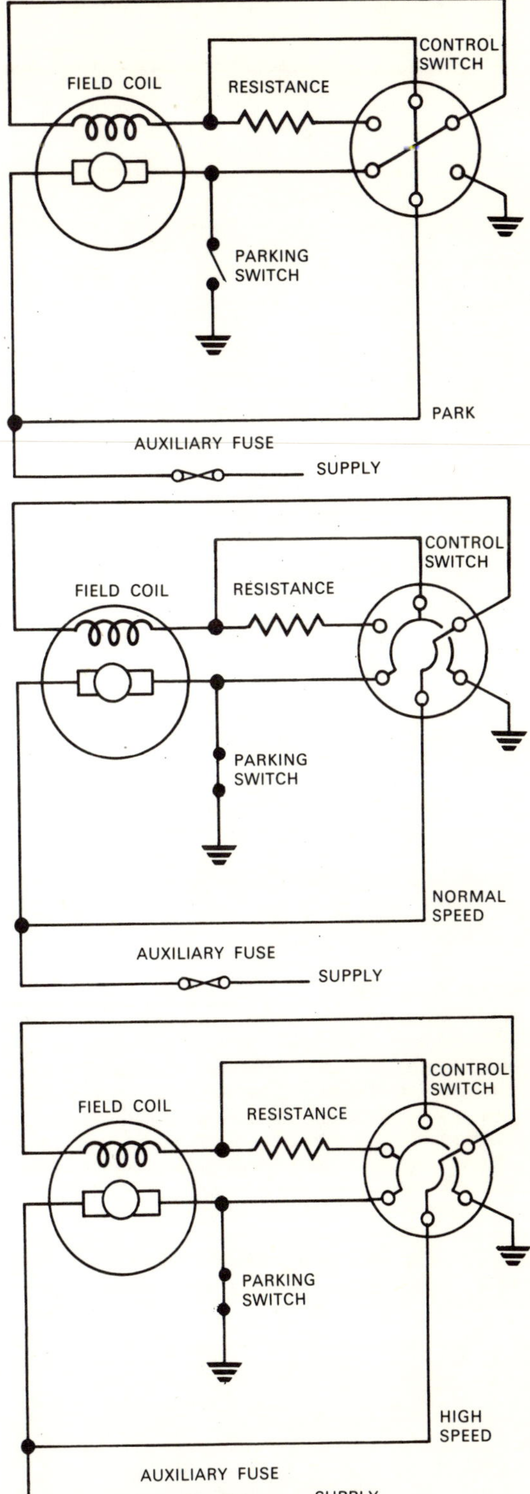

FIG 7:6 Two-speed shunt field wiper motor circuit

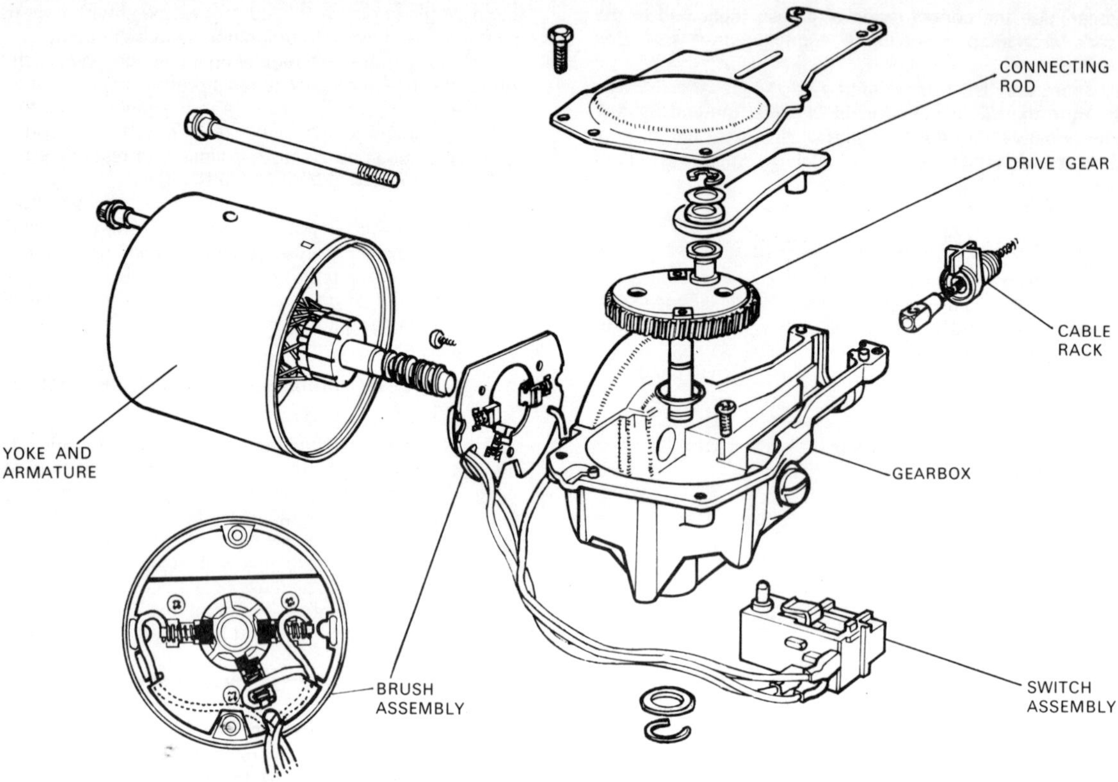

CONNECTING ROD
DRIVE GEAR
CABLE RACK
YOKE AND ARMATURE
GEARBOX
BRUSH ASSEMBLY
SWITCH ASSEMBLY

FIG 7:7 Exploded diagram of a wiper motor

rack drive, by the crank on the main motor drive gear or by a small cam built into the drive gear. It may be found in the rack drive housing, on the drive end plate of the motor or inside the motor terminal block.

Stripping the wiper motor:

Wiper motors are often tucked away in the most inaccessible parts of the car – under the facia or in the top corner of the engine compartment. Refer to the car manual for the method of removal.

On the work bench the procedure for stripping a typical wiper motor is as follows:

1 Before removing components of the wiper motor, score or otherwise mark them so they can be replaced in the right position.

2 Undo the motor securing bolts or screws (they may be at either end of the motor. Older Lucas shunt field (square body) types have a twin brush set at the opposite end of the motor to the drive gear box – pull off the end plate to gain access to the brushes. On some permanent magnet motors the motor casing comes off in one piece and the end plate armature and wiper drive can be inspected as a single unit. On other motors it may be necessary to strip out the drive gear box to gain access to the motor casing bolts. Ensure that the motor's field magnets do not pick up metal particles while the motor is stripped.

3 Inspect the brushes for signs of wear – they should be at least 5 mm long (the high speed brush, if fitted, must not be worn down to the extent that the full brush width is in contact with the commutator). If the brushes are worn replace them – spares are not widely available but will probably be obtainable from a vehicle electrician. A hard grade of solder should be used to reconnect new brushes.

4 Inspect the commutator for pitting or burning. If necessary clean the commutator with fine glass paper.

5 Check the operation of the parking switch using a circuit tester in series with a battery. Renew it if it is faulty.

6 Check the bearings of the motor by placing the armature shaft in the bearing and attempting to rock it. If any play is felt the brass bush bearings will have to be chipped out carefully and new ones pressed into place with a vice. Check that new bushes are available before damaging the old ones. Thoroughly soak new bushes in oil before insertion.

Reassembly is the reverse of stripping ensuring that all parts are replaced in their original relationship to each

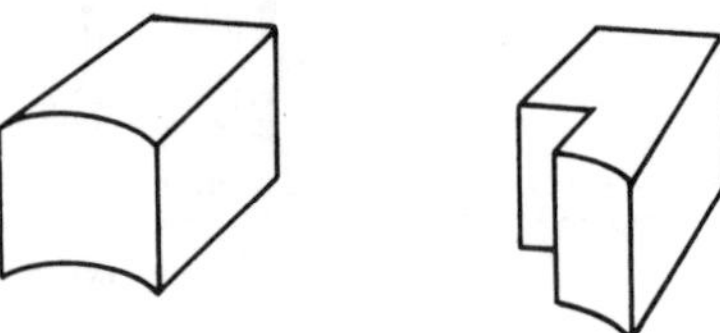

FIG 7:8 Brushes, normal and high-speed (right)

other. Use the correct grade of grease (specified in the car's workshop manual) to lubricate the gear box components.

There may be a screw acting on the tip of the worm gear on the drive shaft – this is to adjust the end float of the armature. Try not to disturb it. If a new armature is fitted consult the workshop manual for armature end float adjustment.

Fault finding in the wiper motor circuit:

Before checking the wiper motor circuit ensure that the car battery is providing enough current (i.e. it is reasonably well charged) and that the wiper blades are not sticking to the glass or windscreen surround. Further checks:

1 Using a circuit tester in series with a battery check the operation of the main wiper switch.

2 Check the continuity of wiper supply wires.

3 If the car's workshop manual gives the current demand of the motor check it with an ammeter in series with the motor.

4 Disconnect the rack or rigid arm drive and ensure the motor operates correctly – if it does the fault lies in the drive to the wiper arms.

Overload protection in the wiper circuit:

Sticking of the wiper blade to the glass (perhaps by icing) or operation of the wipers against a heavy load of mud or snow can overload the wiper motor to the extent that it burns out. A few cars have a thermostatic interrupter in the wiper motor circuit which ensures that if the motor temperature builds up the current supply is switched off. The contacts of the interrupter quickly close once the motor cools down and normal operation is restored.

7:3 Fuel pumps

Electric fuel pumps are electromagnetic devices in which a pumping diaphragm is operated by the action of a plunger free to move inside a coil. When the ignition switch is on the coil is energised and the plunger pulls on the diaphragm drawing petrol into the pumping chamber from the tank. But the plunger's movement also opens the supply contacts and the coil is de-energised. The plunger and diaphragm return by spring action and the petrol is expelled via the outlet valve.

The pump is usually sited on or near the petrol tank (under the car or in the boot) but may sometimes be found on the engine bulkhead. It is supplied with current via the unfused side of the ignition switched circuit.

Fuel pumps are self-regulating in action. When the carburetter float chamber is full the float chamber inlet valve closes and due to pressure in the fuel line the fuel pump diaphragm spring cannot fully return the plunger. As a result the contacts do not close and reactivate the pump until fuel can again flow in the line.

These details and the servicing notes which follow apply to the ordinary pump of the type fitted in a carburetter fuel system. A fuel injection system incorporates a high pressure pump which runs continuously while the ignition is switched on. Usually it is a rotary pump driven by a small permanent magnet electric motor.

Maintenance, stripping and repair of the electric fuel pump:

Many modern electric fuel pumps are sealed units and it is often more convenient to replace the entire unit than to repair it, even when this is possible. The following stripping procedure applies mainly to the SU type of fuel pump. Others vary only in detail.

Carry out pump removal in a well-ventilated space and keep away from naked flames.

1 Disconnect the battery and then the pump's power supply – also the earth lead and insulating rubber cap (if fitted).

2 Disconnect the inlet and outlet petrol pipes – plug the pipe from the petrol tank using a bolt or dowel.

3 Undo the pump fixing bolts or bolt.

4 Undo the terminal nut and remove the plastics end cap.

5 Inspect the condition of the points for burning or pitting – if necessary clean them with a points file or glass paper. This can only be a temporary measure – worn points usually mean replacement of the whole unit.

6 Remove the valve assembly retaining ring. Carefully take out the inlet valve cap, sealing ring and then the gauze filter. Ensure it is not blocked. Remove the valve are carefully wash the valve and filter in petrol.

7 Repeat the procedure with the outlet valve.

8 Refit all components and test the pump in situ. If it still does not operate and the circuit checking procedure in the next paragraph has been carried out to ensure that the pump supply is normal the best solution is to fit a new pump. It may be possible to obtain a new diaphragm and valve parts for some older pumps but it is likely that a failure of these parts will be accompanied by considerable points wear.

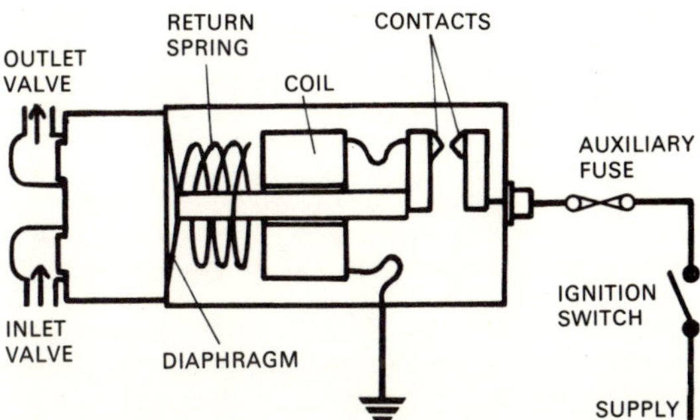

FIG 7:9 Diagram of electric fuel pump

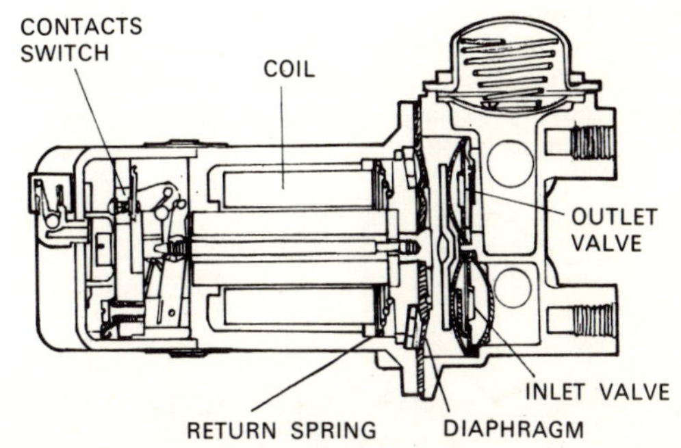

FIG 7:10 Cross-section of SU fuel pump

Checking the electric fuel pump:

1 The pump clicks as it operates. Turn on the ignition switch and listen for a rapid succession of clicks that slows down until the fuel line pressure builds up enough to stop the pump entirely.
2 A further check whether or not the pump is operating is to switch on the ignition and remove the inlet petrol pipe from the float chamber. Petrol should well up from the pipe if the pump is operating correctly; catch it in a suitable container to minimise the fire risk.
3 Check for continuity of the pump's electric supply by disconnecting the supply lead at the pump and connecting a circuit tester in series between the bare wire and earth. The test lamp should glow. If it doesn't, check back along the supply for continuity.
4 Check the continuity of current through the pump by connecting the test lamp in series between the supply lead and pump supply terminal. The light should glow. If it doesn't, remake the earth connection and try the test again. If the pump does not operate now the contacts are probably faulty.
5 Having checked the contacts are operating the fault probably lies in the valve or diaphragm mechanism.

Stuck contact points can sometimes be cleared temporarily by light tapping on the pump body.

7:4 Heated rear windows

Many cars are now supplied with a heated rear window as standard equipment. The heating filament is a special type of printed circuit fused into the glass surface during manufacture. The filaments are quite delicate and it is wise to avoid placing parcels on the rear window shelf in case accidental contact scores or breaks the thin conducting material. Take care when cleaning the inside surface of the window – diamond or metal rings can damage the filament.

Repairs to heated window filaments are best carried out by a garage who use a special kit to seal the broken ends of the conducting material and form a new conducting pathway.

Heated rear windows are high current consuming items (up to 10 amps) and are supplied via a switch (with parallel warning lamp) from the fused side of the ignition switched power circuit. Connections to the window are usually by Lucar spades tightly trapped under the window surround. Take care that these do not bend and break off. On hinged windows the supply wire and earth return are led into the main body of the car in a protective plastics or rubber sleeve – grommets protect the points where the sleeve and wires pass through the window surround and car body.

Circuit checking is simply a matter of ensuring continuity in the supply circuit. Particularly check the insulation of the sleeve mentioned above and that the Lucar connections are firmly made.

Clean heated rear windows with a soft, clean cloth – use of a proprietary windscreen smear solvent or car glass-cleaner is advisable. Do not use an abrasive cleaner (or gritty rag) on the filament side of the glass.

7:5 Heater fan motors

The heater fan motor is often as inaccessible as the wiper motor, tucked way under the dashboard or inside heater trunking. Refer to the car workshop manual for the means of access and removal. The motor is usually a small permanent magnet unit with a conventional fan or radially slotted blower fixed on the drive shaft. It is supplied with current via the blower switch from the fused side of the ignition switched circuit.

It is not usually possible to repair a fan motor – if faulty it should be replaced as a unit. Remember to remove the fan before exchanging the faulty unit as few replacement motors are supplied with fans fitted.

Checking of the motor circuit is confined to ensuring continuity in the supply lead and earth connections. Remember that transposing the connections (or changing the car's polarity) may make the motor run backwards so that the fan blows in the wrong direction.

7:6 Automatic gearbox override switch

Automatic gearbox fitted cars have an override switch to prevent operation of the starter motor except when the lever is in the N or P positions. The switch is connected in series between the ignition switch and starter solenoid. It may be operated by the movement of the automatic gear lever or it may be fitted into the gearbox casing. Refer to the car handbook or workshop manual to find its location.

The switch can fail either open or closed. The symptoms will either be that the starter motor won't operate (there will be no current supplied to the solenoid) or that it will be possible to start the car with the lever in a drive position. The latter failure is potentially dangerous and should be rectified at once.

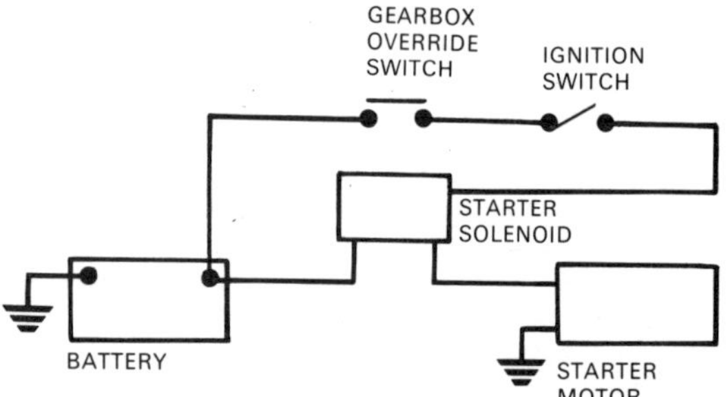

FIG 7:11 Automatic gearbox override switch circuit

7:7 Electric windscreen washers

A small electric pump fitted adjacent to the windscreen washer bottle (or to the bottle cap) is used to pump water for windscreen washing on many cars. The pump is supplied with current via an extra position on the wiper switch (or a separate push button) from the fused side of the ignition switched circuit. The pump is sealed and, if faulty, must be replaced by a complete new unit.

In addition to being fitted as original equipment, such pumps are available as accessories for fitting to cars equipped as standard with manually operated washers. They can be fitted in conjunction with an existing water container so that the switch and wiring are the only modifications required.

CHAPTER 8

Instruments and warning lights

At one time car dashboards were crowded with instruments and lights showing everything from oil and fuel pressure to the battery charging current and engine revs. But car manufacturers began to think these were expensive luxuries so basic models appeared with nothing more than a petrol gauge and a speedometer. Higher priced saloons may have temperature and oil pressure gauges, sports models have rev-counters. Now the facias of today's cars are becoming cluttered with ever more warning lights for low oil pressure, low petrol, choke, handbrake and unfastened seat belts. A few of the car's gauges (like the oil pressure gauge) are essentially non-electrical but in the following sections warning lights and those instruments which are electrical or electronic are explained and if they have an urgent message the clues are spelt out.

8:1 Bi-metal strip instruments

Two basic types of electrical instrument are in use on cars – the bi-metal strip unit and the magnetic type. The bi-metal strip instrument is the cheapest and crudest and it follows that in mass production cars it is the commonest type found. It has two advantages – it is slow reacting so that it will not flicker in response to the car's vibrations and road movement and it is reasonably robust and reliable. This type of instrument is used for temperature gauges, petrol gauges and battery condition indicators.

The instrument is a sealed unit and is rarely worth repairing but a simplified account of its operation is useful.

The needle of the gauge is attached to a bi-metallic strip around which is wound a heating coil. When current passes through the coil the bi-metallic strip heats up, bends and moves the needle with it. The amount that the strip bends, and hence the needle's movement, is proportional to the current flow through the coil.

For temperature and petrol gauges the current supply to the instrument is fed from the accessory fuse which is ignition switched. From the instrument the current passes to earth via a sender unit. In the case of a water temperature gauge the sender unit, tapped into the engine block near the thermostat, consists of a thermistor device. This has a high resistance at low temperatures and the resistance falls as the temperature rises. Thus at higher temperatures the current flowing through the gauge rises and the needle is deflected more.

In the case of the petrol gauge, a sender unit fixed into the side or top of the petrol tank is used. The unit consists of a float on an arm which is attached to the moving contact on a variable resistor. As the petrol drains out of the tank the float falls and it is arranged that the resistance is raised. This lowers the current flowing through the instruments and the needle deflects downwards.

This simple principle of operation would be very accurate if it were not for one additional factor – the car's system voltage goes up and down as the generated voltage increases and decreases with engine speed. The gap is as much as 2.4 volts between battery and full generator voltage if the car has an alternator. Of course the higher the voltage the greater the current that would flow in the instrument heating coil giving rise to considerable inaccuracies in readings.

The answer is the voltage stabiliser unit used exclusively to limit the voltage applied to bi-metal type instruments.

The voltage stabiliser is another bi-metallic strip application. But instead of moving a pointer the stabiliser

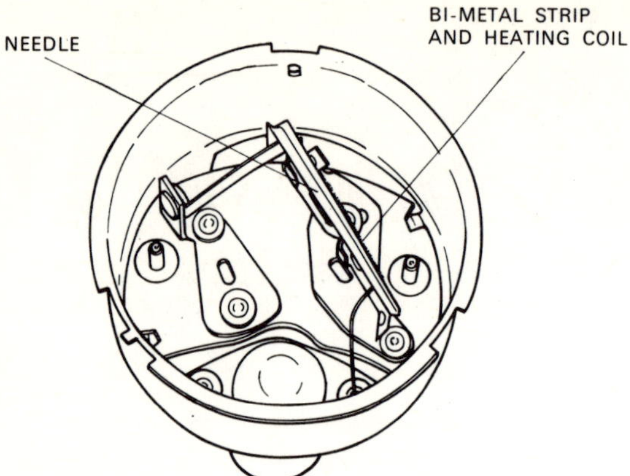

FIG 8:1 Mechanism of bi-metal instrument

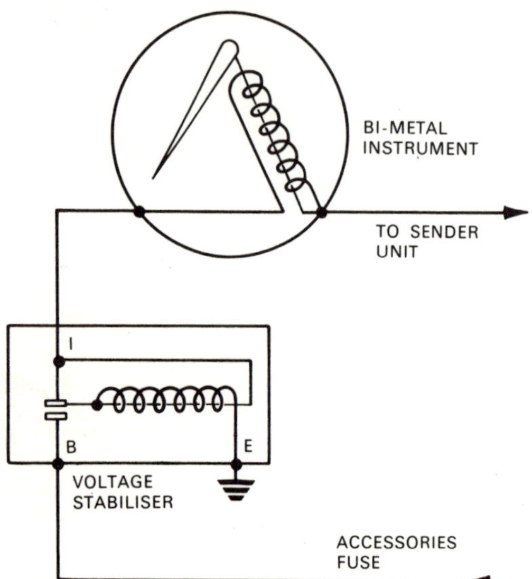

FIG 8:2 Circuit of bi-metal gauge with stabiliser

strip's bending parts two contacts and cuts the current supply to itself and to the instruments. The strip then cools down, closes the contacts and restores the supply. The rate at which the stabiliser operates depends on the voltage output from the battery and generator – it is a relatively slow cycle of events compared to the voltage regulation in the control box. Since the instruments themselves have a sluggish action, momentary rise and fall of the voltage has no effect on the reading – it is the average voltage that counts. Most stabilisers are designed to give an average voltage of 10 volts.

8:2 Magnetic instruments

Older cars were fitted with magnetic instruments – the difference between these and the bi-metal type is easy to spot. The magnetic instruments give an instant reading when the ignition is switched on – bi-metal types

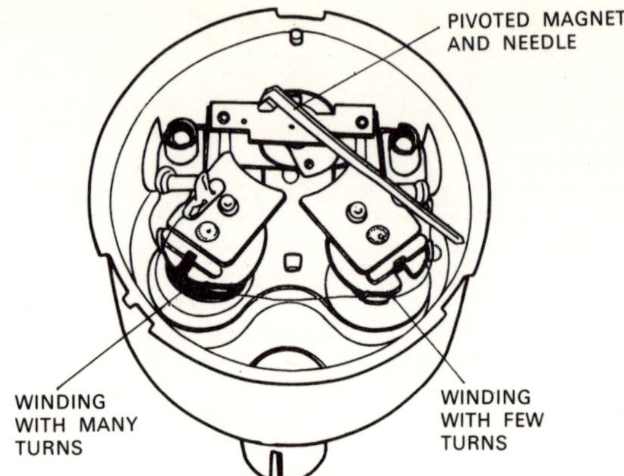

FIG 8:3 Mechanism of magnetic instrument

have to warm up and the gauge deflection occurs very slowly.

Magnetic instruments contain two coils, one with a few less turns than the other, arranged each side of the needle which is pivoted and balanced against a coiled hairspring.

Current from the accessory fuse enters the instrument at a centre tap between the two coils. It flows through the smaller coil to earth and through the larger coil to the sender unit (temperature sensor or petrol tank float). The lower the resistance of the sender unit the nearer the current flowing through the larger coil comes to equalling the current flow through the small coil direct to earth. Even though the current in the sender coil is lower the larger number of windings ensures that the magnetic effect it creates overcomes that of the smaller coil and attracts the needle across the scale. No voltage stabiliser is required for this circuit because the greater magnetic effect created by higher current flows at increased voltages is evenly applied to each coil.

8:3 Fault-finding and repair

Petrol gauge:

To test the gauge disconnect the wire from the sender unit on the petrol tank. (Access to the tank may be via the boot floor, side, or rear panel, under the car or under the rear seat.) With the ignition on, connect a circuit tester between the end of the wire and a good earth point for a second or two. The lamp should light to show the gauge circuit is continuous – the gauge will also move, so arrange that a helper watches it. If this test is negative repeat it at the back of the instrument to ensure the connecting wire is continuous.

If the fault proves to be in the sender it has to be replaced. This should be possible without moving the petrol tank. Disconnect the battery, drain the tank of as much petrol as possible. Work in a well-ventilated space and ensure that there are no naked lights or potentially arcing electrical connections anywhere near.

Three types of petrol gauge sender fixing are widely used – screws on a retaining ring, interlocking lugs or a coarse screw (like a jam jar lid). Carefully undo the fixing and remove the faulty unit.

Clean off the old gasket materials, fit a new gasket (it

is a good idea to use a proprietary gasket sealing compound suitable for petrol contact) and fit the new sender unit, reconnecting the sender lead. Ensure that the fixing is as tight as possible. Do not reconnect the battery or start the car until all petrol around the work area has evaporated.

If the instrument itself has failed (less common) the job of replacement depends very much on the type of instrument fitted. Many gauges are clipped or otherwise fixed onto the back of the speedometer so the dial shows through the speedometer face. Some older units are easily replaced, others will have to be taken to a vehicle electrician or an agent for the make of car. Sealed instrument modules and printed circuit connections make the job harder – again a vehicle electrician's help is called for. The easiest instrument to replace is the separate gauge type. This can simply be removed from the facia and a new instrument fitted into the mounting.

Temperature gauge:

The commonest fault in the temperature gauge system is at the sender unit, which although robust, operates in far from ideal conditions of fluctuating heat. Deposits of rust, dirt and water scale sometimes affect its operation. Check the continuity of the gauge circuit from the wire at the sender to earth and also check the continuity through the sender using a small battery in series with the test light. The temperature operation of the sender can be checked by unscrewing it from the engine block (which may allow some coolant to escape), rigging a lead to the known good indicator and a second lead from the body of the sender to the car body. Dip the sender in a bath of near boiling water – the gauge should read hot.

A new sender is easily fitted in place of the old one – a wipe of gasket sealer or high temperature grease on the threaded shank aids watertight sealing.

The job of gauge replacement is subject to the same restrictions as for the petrol gauge.

Voltage stabiliser:

A fault in the voltage stabiliser can be spotted if both bi-metal gauge readings are erratic or if by eliminating possible faults in the gauges, wiring and senders this is the only possibility. Some voltage stabilisers are mounted inside a sealed instrument unit; some are simple bolt on items. Vehicle electricians have special equipment to test this unit – it is worth asking for a check before buying a replacement. Observe the installation instructions for the unit – some are very sensitive to the angle at which they are mounted.

Magnetic gauges:

Testing procedures are the same as for bi-metal gauges to eliminate possible faults in the sender unit. By far the most common fault in the gauge itself is a bad earth connection that lowers the current flowing through the balance coil and allows the sender connected coil to have undue influence on the needle. The signs are very high or erratic readings. Check the earth connection and if necessary provide a good earth by means of a thin braided wire strap or lead secured to the metal instrument body.

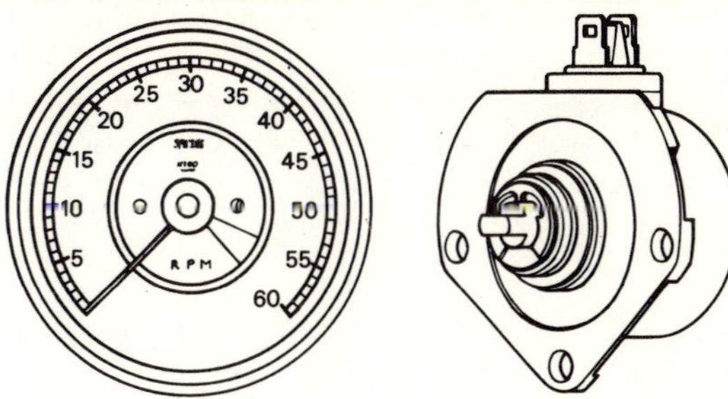

FIG 8:4 Moving coil tachometer and sender

8:4 Tachometer or rev-counter

A very useful instrument, both for tuning and gauging the correct moment for gear changes, is the tachometer or rev-counter. Two kinds of rev-counter are in common use – the moving coil type, fitted as standard equipment only, and the impulse tachometer, available as a standard or accessory item.

Moving coil tachometer:

Two units make up this rev-counting system – a small alternating current generator coupled to the engine's crankshaft or camshaft and an instrument head.

The ac generator produces a voltage proportional to the engine revolutions of approximately 1 volt per 100 rpm. The instrument head to which it is connected by two wires, is simply a moving coil voltmeter.

Both units are sealed and if found to be faulty they have to be returned to the instrument manufacturers.

The only checks that can be made are to ensure that all the circuit connections are tight. If an ac voltmeter is available (multimeter type) the generator output can be tested and checked against an accurate tachometer.

Moving coil tachometers are completely independent from the vehicle's electrical system (except for the instrument lamp connection).

Impulse tachometer:

An impulse tachometer contains circuitry which counts the low tension distributor switched impulses to the ignition coil, divides the pulses by a factor to adjust for the number of cylinders in the engine and transmits the time based result to a conventional moving coil instrument. The pulses may be sensed magnetically from a loop in the extended lead between the contact breaker and the ignition coil. The loop is formed inside a plastic cased soft iron core sensing unit which protrudes from the back of earlier instruments but is incorporated inside more recent designs.

Standard impulse tachometers have a single terminal: earth is via the instrument casing. Accessory instruments usually have a terminal block with up to three connections (one may be for a 6 volt system) to allow fitting to cars of either polarity. The instruments are sealed units which are usually specific to 4, 6, or 8 cylinder engine applications.

Little can be done to check an impulse tachometer's operation apart from ensuring that all circuit connections are clean and tight, that the impulse loop is correctly made in the sensing unit, and that all leads are unbroken.

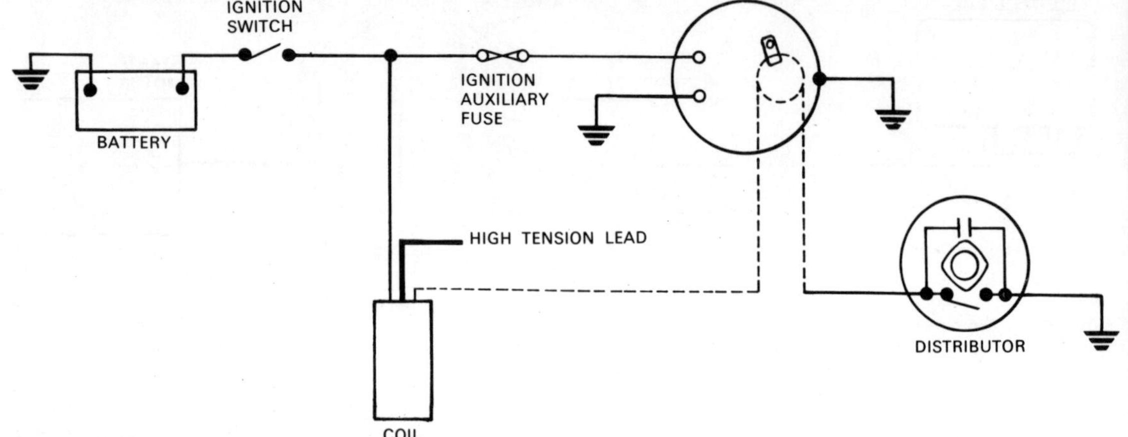

FIG 8:5 Impulse tachometer circuit

8:5 The ammeter

Ammeters are fitted as standard equipment on some more expensive cars (they were a standard feature of older car facias) and are often the first choice of the accessory instrument buyer. The ammeter reading shows the amount of current by which the battery is being charged or discharged. Thus the ammeter dial has a central zeroed needle with graduated marks each side corresponding to amps discharged (−) and charged (+). The usual scale deflection is ± 30 amps.

An ammeter has two connections. Inside the instrument body the connections are joined by a two or three turn loop of very thick copper wire which is arranged adjacent to a pivoted permanent magnet on which the needle is fixed. The needle is usually damped by small springs so it naturally rests at the centre zero position. The ammeter is normally connected between the starter solenoid terminal and the charging and supply leads secured on the terminal or connected in series with the lead from the control box (terminal A1 or B) to the solenoid's battery terminal. (See **Chapter 9** for accessory ammeter installation.)

The entire current flowing to and fro from the battery and the generator passes through the loop of wire in the ammeter. The result is a magnetic field of constantly changing strength and polarity which attracts and repels the permanent magnet in proportion to the amount and direction of the current. The needle reproduces these magnetic movements on the ammeter scale.

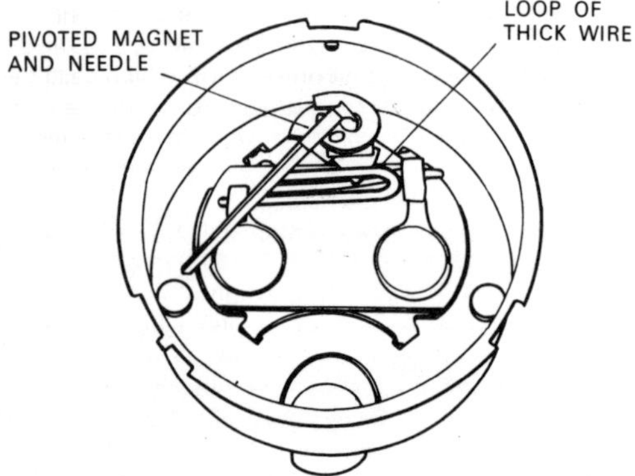

FIG 8:7 Internal components of an ammeter

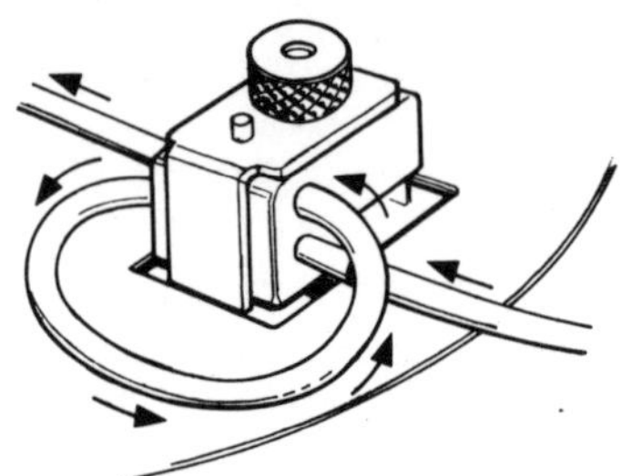

FIG 8:6 Tachometer impulse loop sensor

Ammeter fault-finding:

A break in the ammeter connections results in total electrical failure (apart from the starter motor, the only unit with its own electrical supply – although the solenoid will not operate). Retighten all ammeter connections. If the car and the instrument now work it is best to completely remake the circuit ensuring that such a failure cannot happen again.

A resistive but unbroken connection in the ammeter circuit will be betrayed by heating when the ignition is on and a heavy current demand circuit (like the headlamps) is switched on. Again all the circuit connections must be cleaned and remade.

A break inside the instrument will again result in vehicle electrical failure – disconnect the ammeter from the circuit and reconnect the charging circuit wires to the battery terminal of the solenoid to get going again. In fact this is a very rare fault. The more usual instrument failure is a short to earth inside the casing in which case the battery will rapidly discharge through the wire to the instrument which will overheat – the instrument itself will be irreparably damaged. A short at any other part of the

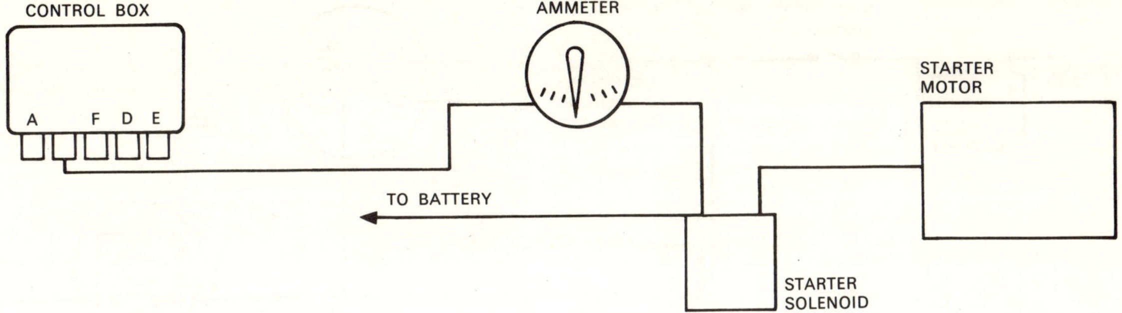

FIG 8:8 **Ammeter connections**

ammeter circuit will have similar disastrous consequences.

If the car is operating correctly but there is no needle response the needle mechanism has probably broken and the gauge will have to be replaced.

Ammeters are usually very reliable instruments which are extremely sensitive to the car's electrical condition – proper interpretation of the ammeter's readings (see **Section 8:8**) can save a great deal of expense.

8:6 Battery condition indicator or voltmeter

Bi-metal strip gauges can also be used as voltmeters and in this application a voltage stabiliser is not required because it is the fluctuating battery and generator output that is being measured. The instrument is sometimes called a battery condition indicator – a bit of a misnomer because although it shows battery voltage when the ignition is first switched on, with the engine running it is the voltage of the generator output that is read.

A voltmeter of this kind is connected in parallel between earth – a suitable point on the car body – and an ignition switched live point. This may be a spare terminal on the ignition switch itself or any other point at which a direct battery supply is received via the switch. A useful position in the instrument panel area is the spare terminal on the battery side of the voltage stabiliser.

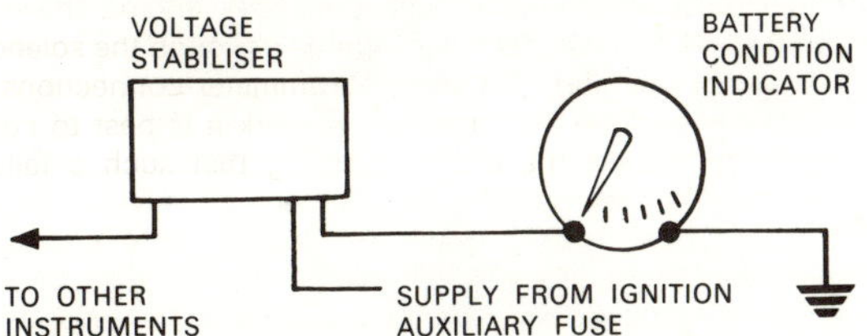

FIG 8:9 **Battery condition indicator circuit**

The crude bi-metal instrument has to be wired to the ignition switch because it is itself a small current user – leave the car for a while with it permanently connected across the battery and the leak would drain away battery power. Unlike good quality magnetic voltmeter instruments used for circuit testing the scale of the car voltvoltmeter does not start at zero – it is a short scale instrument reading from 10–16 volts.

Normal reading with ignition switched on should be in the region of 12 volts – up to 14 volts should be shown when the engine is revving (see **Section 8:8**).

Voltmeter fault-finding:

The possibility of erroneous readings can only be checked by using a good quality voltmeter connected across the same points. A resistive voltmeter connection will reduce the voltage at the instrument's terminals – check to ensure all connections are tight and clean.

Failure of the instrument will not normally affect the car's running unless it is a short circuit. A short circuit anywhere inside the voltmeter or along its connections will burn out the wiring (usually a light grade of wire) and cause instrument damage.

8:7 Warning lights

Oil pressure:

A battery supply from the ignition switch is permanently connected to the oil pressure warning light. The earth return is completed via a pressure sensitive switch which is screwed into the engine block at the point where it is in contact with a feed from the oil pump. The contacts are closed when the engine is stationary so the lamp glows when the ignition is first switched on. As the engine begins to turn and the oil pressure builds up the contacts separate and the light extinguishes. It should not come on again while the engine is running – even at idling speed the oil pressure should be sufficient to keep the contacts parted. Unfortunately the pressure at which the contacts will close is very low, 10 to 15 lb/sq inch. Unless there is a sudden failure of oil pressure (in which case the light provides a timely warning of impending engine seizure) it is possible for the engine to run for some time at oil pressures little more than the switch setting, with inevitable increases in wear.

Check the operation of the light by removing the lead from the sender unit and touching the connector on the engine block. The lamp should light. To check the sender's pressure operation connect a circuit tester between the end terminal and a live supply – when the engine is revved the test lamp should extinguish.

Replacement of the warning lamp is often not a simple matter on modern instrument modules but on older cars it is usually possible to gain access to the lamp's socket fitting.

Some older cars (notably Austin/Morris) have a pressure differential warning light which detects an undue pressure drop across the oil filter – when it is lit it indicates that the filter is partially blocked. The sender is located in the top mounting of the filter bowl. This light does not come on when the ignition is first turned on, so bulb failure may well go unnoticed. Check by removing the lead from the sender unit and earthing it: the lamp should light.

Main beam warning light:

All cars are fitted with a light connected in parallel with the main beam lighting circuit to show when the main beams are in use – the lens or filter colour is usually blue or green.

Indicator warning light:

A green or orange filtered lamp (or lamps) is fitted to show the operation of the indicators (see **Chapter 6** for variations in fitting).

Brake warning lights:

Various types of brake warning light are fitted to some cars. The simplest is a lamp (usually red) to warn that the handbrake is on. This is operated by a switch connected to the handbrake lever.

A few cars have a facility for brake pad wear warning lights operated by contacts buried in the brake pad material. When the pad wears down to the level of the contacts they connect with the brake drum or disc and complete the warning lamp circuit to earth.

Several countries have now adopted laws necessitating the fitting of brake pressure warning lights in conjunction with dual circuit braking systems. A sender unit monitors the difference in pressure between the two parts of the system; the lamp illuminates when insufficient brake pressure is available in one half. There also has to be a means of checking the lamp circuit. The usual solution is to mount the lamp inside a rocker switch – when pressed the switch bypasses the sender and the light illuminates to show it is functioning correctly.

Brake fluid level warning lights can be bought as an accessory. They are operated by a float switch unit screwed to the filler cap of the hydraulic fluid reservoir. A similar device can be used to check the clutch fluid level.

Low fuel level warning light:

Supplementing the fuel gauge on some cars is a warning light which senses a low fuel level – it is also possible to buy this unit as an accessory. The warning light circuit operates from the normal petrol gauge sender but utilises a bonus factor of the instrument's voltage stabiliser. Peak voltages from the stabiliser rise as the petrol gauge circuit resistance increases. This is because the reduced current flow through the gauge and stabiliser heats the bi-metal strip much more slowly – thus the points stay closed longer and the voltage peaks rise.

A sensor unit monitors the waveform of the voltage stabiliser output and when the voltage peaks reach a certain level, triggers the lamp.

Choke warning light:

The choke is often necessary to start the car but its use for extended periods will cause plug fouling, cylinder wear problems and greatly increased petrol consumption. One way manufacturers are combating this is the fitting of a choke warning light. Usually this light is simply controlled by a switch attached somewhere along the choke cable linkage.

Added sophistication may be provided by a second switch, in series, that is temperature actuated. The temperature switch unit may be installed on the exhaust manifold or in the radiator header tank but its effect is similar – it delays the operation of the warning light until the engine is sufficiently warm to dispense with the choke.

Seat belt warning lights:

It is mandatory in America to have a seat belt warning light system coupled to an audible buzzer. Some cars are appearing in Britain with this system fitted (notably Volvo) but with the buzzer deleted. Switches controlling the system are fitted to the seal belt centre mounting and to the seat squab at each side of the car. The weight of driver or passenger sitting on the seats actuates the warning light with a red legend 'fasten seat belts' – there is usually a flasher unit (Volvo use the direction indicator flasher) to add emphasis to the signal. Slotting the seat belt into the centre mounting cancels the signal.

Bulb failure warning lights:

There are a number of ways of providing a dashboard signal for the failure of a bulb in the lighting circuits.

The most common way is to connect a current sensor into the supply leads to each bulb in the case of stop-lights or arrange two sensing devices so that they are separately in circuit with the front and rear lights.

The current sensor is a bi-metallic strip wound with a heating coil. Movement of the bi-metallic strip under the influence of the heating effect of the current passing to the lights, operates contacts connected to a warning light on the dashboard. The warning light will glow momentarily as the relevant lighting circuit is switched on – this is a convenient check that the circuit is working. The warning light will extinguish as the strip heats up and the contacts part. Failure of a bulb reduces the current flow in the circuit to the extent that insufficient heat is generated to keep the contacts open and the warning light will glow continuously.

Accessory kits employing this type of sensor are marketed by Smiths Industries. They are a useful addition to the car's safety equipment.

Volvo have designed a more sophisticated bulb failure sensor. It is a magnetic switch or relay. The supply leads to all the lights on one side of the car are connected to one winding of the relay. The lights on the other side of the car are supplied via a similar coil on the relay core which is wound in the opposite direction to the first coil.

When the lights are switched on, the current flowing to the lights on each side of the car set up equal and opposite magnetic fields in the relay's core. The net effect is that there is no magnetic influence on the relay contacts which are connected to a warning light. However when one bulb fails the current flowing in one

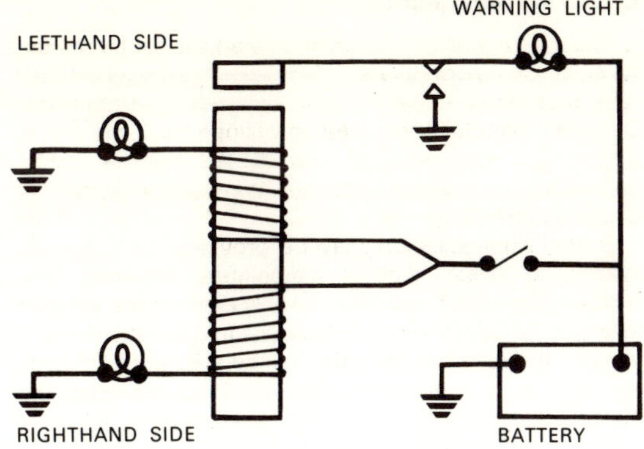

FIG 8:10 Volvo bulb failure sensor system

of the coils is reduced, allowing the magnetic field of the other coil to dominate the relay contacts – these close and the warning light glows.

Fibre optics, a means of transmitting light for long distances along tightly bound bundles of glass fibres, is another means to sense bulb failure. One end of a fibre optic light guide is fixed into the reflector of the side, rear, head or stop light and the guide is led through the car to a central warning light cluster where the free end is inserted in a small lens unit. The warning lights will glow by transmitted light all the time the car's bulbs are illuminated. This type of bulb failure device is available as an accessory.

8:8 Reading instruments and warning lights

Instruments and warning lights give clues about the engine's performance that, if heeded in time, can prevent serious damage occurring and save costly repairs.

Ammeter:

The ammeter shows the rate of charge and discharge of the battery. When the engine is first started and the car is travelling over 25 mph the ammeter should show a charge (+) reading of up to 30 amps. The exact reading depends on the output of the charging system – dynamos will usually give charge readings between 15 amps and 20 amps, alternators can deliver a higher current.

After a few minutes the charging system's control circuitry comes into operation and the charge falls to 0–5 amps.

The ammeter should not show a discharge (−) reading while the engine is running at over 2000 rev/min. Both dynamo and alternator charging systems are designed to cope with the full electrical load of the car's ignition and auxiliary equipment and provide the battery with a minimal charge. Check that the generator is working efficiently by switching on all the car's equipment, especially headlights and heater fan motor, revving to about 2000 rev/min (or cruising at over 30 mph). The ammeter reading should be a steady 0–5 amps charge.

Dynamos operate with a very small margin of ability to power more than the car's standard electrical equipment. The fitting of accessories with a high current demand – a 90 watt, $7\frac{1}{2}$ amp heated rear window, for example – may raise the car's current consumption to a level at which the dynamo cannot charge the battery. The result is a discharge (−) reading on the ammeter when the full load of standard and accessory equipment is switched on. There will also be a heavy discharge from the battery when the car is stationary or crawling in traffic.

From the level of discharge it is possible to gauge if the car's current consumption is within reasonable limits. For instance, it is unlikely that all the car's equipment will be switched on at one time. It may be possible to forego the comfort of the heater fan for the sake of brief heated rear window operation. Should it be necessary to switch off items like the car's headlights to give a charge reading on the ammeter the electrical system is much too overloaded for safety. Generally speaking it is unwise to run the car with a continuous discharge reading of over 1 amp for any length of time.

Alternators are much better able to deal with the current demand of cars fitted with accessories – in fact they started to appear on cheaper cars when heated rear windows, high wattage headlamps and other current demanding improvements were introduced as standard equipment. Nevertheless the alternator only has a limited capacity to cope with the demand of additional accessories and the ammeter can show the same symptoms of overload as on a dynamo fitted car. One other factor in favour of the alternator is that it will satisfy a high level of current demand at lower engine speeds – therefore in traffic the discharge recorded by the ammeter will be of a lower order than that arising in a dynamo system.

If the charging system normally copes with a heavy load of electrical equipment, but begins to show discharges under certain conditions of engine speed the most likely cause is a slipping fan belt. Tighten it and check that a correct charge reading can be obtained on the ammeter with the engine revving and most of the electrical equipment switched on. If the charge is not restored the fault will lie in the generator or control box. Sticking or worn brushes may produce intermittent discharge indications on the ammeter or a flickering charge/discharge reading.

The ammeter may also be used to track down faults in individual units on the car. For instance, when the wipers are operated on a wet windscreen (engine stationary) the ammeter should show a steady discharge reading perhaps with a slight kick of the needle at the end of each wiper stroke. Fluctuation of the needle while the wipers are in mid stroke points to a sticky wiper drive or, a worn commutator or brushes in the wiper motor (see **Chapter 7, Section 7:2**). Operating the indicators, each side in turn, should produce equal discharge readings as the lights come on. A higher or lower reading from one side's indicators can mean a faulty earth, bad connections in the circuit or a blown bulb. It is not usual for the ammeter needle to flicker – it normally gives steady readings. Flickering is usually caused by a bad connection being made or broken by the vibration of the car. Switch on each of the car's systems in turn to find the one that causes the needle's flicker.

Few cars are fitted with electrical instruments but they are very useful accessories. Experts argue which instrument is the most useful to fit when it is only possible to fit either an ammeter or a voltmeter. On balance it is considered that the single most useful indicator is the ammeter since it provides a check on the generating system – the most expensive and potentially most damaging faults can occur here and the ammeter's reaction to a fault is almost instantaneous. Although the voltmeter primarily monitors what is happening to the battery, it does react, relatively slowly, to some charging system faults. So the complete answer to this problem is that the best monitoring of the electrical system can be achieved by fitting both instruments.

Voltmeter or battery condition indicator:

With the ignition switched on but with all the rest of the car's electrical loads switched off the voltmeter should read about 12 volts. A slightly higher reading (up to 13 volts) may be obtained with a fully charged battery.

When the engine is running the voltmeter reading rises to show the voltage produced by the charging system. This will normally be in the range 13 to 14.4 volts depending on the type of charging system. A higher reading than 15 volts means that the battery is being overcharged – the control box voltage setting or the alternator's voltage regulator should be investigated.

A lower reading than 12 volts with the engine stationary shows that the condition of the battery is below its correctly charged potential. Charging the battery (see **Chapter 3**) may produce a satisfactory voltmeter reading. If after full charging the voltage is still below 12 volts the battery is beginning to deteriorate.

Readings lower than 12 volts while the car is running may mean that the battery is being flattened because the generating system can't cope with the car's electrical loads. If a low reading is accompanied by glimmering of the ignition warning light or its reluctance to extinguish it is possible that the fault is a slipping fan belt. It is also possible that the control box voltage regulator setting is out of adjustment, or that the generator requires overhauling.

Ignition warning light:

As described in **Chapter 3** the ignition warning light indicates when the generator is producing a voltage equal to, or higher than, that of the battery and is thus creating an electrical pressure which enables it to charge the battery. Simply, if it is on, the generator is not providing a high enough voltage to charge the battery. The light should illuminate when the ignition is switched on and as the engine starts it should go out.

On some dynamo-fitted cars the light will just stay illuminated with the engine idling. But it must go out as soon as engine speed rises above idling.

If the light comes on when the car is moving the commonest reason is a broken fan belt. If the fan belt proves to be intact and at the correct tension, generator or control box faults should be suspected.

Never continue to run the car with the ignition warning light showing – at best the battery will quickly be flattened, at worst the engine will overheat.

A flickering ignition warning light can indicate brush or commutator faults. Failure of the light to extinguish immediately the engine is revved is most likely to be caused by a slipping fan belt.

Water temperature gauge:

The water temperature gauge reading should rise steadily up to the normal coolant temperature level over the first few miles of a journey. The normal reading varies from engine to engine and is dependent on the pressure at which the system operates and whether the cooling is by means of an electric or engine fan. It will usually be between 80 deg. C and 100 deg. C.

Failure to reach the normal reading after a few miles may mean the thermostat is stuck open.

Higher readings than normal may result from a thermostat stuck closed, failure of the electric cooling fan, a burst hose or a leaking or blocked radiator. Temperature rises on the road must be investigated as soon as possible. The result can be damage to the cylinder head and gasket – if all the coolant leaks out of the system the engine can overheat to seizure. Read the water temperature gauge in conjunction with the ignition warning light – a temperature rise with the ignition light on while running is probably due to a broken fan belt.

Oil pressure warning light:

The oil pressure light should extinguish as soon as the engine is started. If the car has covered a high mileage the light may flicker at idling speed when the engine is hot, but it must go out as soon as engine speed rises above idling. If it fails to do so the engine's oil level may be low, there may be a leak in the oil system, bearings and other vital lubrication points may have worn enough to prevent the system reaching operating pressure, or the oil pump may require maintenance.

If the light comes on when the car is running, stop immediately for investigation. Failure to do so will almost certainly result in the engine's seizure. First check the engine oil level and then for obvious signs of leaks. There are several external points in the lubrication system that can fail – for instance the sump gasket, the point where the oil pressure relief valve is inserted, the connection of the warning light or oil pressure gauge sender and the filter mounting.

Tachometer:

The tachometer or rev-counter gives a straight readout of the engine's crankshaft speed. The impulse type senses the low tension current from the distributor to the ignition coil. If the engine is misfiring and the tachometer reading is erratic, investigate the action of the contact breaker and the capacitor as there may be discontinuity of the pulses to the coil.

In normal running conditions the tachometer can make an important contribution to fuel economy. On most cars, limiting engine revolutions to the 2000–3000 rev/min band will ensure that the engine is used most efficiently. Occasional revving into the orange warning band of a tachometer for extra overtaking performance is permissible although frequent use of such high engine revolutions will be uneconomical and accelerate wear. Never rev past the red line or into the red tachometer band – this will cause engine damage.

CHAPTER 9

Fitting radios, tape-players and other accessories

At many garages and high street parts shops the motorist is presented with a bewildering array of accessories which cater for almost every in-car need. They range from anti-theft devices through extra lighting to radio and tape-player systems. There are many worthwhile accessories that can add safety and convenience to motoring, relax the driver and make the car easier to drive. There are also many badly designed and made accessories glossily packaged to trap the unwary motorist.

This chapter describes some of the most popular and useful accessories available for fitting to cars, details the way in which they should be fitted to obtain the most efficient operation and points out some of the traps in the accessory market.

Particular attention is paid to the installation of radios and tape-players. These increasingly popular entertainment accessories can do a lot to relieve the tedium of car journeys and, by relaxing the driver, promote safer motoring. Radios in particular perform a very useful function as more and more radio stations, local and national, are broadcasting traffic information. Correct installation and interference suppression is important as the cacophony of a poorly fitted radio can be a dangerous distraction.

For the future, government scientists are considering the installation of a network of small transmitters (possibly with aerials buried under the road surface) that will provide immediate and specific warnings of traffic hazards in the car's vicinity. A tiny in-car receiver is envisaged that will be able to cut into the normal broadcast or tape programme that the driver is listening to, delivering the message over the radio or tape-player amplifier and speaker system. Owning a properly fitted and maintained radio or tape-player will thus become an increasingly important part of safe and convenient motoring.

Before reading the section relevant to fitting a particular accessory it is advisable to read **Chapter 2** on electrical wiring techniques and good workshop practice.

9:1 Connecting accessories

All cars have at least one point in the electrical system where it is possible to fit the additional electrical wiring to power accessories. These points fall into four categories:

1 Spare terminals on the fuse box connected to the ignition switched fuse.

2 Spare terminals on the fuse box connected to the battery auxiliary fuse – these provide a continuous electrical supply that is not switched by the ignition switch.

3 Spare terminals on the ignition switch – modern switches may have an accessory position to which the spare terminal is connected. Older switches may have a spare terminal connected by an internal link to the main switched terminal. There is not usually any fuse protection in this circuit.

4 Direct connection to the battery via the battery terminal itself, a terminal on the starter solenoid or a spare terminal on the unfused side of the fuse box at the battery auxiliary fuse position.

Where the accessory power supply is taken from must to some extent depend on the available alternatives. In some cars the only positions available for supply may be the battery itself or the fuse box. Others may present all four alternative possibilities for connection. With this in mind there are a few more guide lines that will enable the selection of the best position.

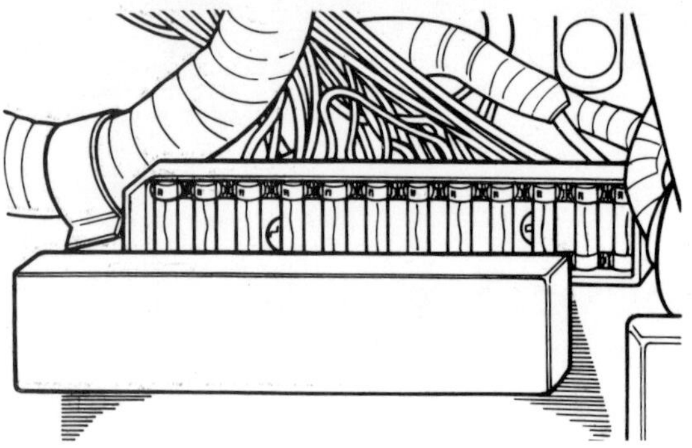

FIG 9:1 Fuse box

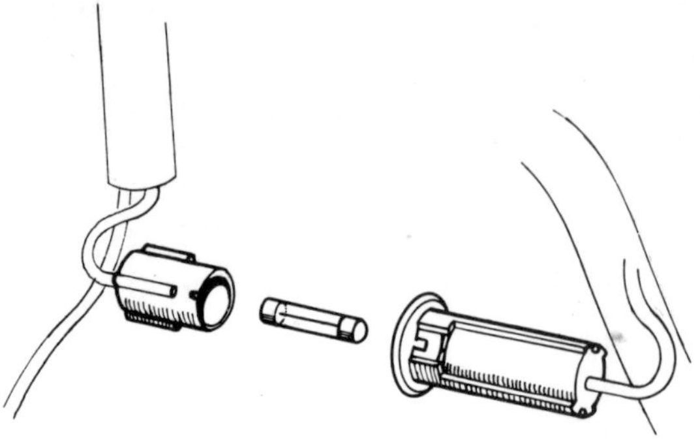

FIG 9:2 Line fuse holder

Some accessories, like an electric clock, must have a constant power supply even when the ignition is switched off – therefore they must be connected to the battery terminal (or any point connected to it) or the battery auxiliary fuse terminal. Most types of anti-theft device also require a constant supply and so must be connected to one of these points.

It is desirable for some accessories to be operable with the main ignition circuits switched off. A radio, for instance, may be used for long periods when the car is not running. The best solution to powering these accessories is to connect them to the special accessory terminal found on modern ignition switches. Connected in this way there is no possibility of leaving them switched on when the key is withdrawn but their use does not involve the additional battery drain of the ignition coil current.

If this position is not available a choice must be made whether to connect the accessory to the main ignition switched terminal or to any of the other available positions.

Consideration must also be given to the power of the accessory to be fitted. Accessories with a high continuous current demand, such as a heated rear window, should be fitted to an ignition switched position (preferably the terminals on the ignition auxiliary fuse) because to leave them on accidentally would rapidly drain the battery. However, some high current demand items like cigar lighters and air horns do not operate for very long periods at a time and these are best connected to the battery auxiliary fuse.

Accessory lights can have quite a high current demand but they may be used as warnings or to give necessary light when the car is stationary. It doesn't matter too much that fuse failure would deprive the car of auxiliary lighting (there is probably no fuse protection in the main light circuit so lighting should always be available) so foglights and spotlights are best connected to the battery auxiliary fuse. Warning lights should be used as a reminder to switch these lights off.

Smaller lights, like the reversing lamps, should be connected to the ignition switched fuse or the main ignition switch terminal.

Fuses in the accessory circuits:

It is always wise to fit a fuse in an accessory circuit. In the case of expensive units like radios and tape-players this provides some protection against damaging surges of current. However, the main object is to prevent short circuiting or other faults in accessory circuits from incapacitating the car's main circuits.

Fuses can be connected into the circuits in line fuse form or a subsidiary accessory fuse box can be obtained and mounted in a convenient position on the engine compartment bulkhead or behind the facia.

As a general rule fit the fuse in the circuit at the nearest convenient point to the connection of the accessory with the car's existing circuitry. This provides the maximum protection against short circuiting throughout the length of the accessory circuit. Always bear in mind that the fitting of accessories to either the ignition switched fuse or the battery auxiliary fuse may prove to be the straw that breaks the camel's back. In other words, continuous operation of all the car's normal electrical equipment and additional accessories connected through the main fuse box may overload these fuses.

To ensure that this does not occur, calculate the total current demand of the circuits connected to the fuse – most car workshop manuals will give the individual power or current ratings of each piece of electrical equipment. If these are not obtainable seek the advice of a vehicle electrician or use an ammeter connected in series with each piece of equipment in turn to determine the exact current demand.

Compare the total obtained to the rated value of the fuse. Remember that the fuse may be labelled according to the old convention, in which case the marked current must be halved to find the continuous working current (see **Chapter 1, Section 1:7**).

If the current demand through the fuse is greater than its working value a subsidiary fuse must be used in parallel to take the additional loads.

In the case of the battery auxiliary fuse remember to allow a generous margin on the current calculated to account for the intermittent use of the horn and other high current demand items like the cigar lighter. For instance, the continuous demand on a battery auxiliary fuse of working value 17 amps may be 10 amps. The margin of 7 amps might be exceeded for short bursts of the horn but any additional accessory load would bring the total current when the horn is in use well over the working value. At best this will shorten the life of the fuse considerably – at worst the fuse could blow every time the horn is used.

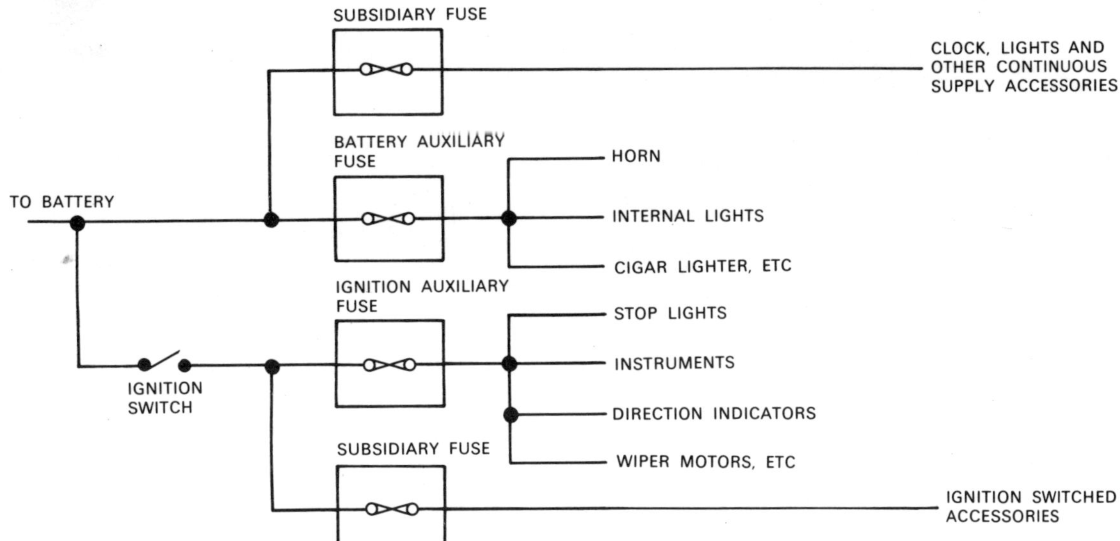

FIG 9:3 Circuit for subsidiary fuses

Individual line fuses or those in a subsidiary fuse box should be of a value close to the continuous working current of the electrical unit supplied. For example: a $7\frac{1}{2}$ amp heated rear window should have a 10 amp fuse; tape players (particularly eight track types with a track selection button) will need a 5 amp fuse as they demand up to 4 amps; radios are usually supplied with a 3 to 5 amp line fuse.

Wiring:

Various thicknesses of wire are designed to carry a certain amount of current without overheating and without causing too high a voltage drop. Consult the wiring grade table in **Chapter 2** to find the minimum thickness of wire for each current carrying application.

Circuit connections for accessories:

Whenever possible use Lucar connectors for accessory wiring to the unit itself and to the fuse box or ignition switch. This is not always possible – some units have tag connections. The only disadvantage of tag connections is that they may become loose with the car's vibration – ensure they are tightly made.

Connections into existing circuit wiring or junctions between accessory wires should be made with bullet connectors. Low current demand accessories may be connected to existing wiring with Scotchlok or similar insulation penetrating connectors (see **Chapter 2**).

9:2 Radios

There are an enormous number of different types of radio on the market. The current price range is between about £10 and £100. The majority of sets offer reception of Medium Wave and Long Wave frequencies. Cheaper sets may only receive Medium Wave stations. However, there are an increasing number of local BBC and commercial (IBA) stations transmitting frequency modulated (FM) signals in the very high frequency (VHF) wavelengths. There are now many car radio sets on the market that will receive VHF stations. The latest development in radio is the transmission of stereo signals – the most expensive car radios will decode these signals to give stereo reception on the move.

Cheaper sets give poorer reception and less differentiation between the signals of transmitters with nearly similar wavelengths. Generally they are only suitable for listening to high strength broadcasts in areas of good reception. The more expensive the set the better the quality of reception and the greater the differentiation between stations. Some more expensive sets have special circuitry to ensure that the radio tuner remains locked to the signal from a particular transmitter whatever the variation in signal strength and error in the tuning mechanism. A radio can, for instance, drift off the tuned station as its transistors become heated or simply by the vibration of the radio mounting.

On the move, push-button tuning is an advantage – it isn't safe to be turning a tuner and glancing at the radio dial while driving. This is a factor to be borne in mind when selecting a set.

Remember that a set is not complete without loudspeakers – some cheaper sets are sold without them and they can cost about half as much as the set.

A few dual-purpose car radios are available that can be removed from the facia mounting and used as ordinary portable sets. Special connectors at the rear of the set plug into sockets to connect with the car's electrical supply and aerial. When the set is taken out of the car its internal aerial and batteries take over. It is unfortunately true that these sets do not necessarily perform particularly well in either type of use. However, they do have the advantage that they can be removed from the car for security – radios and tape-players are thieves' prime targets.

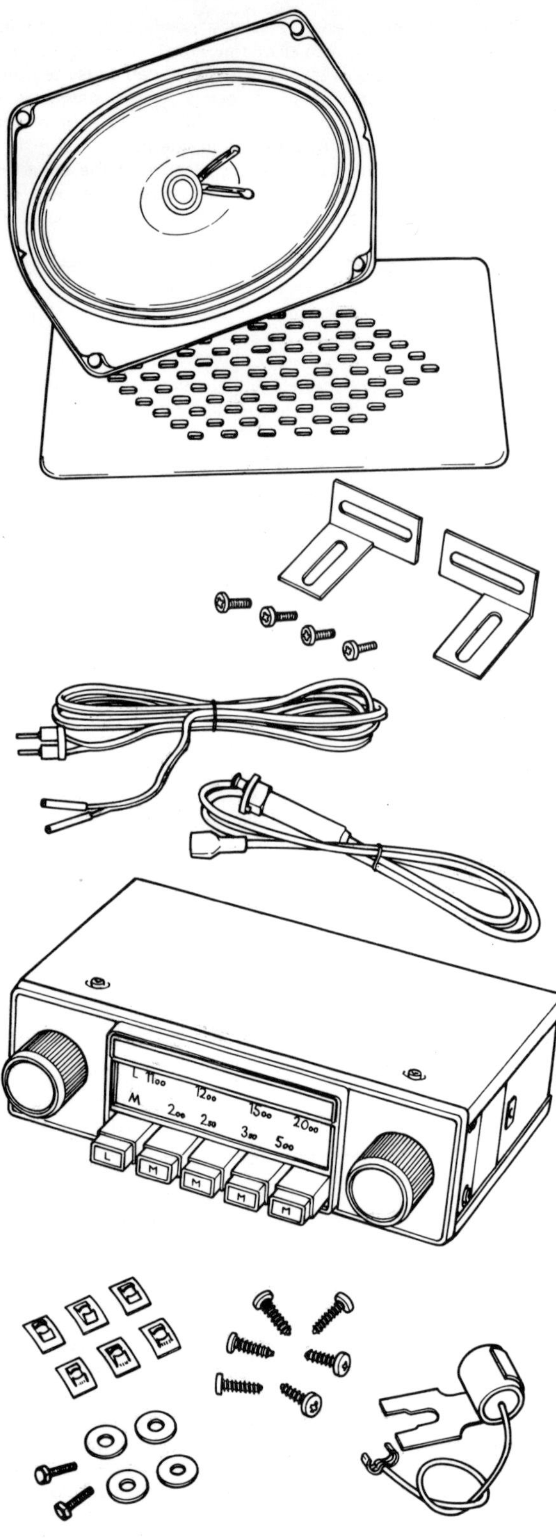

FIG 9:4 Radio, speaker and fitting kit

Fitting kits:

Most of the well-established companies selling car radios (for example, Motorola, Phillips, Radiomobile) offer special fitting kits designed to simplify the fixing of a radio in a specific model of car. The kits consist of brackets, facia panels and the required number of bolts, nuts and washers. These kits are generally very expensive in relation to the cost of the radio itself.

It is wise to examine the materials offered in the fitting kit before purchase. With a little ingenuity, scrap metal, spare bolts, etc., from the tool box it is often possible to provide a perfectly satisfactory mounting for the set at practically no cost.

Aerials:

A car radio aerial is another extra purchase to be made when buying a car radio. It is almost impossible to tell a good aerial from a bad one, even on close inspection. Price can be the only guide. The higher the price the better the quality of workmanship and the longer the aerial will last, as a general rule.

There are various types of aerial. Telescopic types, with or without a locking device to prevent malicious tampering, are the most popular kind. There are roof mounting types and whip aerials which consists of a fibre glass, metal-cored rod, spring mounted to the car body.

A more expensive aerial is the electrically operated type. This is controlled by a separate switch or may be connected in such a way that turning on the radio activates the aerial motor. Before purchasing an aerial of this type ensure that there is sufficient clearance at the mounting point to accommodate the extra length of the motor body.

Steer clear of stick-on windscreen aerials or those fashioned into a licence disc. They will not give good reception characteristics.

WARNING. When purchasing radio equipment ensure that the set is of the same polarity as the car. The majority of car radios are produced for fitting to negative earth vehicles – a few sets are available in positive and negative earth versions. Some radios are provided with a polarity changeover switch which must be set to the car's polarity before fitting is attempted.

9:3 Fitting a car radio

A fitting position for the car radio is often provided by the car manufacturers. It is usually an aperture on the facia blanked off by a trim plate which can quite easily be levered or pulled off. If this position is not provided the manufacturer may be able to supply a special radio console. This may be designed to fit at the centre of the facia or over the transmission tunnel. Consult the car's handbook or main agents to find out if fittings like these are available.

Smaller cars may not have special radio mounting points, in which case a suitable position must be selected for the unit.

Bear in mind the following guide lines when mounting a radio:

1 The radio controls should be accessible to the driver when he is seated in his normal driving position – to fix a radio out of the driver's reach can distract his attention from the road.

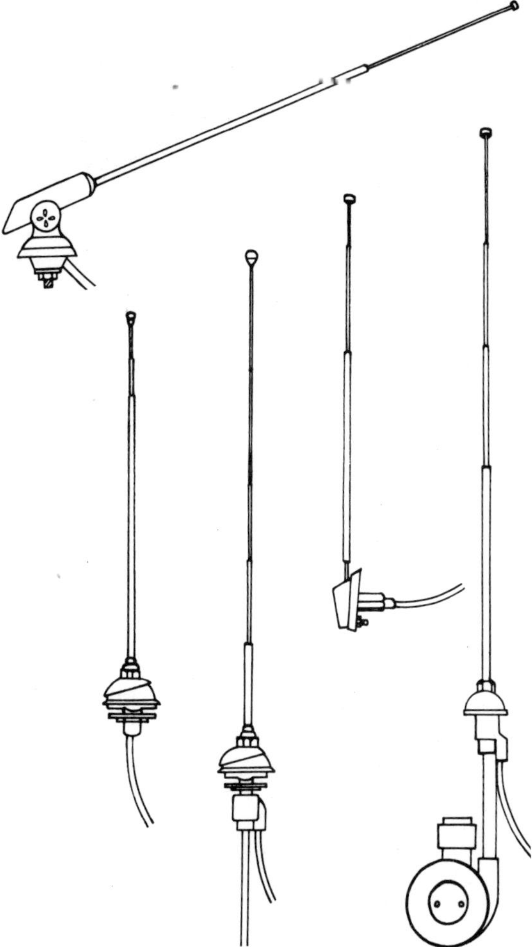
FIG 9:5 A selection of radio aerials

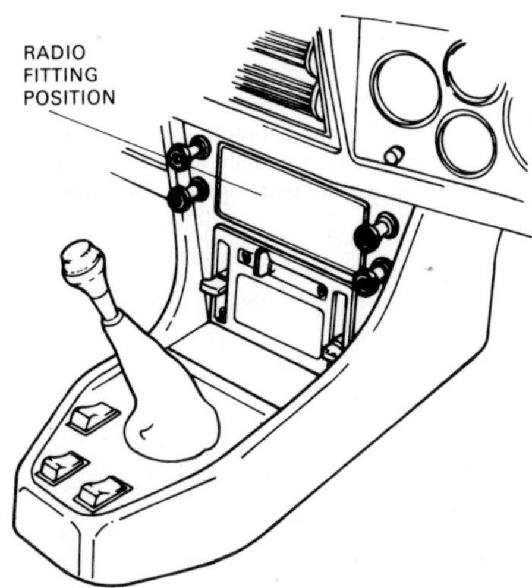

FIG 9:6 A typical radio mounting position

2 Avoid fitting a radio in such a position that it could cause injury to the driver or passenger in an accident – sets under the parcel shelf at knee level can cause terrible lacerations to the legs and knees. Don't fit the set in a position on the façia where the head of the driver or passenger could contact it in an accident.

These strictures will generally mean that the areas of mounting are confined to the centre parts of the facia, on the parcel shelf (but not right at the lip), or in a central console.

3 If the set is not fully enclosed in a metal case try to fit it as far away as possible from sources of interference like the windscreen wiper motor and the instrument voltage stabiliser.

Many radios, specially designed to fit into the facia, have a front plate that can be removed by pulling or levering off the volume and tuning knobs and undoing small screws or locking nuts on the control spindles. These may provide a means of fixing the set direct to the facia or on an adaptor plate which replaces the blank removed from over the radio recess.

Insert the set into the recess ensuring that wires and cables behind the facia are not fouled or snagged. If there are brackets in the fitting kit to secure the rear of the set, supporting its weight or preventing vibration, these must now be placed in position to determine whether holes will have to be drilled for the fixing screws. Sometimes it is possible to use existing bolts or screws to secure the bracket – holes in the bracket may line up with holes already drilled in the bulkhead or facia.

If it is necessary to drill new holes under the facia a flexible extension to a power tool may make drilling inaccessible corners a lot easier.

When the bracket is fitted secure the set to it and replace the front plate or adaptor plate, firmly clamping the set to the facia.

If the car has no special radio position or it is not possible to fit the set in this location it will almost certainly be necessary to drill holes at the selected position. Avoid damaging under facia wiring when drilling.

Radios must be bolted or screwed to a metal part of the facia that is well connected to the main bodywork of the car as on most sets the earth return is via the metal casing. If the facia is plastic and there is no possibility of connecting the casing or a fixing bracket to bodywork metal, a stout metal earthing strap or thick wire must be connected between the radio and a good earthing point (see the following section on connecting the set and **Section 9:4** on interference suppression).

The same provision must be made if the set is to be fitted into a console made of a non-metallic material.

Connecting up a radio set:

Most car radios have only one supply lead – the earth return is via the metal radio casing which should be in good contact with the car bodywork. The supply lead should have a 3 to 5 amp line fuse – these are usually supplied with the radio. Fit a fuse if one is not supplied.

Connect the supply lead to: **1** the special accessory terminal on the ignition switch (or a connector provided under the facia that is wired to this terminal – see car handbook) or, **2** to the ignition auxiliary fuse position on the main fuse box.

Fitting a car aerial:

For the optimum position of a car aerial refer to the information on interference suppression in **Section 9:4**, but for reasonable aerial performance and convenience it may be suitable to fix it on the nearside front wing. (Avoid fitting an aerial on the offside front wing as this may obstruct vision). See the aerial manufacturer's instructions for the exact details of aerial fixing – the following instructions are a general guide:

1 Having selected the fixing position check that there is enough clearance between the lower end of the aerial and the tyre when the suspension is at its lowest. Far too many people neglect this elementary precaution.

2 Protect the car paintwork against scratching and slips while drilling by sticking masking or other adhesive tape around the site of the hole. Mark the exact spot for the hole to be cut with a centre punch.

3 Hole cutters for use on metal are of various types. Choose one that will cut a hole for the threaded shank of the aerial so the shank fits as tightly as possible. Drill a pilot hole and then use the cutter.

Car steel is thin enough to make a hole by cruder means if necessary – drill small holes close together and using a round file, enlarge the hole to the required dimensions. This saves the purchase of a cutter for a single job. Use a soft brush to remove filings or drill swarf.

4 Thoroughly clean underseal, paint and dirt away from the metal on the underside of the hole – about $\frac{1}{8}$ to $\frac{1}{4}$ inch all round the hole is sufficient (some underseals will dissolve in petrol).

5 If the paint coat around the upper side of the hole is chipped or broken retouch with zinc paint or red lead primer and universal primer – this protection can also be applied to the bare metal edges of the hole.

6 After the paint has dried, fit the aerial carefully noting the order of washers and spacers given in the manufacturer's instructions. Tighten down the securing nuts very carefully as overtightening can damage the plastics parts of the aerial casing.

7 Drill whatever holes are necessary to pass the aerial coaxial lead into the car's interior. If the aerial is being fitted in the front wing the best way is to drill a hole from the passenger footwell into the wing. Avoid passing the aerial lead through any part of the engine compartment. Remember that the hole must be made large enough to accommodate a grommet as well as the cable. Ensure that the aerial cable will not foul heater and ventilation controls, bonnet opening levers, or pedal linkages.

8 Apply underseal or a thick layer of grease to the aerial joint on the underside of the wing ensuring that all bare metal parts are well covered.

Selecting and fitting loudspeakers:

The quality of sound from a radio is influenced as much by the siting and mounting of the speaker (or speakers) as by the quality of the set itself. Most car radios are supplied with a matching speaker of the correct resistance characteristics ($2\frac{1}{2}$ ohms or, more usually, 8 ohms). Radios intended for fitting specific cars may have a speaker designed to fit the car's speaker mounting.

If a speaker has to be purchased separately from the radio make the following checks:

1 Ensure the speaker is of the correct resistance for the radio – the instructions will give the specification.

2 If the car has a speaker aperture provided by the manufacturers check that the speaker will fit it.

The radio's manual will also indicate whether or not it is possible to fit twin speakers to give more even sound distribution and quality.

Speakers should be supplied with a metal or plastics grille and a thin baffle board or cork gasket to prevent resonating parts of the unit contacting the car's bodywork (this can give rise to annoying rattles).

Many car manufacturers provide special speaker mounting positions. These are located in the following places: **1** in the centre or at each end of the rear shelf (usually accessible from the boot); **2** in the top or at the sides of the facia; **3** in the front or rear door trim.

It is often necessary to remove trim panels to find the mounting points – some searching may be saved by consulting the car's main agents.

If no mounting positions are provided, speaker units are available ready mounted in small consoles for fitting to the rear shelf.

There is, however, an advantage to mounting the speakers in holes cut into the rear shelf – the boot can act as an excellent sound box endowing the bass notes with added depth. Use a Monodex or similar metal cutter to make a suitable aperture in the shelf.

The cavity inside car doors also enhances bass notes and, even if there are not special cut-outs for speakers behind the door trim, there may still be adequate space for correct fitting. Ensure that in the position selected the speaker does not prevent the operation of the windows or the door opening and locking mechanism. Fit speakers as high in the door panel as possible – sound may be absorbed and muffled by the car's upholstery if the units are fixed too low.

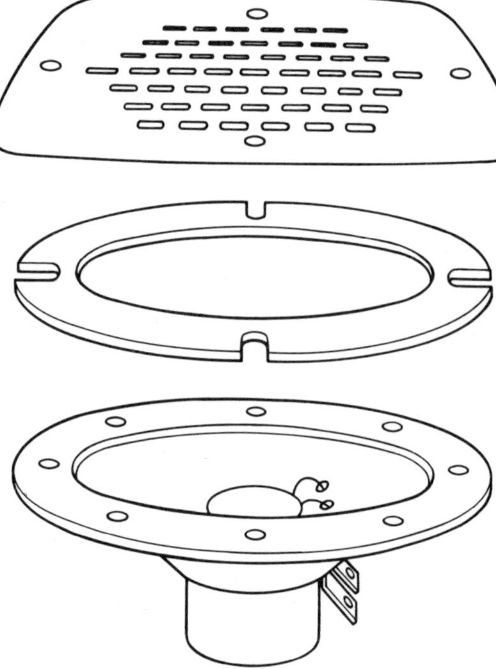

FIG 9:7 Components of a speaker assembly

When the speaker position has been selected drill holes around the rim of the speaker aperture which corresponds to the holes in the speaker rim. Position the speaker and baffle board or gasket under the aperture and fit the grille so its studs pass through the aligned holes. Tighten the retaining nuts down evenly all round the speaker – they should not be overtightened as they may distort the rim of the unit or sever the studs from the grille.

Some speaker assemblies (especially those with plastics grilles) are fixed into the aperture with self-tapping screws: they may locate into threaded clips.

Unless some form of electrical connector is supplied for the connection of speaker leads they should be soldered in place on the speaker tags. Run the lead to the radio via grommeted holes in the panel behind the rear seats and under the carpets to the front of the vehicle. Tape the lead to the floor to reduce damage by abrasion.

Door-mounted speakers present special problems of lead location. The lead must pass between the door and the car body at a point where there is no possibility of pinching. There must be sufficient slack in the lead to allow for door opening. Protect the exposed length of lead with a flexible plastics or rubber sleeve (screen wash tubing is ideal) making sure that each end of the sleeve is firmly located in the grommets on the door and vehicle body.

WARNING. Never operate a car radio without the speakers connected. This can damage the output stage of the radio's amplifier circuit.

Trimming the aerial signal:

Many radio sets have a small control known as the aerial trimmer. This is usually a small screw adjuster located under the radio's front panel or at the rear or side of the set. This adjuster is provided as a means of matching the radio to the signal characteristics of the aerial.

In cases when this control is sensitive to earth contact with the human body via a screwdriver blade, or when shorting on the radio's metal casing must be avoided, the manufacturer provides a special trimming tool – a plastics or wooden screwdriver.

To set the aerial trimmer, plug the aerial into the set, switch on the radio and tune to a weak station around 200 metres (1400 kHz to 1500 kHz) on the Medium waveband. Using the special tool or a small screwdriver, turn the adjuster until the best reception of the station is obtained. The radio will now be tuned for optimum reception of all stations.

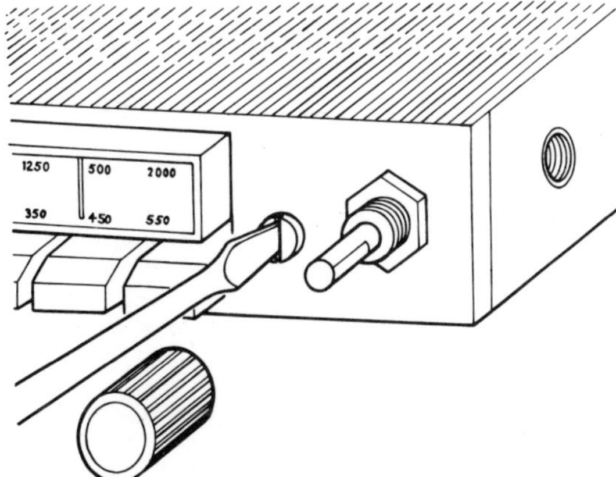

FIG 9:8 Typical aerial trimmer adjustment

9:4 Radio interference suppression

Radio sets may give perfect reception of many stations from the moment they are installed but almost certainly the reception of weaker stations will be interrupted by crackles, screeches and whistles. These are the sounds of radio interference which can totally obliterate broadcasts from weak stations and seriously mar the quality of programmes from stronger transmitters. Interference is caused by stray magnetic fields emitted by all the car's electrical units. The fields generate tiny alternating current pulses in almost any conductor which lies inside their magnetic range. These tiny pulses of current can enter the radio set in a number of ways – via the supply lead, the aerial or they can even be generated in the internal wiring of the set itself. The result is audible interference.

Prime offenders for interference are the car's ignition circuit components, the dynamo or alternator, wiper motors, indicator flashers, the control box and the instrument voltage stabiliser. In addition interference can arise almost anywhere that one electrostatically charged mass or conductor is situated close to another charged mass or conductor with no physical bond between them. A common example is the wheel, charged to a high voltage by flexing and friction – the charge attempts to leak to the barely charged car body and in doing so creates a magnetic field resulting in interference.

Fortunately some efficient means of preventing the emission of stray magnetic fields and stopping the tiny alternating currents reaching the radio set are available:

Capacitors. Like the capacitor in the distributor, radio interference prevention capacitors won't allow a direct current to flow but they will dissipate the energy of alternating current.

Resistors. Resistors damp the to and fro flow of small alternating currents down to a frequency where they no longer interfere with radio reception but, in the high tension side of the ignition circuit in which they are used, don't restrict the passage of direct current too much.

Chokes. Another way to damp out the oscillation of alternating currents is to use a choke. This device is like a one-sided transformer – there's no secondary winding and the energy of the alternating current is dissipated in the cyclic creation and collapse of a magnetic field in a tiny core. The direct current supply passes through the winding unhindered.

Earthing. Short-circuiting the interfering currents created in otherwise non-electrically active components like carburetter linkages and choke cables to earth by means of a connecting strap effectively puts a stop to any further radiation of magnetic fields.

Earthed metal screening. Magnetic radiation can't pass through an earthed metal screen provided it is continuous all round the magnetic source. The best magnetic screen is the car body itself – much of the interference radiation from under-bonnet components never gets further than the engine compartment. The metal radio case acts in the same way – preventing radiation getting in.

Tracking down the causes of interference:

Symptom	Source
Ticking noise varying with engine speed and ceasing when ignition is switched off	Spark plugs, distributor, high tension cables
Whining sound increasing in pitch with engine speed	Dynamo or alternator
Sizzling or rapid spitting sound at engine speeds over 1500 rev/min	Control box voltage regulator
Regular bursts of a buzzing sound occurring with greater frequency as engine speed increases	Instrument voltage stabiliser
Buzzing or crackles when various equipment is operated	Motor interference – wipers, heater, windscreen washer, identifiable by switching each unit on separately
Ticking at frequency of indicator flasher	Indicator flasher unit
Sizzling sound present only on dry roads	Electrostatic tyre noise

Fitting suppression equipment:

Most items of suppression equipment are available separately, or in kit form, from accessory shops and vehicle electricians. Capacitors are usually available in 1 mfd and 3 mfd capacities – any other rating means a visit to a specialist shop. Some difficulty may be experienced in obtaining radio frequency suppression chokes for fitting in supply leads – consult a vehicle electrician.

For successful interference elimination the whole of the vehicle's electrical system must be in good order; terminals and connections must all be tight, leads must be in good condition and spark plugs must be correctly gapped. Pay particular attention to the earthing of the set to the car body – make sure by fitting an earth strap from a sound earth point to the radio casing. Ensure that the aerial mounting is making good earth contact with the car body.

Make a simple check on the way the interference is getting to the radio by disconnecting the aerial from the set. If interference can still be heard it is being conducted through the set's supply lead – fit a choke in series with the supply.

This may not be sufficient on alternator fitted cars – see if supplying the radio direct from the battery eliminates alternator whine.

If the interference is aerial-borne and the methods used so far have not worked, each noise will have to be dealt with at source.

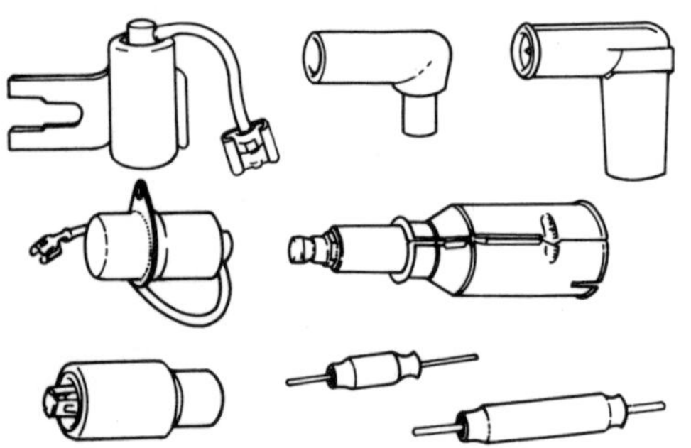

FIG 9:9 **Interference suppression equipment**

Ignition system:

Carbon impregnated rayon high tension leads should provide sufficient damping resistance on the HT side of the ignition circuit. However, these leads are notoriously faulty. If they are suspected as a source of trouble replace them with ordinary copper strand leads and use resistor plug caps plus a line resistor in the lead from the ignition coil to the distributor. Sets of caps with an in-line resistor are available from accessory shops.

Suppress the ignition coil with a 1 mfd capacitor connected between the SW terminal ('+' on negative earth cars) and earth.

Do not use an ignition coil suppression capacitor if a transistorised or capacitor discharge ignition system is fitted.

Generators:

Dynamos can be suppressed by connecting a 1 mfd capacitor between the D terminal and earth. **Never connect a capacitor between the F terminal and earth.** Alternators with separate voltage regulators require a 1 to 3 mfd capacitor connected between the B terminal and earth. Do not fit a capacitor to an alternator with an internal (ready suppressed) voltage regulator.

Control box:

Connect a 2 to 3 mfd capacitor (preferably of the bypass type) between the A1 or B terminal of the control box and earth.

Motor units and solenoids:

Field winding motors require a good earth connection by strap from the motor housing to a suitable body part. This may not be sufficient, so in addition use a 1 to 3 mfd capacitor connected between the supply terminal and earth. Permanent magnet motors require a choke in each lead to the unit – in the case of two speed wiper motors this may mean the installation of up to seven chokes to complete the suppression.

Voltage stabiliser and flasher units:

A 1 mfd capacitor connected to the battery side of these two units should suffice provided that the cans surrounding the mechanism are making good earth contact.

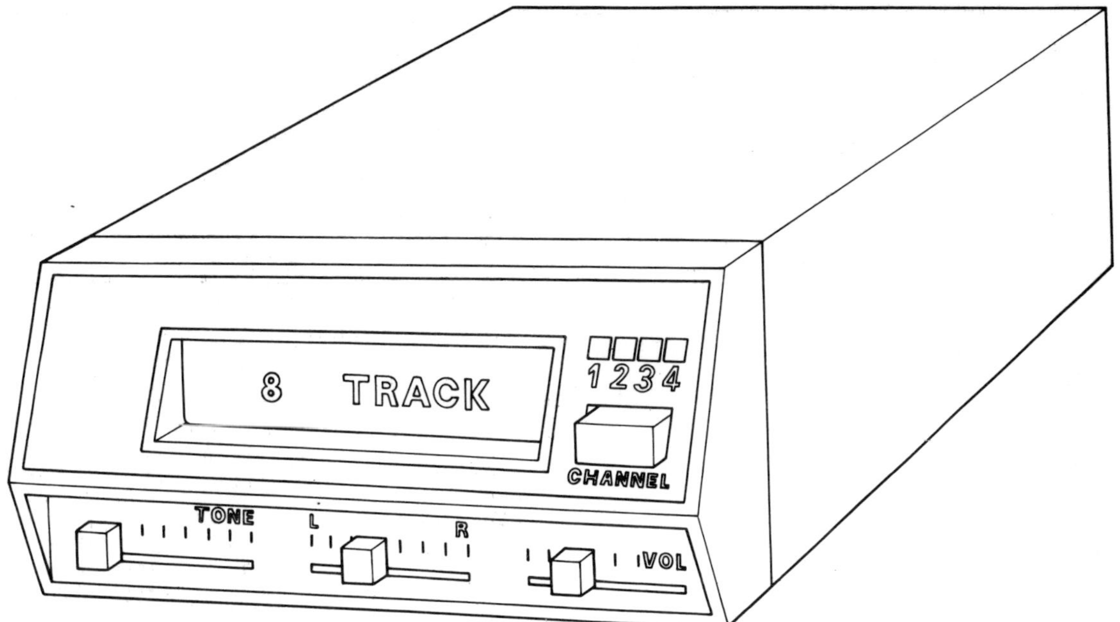

FIG 9:10 Tape player unit

Electrostatic wheel interference:

This type of interference is becoming less of a problem but if it is suspected (the particular clue is absence of interference in wet weather) the car should be taken to a vehicle electrician to have wheel to axle contact springs fitted.

Earthing:

Ensure that all parts of the engine compartment that can move in relation to one another and that are not usually considered part of the earth return system are connected to the car body or the engine with earthing straps. Particularly, connect carburetter linkages and cables and the bonnet lid to earth.

Additional measures for good VHF reception:

It may be necessary to suppress the high tension ignition circuit further by fitting shielded plug caps. These are small metal shrouds with earth connections that cover the spark plug cap. If all the usual methods, above, have been tried and VHF reception is still badly marred by interference consult a specialist in car radio fitting.

Suppression on fibreglass bodied cars:

As fibreglass (GRP) bodied cars do not have a metal shield around the sources of interference in the engine compartment, full suppression of these vehicles involves sticking aluminium foil over all under-bonnet surfaces. Rivet or clamp earthing straps to connect between each section of foil (particularly between the bonnet lid sections and those on the bulkhead) finally connecting each strap to the car's metal chassis or the engine block. Normal suppression measures can then be taken. It may be necessary to enclose the radio in a metal casing – especially if it has a plastic body. This earthed screen around the radio will arrest interference radiation from electrical components outside the engine compartment. Ensure that the base of the aerial is properly connected to earth both by foil screening of the area to which it is mounted and by a stout earth strap.

9:5 Tape-players

Modern tape-playing devices present few of the problems that radio fitting and interference suppression can bring. However there are a number of factors which must be born in mind when selecting and mounting tape-players.

The same general relation between the quality of the sound output and price exists with tape-players as for radio sets – the more a player costs the better the results are likely to be and the more facilities (like fast wind in both directions and four speaker connections) are built into the unit. Combined radio and tape-player units are available.

There are two distinct systems of tape-player being sold today – the cartridge and cassette types. A summary of their operating characteristics is useful.

8-track cartridge:

The cartridge itself is a plastics tape magazine in which the tape is contained in endless loop form. The tape has four magnetic recording bands on it – each band has a right and left hand stereo track. Cartridge players have a moving pick-up head which adjusts in height above the deck to pick up each track in turn. This height adjustment is performed automatically but there may also be a manual track change button. Each track will play for about 10 minutes. Sets do not have a fast wind facility because:

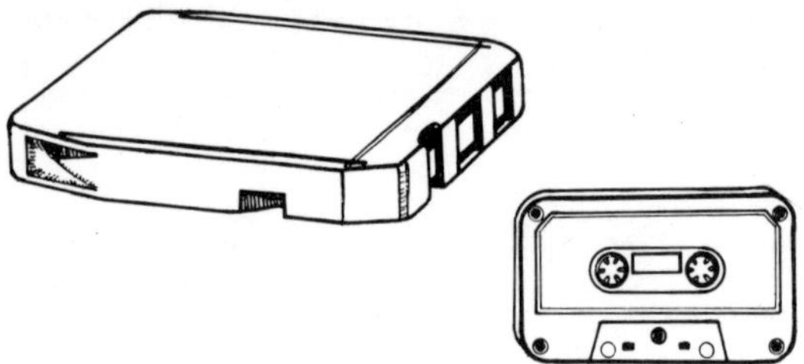

FIG 9:11 Tape cartridge (left), cassette (right)

1 the looping of the tape in the cartridge is a process that cannot be speeded up too much and 2 the maximum waiting time for a track to replay is the length of one loop of the tape, that is about 10 minutes.

There are some disadvantages to the operation of cartridges. They are generally less mechanically reliable than cassettes (mainly because of the friction characteristics of the tape looping mechanism). As the tape is driven by a friction roller they are prone to drive slip and friction problems. The tape has a higher degree of freedom to move at the pick-up interface so problems of aligning tracks with the pick-up occur – some 8-track players have a fine pick-up adjuster to ensure maximum signal strength and elimination of the signal from adjacent tracks.

Cassette:

Generally there is a wider choice of music and other programmes (language courses, for example) recorded on cassettes. These are slim tape packs containing two reels which are positively driven by the player unit. The tape is narrower than the 8-track type – there are two bands of recording with, in the case of a stereo system, two stereo tracks each. Cassettes are available containing different lengths of tape, total playing time varying from one to two hours. Most sets have a fast wind facility to allow relatively quick selection of the desired recording.

The only real disadvantage of cassettes is that it does take more of the driver's attention to operate the winding facility for selection of recordings. In addition the cassette needs to be turned round in the right way to obtain the next side of the tape. However there are generally fewer mechanical problems with cassettes and location of the pick-up in relation to the track is fixed to maximise signal strength and prevent interference from the adjacent tracks.

Siting of a tape-player and speakers:

The same safety restriction on mounting units where there is a possibility of driver or passenger contact in an accident apply to tape-players as to radios. It may be even more important in the case of a tape-player to have the unit well within the driver's reach. The added distraction of selecting a cassette and inserting it into the unit can cause accidents.

Few cars have accessory apertures large enough to accommodate a tape player (although cassette units in particular are being made smaller as development proceeds) so neat installation very often means the purchase of a special console that will fit at the centre of the facia or over the transmission tunnel.

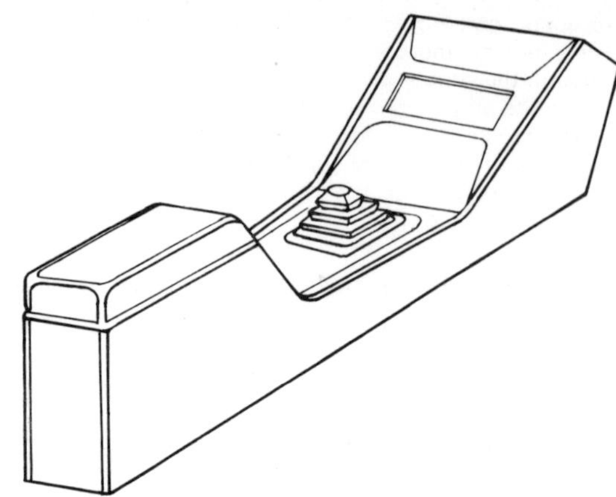

FIG 9:12 Centre console with radio mounting

Two speakers must be fitted with a tape-player to provide stereo reproduction and these should be as widely separated as possible within the confines of a car. Refer to the radio fitting section, earlier in this chapter, for the range of possible positions.

There is an additional problem in siting a tape-player – these units are generally more attractive to thieves than radios. It is a good plan to site both the tape unit and speakers where they will not attract undue attention in a casual glance over the car's equipment.

Fitting a tape-player:

Tape-players can be bought for positive or negative earth systems – ensure that the correct type has been purchased. The casing must be mounted to bodywork metal to provide a good earth connection and, as players usually weigh more than radios (and they are more sensitive to vibration), it is essential that a rear mounting bracket is used. There are few special fitting kits developed to mount tape-players in particular cars – the unit usually comes with some form of adaptable bracket.

A 5 amp line fuse should be connected in series with the supply lead. It is very important that the supply lead be connected to an ignition switched terminal on the fuse box or on the ignition switch itself as tape motors run silently and there may be no clue that the unit has been left switched on once the tape is withdrawn.

Speaker fitting is the same as for radios. Sound quality depends very much on the resonance characteristics of the location in which the spakers are fitted. Considerable enhancement of speaker performance can be gained by ensuring that the units are firmly secured to the car body and that there is no possibility of resonating speaker parts touching body metal. Make sure that each speaker is connected to the correct output channel on the tape-player – stereo sound has a right and left hand channel and the stereo effect is destroyed by swapping the channels over.

Interference on tape-players:

Radio-frequency interference is not a great problem with tape-players as the circuits simply aren't designed for reception and tuning of transmitted signals. However, some engine induced noise may be fed to the unit through the supply wire and this may become amplified within the player to the extent that it mars listening.

The problem will probably be eradicated by fitting a suppression choke in the supply lead. If not, suppression may have to be carried out as for a radio, paying particular attention to the generator circuit.

Care of tape cassettes and cartridges:

Favourite cassettes and cartridges can quickly amass inside the car and the most common tape care problem is keeping some order in the collection. Here are a few guidelines to prolong tape life:

1 Keep tapes away from sources of magnetism like wiper motors (these may be adjacent to the glovebox) and loudspeakers. Any magnetic field around a permanent magnet can erase the tape's systematically ordered magnetic tracks.

2 Tapes and cassette and cartridge bodies are sensitive to heat – don't store them near heater vents or over the transmission tunnel. Remove tapes from the car on hot sunny days.

3 Cassettes and cartridges can be protected from damaging dirt and abrasive grit by storage in a specially designed container. This box or file is also a good way to keep tapes in order.

4 Cleaning cartridges, containing a short length of special tape, can be used to clean the pick-up and friction drive wheel of 8-track players but both types of player will need periodic cleaning of the interior. Tape dust and fluff or fibres builds up around the drive units and pick-up – an aerosol de-duster or compressed airline can be used to blow dirt away. If necessary a soft camel-hair brush can be poked through the tape-player aperture.

5 If the car is kept outside at night or it is left for long periods, remove tapes from the car to prevent moisture build-up in the cassettes or cartridges.

6 Never leave tapes in the player overnight.

9:6 Anti-theft devices

The car is a vulnerable target for thieves and the added attraction of radios, tape-players and other easily removable accessories increases the chance of a break-in.

The simplest electrical anti-theft device is the ignition immobiliser. This consists of a wire from the ignition coil CB contact to a switch, well concealed under the facia. A short link wire earths the other terminal of the switch.

The effect of this device is to short circuit the contact-breaker points and render them ineffective. It is a measure that will defeat few determined and experienced thieves but it is a useful first line of defence against the joy-rider.

Better protection is afforded by fitting an alarm unit that operates the car's horn or, even better, an independent siren if the car is disturbed while parked.

A typical alarm unit consists of a vibration sensitive pendulum or spring that if set into motion operates a relay which switches on the horn. The relay is of the type that maintains current flow even if the stimulating current from the sensor contacts is discontinued – to prevent battery drain there is usually a bi-metal strip timing device in series with the relay which switches off the alarm after a pre-determined period. The alarm system is activated by a key switch located in such a way that the terminals are inaccessible from outside the locked vehicle.

Individual fitting instructions for alarm kits vary but the following rules should be observed to ensure efficient operation and the provision of maximum protection:

1 Tune the sensitivity of the sensor unit very carefully – some are very temperamental and cannot distinguish between a cat landing on the bonnet, vibration from passing lorries, wind disturbance and a thief. To avoid causing a nuisance while tuning the unit connect a test lamp across the horn terminals on the unit (or between the single horn terminal and earth).

2 Set the time control for at least 25 seconds but not more than 45 seconds of horn blast.

3 Site the lock switch in as well concealed a position as possible. A good place is inside the petrol filler flap provided that the tank is sealed with a separate filler cap.

4 Wire additional switch units on the door pillars and boot and bonnet surrounds – ordinary courtesy light switches should be used and they should be connected in parallel with the vibration sensing unit so that any or all of the thief's actions will set off the alarm.

5 On most cars the horn wires or terminals are readily accessible from outside the car. Ensure that the thief cannot disconnect the horn by either fitting an enclosure around the rear of the horn or wiring the alarm unit to a separate horn or siren placed in an inaccessible position.

6 Always remember to switch the device on when the car is left unattended.

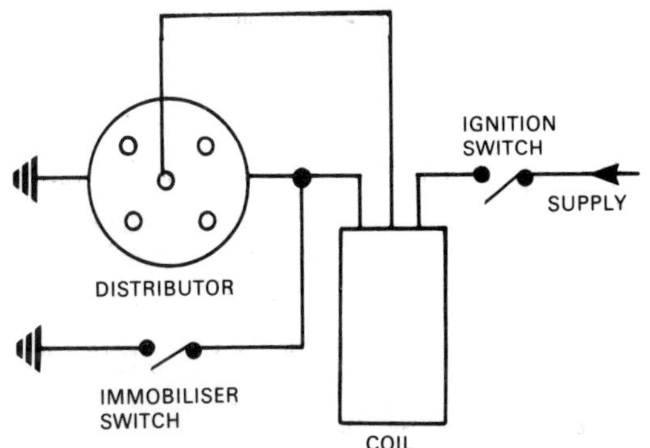

FIG 9:13 Ignition immobiliser circuit

9:7 Auxiliary lighting

Foglights, spotlights and reversing lamps are popular additions to the car which increases night-time driving safety and ease the task of driving in foul weather.

Foglights:

A foglight must be mounted low down on the front of the car so that the sharp cut-off at the top of the light beam is well below driver's eye level. To be fully effective a pair of foglights should be fitted – a pair can be used with the headlights extinguished in fog and driving snow according to the law. But the lamps must be fitted within the areas defined by the law for headlamps (see lighting – **Chapter 6, Section 6:5**).

A single foglight cannot be used on its own and its

performance will be limited by the light scattered from the dipped headlamps.

There are two good positions to mount foglights – on the bumper or front apron or on special brackets (obtainable from accessory shops) which are secured to the front grille. If possible avoid fitting lamps below the front bumper where they are likely to be damaged in parking or by flying stones.

Most lamps are supplied with a fitting kit containing the correct number of bullet connectors, a switch, and sufficient wire of the correct current carrying grade. If these components are not supplied ensure that the wire used for fitting is suitable for carrying a continuous current equal to the demand of both lamps. If they are 60 watt units, the total power will be 120 watts and the current will be 10 amps.

Wiring should be carried out according to the instructions in **Chapter 2** – apply additional protection to connectors behind the front grille by wrapping each one with plastic tape to prevent the ingress of dirt and moisture. The light switch should be firmly secured to the facia on a subsidiary switch panel or in a hole cut into a free part of the instrument panel.

Connect the supply lead to the switch to the battery auxiliary fuse box terminal. But bear in mind that a current load of up to 10 amps might overload this fuse and it may be necessary to fit a relief fuse-box as described earlier in this chapter. It is a wise precaution to connect a small warning lamp in parallel with the lead to the lamps – foglights are often provided with covers so you may not notice if they have been accidentally switched on.

Spotlamps:

As a spotlamp is fitted to extend the range of the car's normal lighting it is realistic to fit only one of these units. A single spotlamp can be fitted anywhere at the front of the car provided it is not more than $3\frac{1}{2}$ ft from the ground and below 2 ft from the ground. The best position for the lamp is probably at the offside of the car with its beam directed towards the nearside to pick out the kerb. Wiring is the same as that for foglamps.

A single spotlamp must only be used when the headlamps are also in use (see **Chapter 6, Section 6:5**).

Reversing lamps:

White or yellow lights of a power not exceeding 24 watts can be fitted to make the task of reversing much easier (see the regulations on reversing lamps in **Chapter 6, Section 6:5**).

Manufacturers often supply a reversing lamp kit which incorporates a specially designed gearbox fitting switch. Consult the main agents for the car to find out if this is available.

If there is no gearbox switch available, reversing lamps can be wired to a facia switch – but the law states that a warning lamp is essential to tell the driver when the reversing lamps are on. The warning lamp should have a red or green filter or lens.

Wiring precautions are the same as for other auxiliary lamps but in this case it is best to take the lamp supply from an ignition switched fuse position. If a gearbox switch is fitted ensure that the leads are secured well away from the hot exhaust pipe.

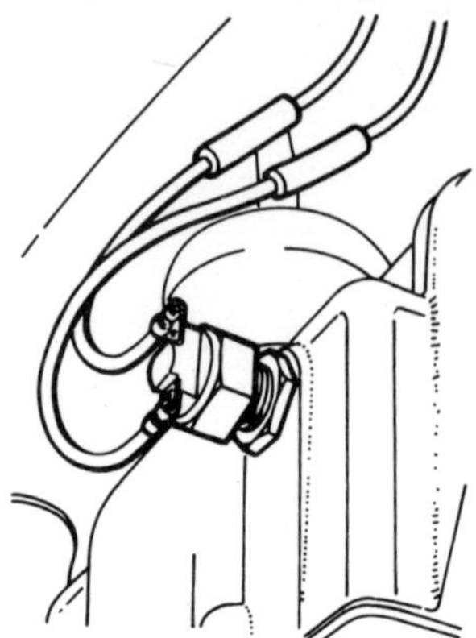

FIG 9:14 Reverse light gearbox switch

Hazard warning lights:

A hazard warning light kit consists of a heavy duty flasher unit which is connected into the indicator light circuit in such a way that it bypasses the indicator switch and normal flasher unit. The supply to the hazard warning system should be taken from a direct battery supply point such as a fusebox terminal on the battery side of the battery auxiliary fuse. Thus the lights can be used when the vehicle is totally immobilised.

Fitting of hazard warning lights should be performed with very careful reference to the car's circuit diagram. Keep leads to and from the unit as short as possible to cut down on the wiring clutter that can arise from fitting such a unit. Kits are usually supplied with appropriate insulation piercing connectors to make contact with the existing wiring in the indicator circuit.

Install the hazard warning light switch (usually an integral part of the unit) in a prominent position on the facia, instrument panel or subsidiary switch panel.

9:8 Auxiliary instruments

For the motorist who wants to know more about the things that are happening to the engine or the electrical circuits additional instrumentation is a necessity. Instruments are best installed on a subsidiary instrument panel placed as near as possible to the driver's line of sight – as near to windscreen level as practicable. It may be thought more convenient and stimulating to include the fitting of additional instrumentation at the same time as customising or facelifting the car's existing instrument panel or facia. A few general notes on instrument installation and wiring will aid the design of an easily read and correctly working instrument panel.

Ammeters must be wired between the main battery supply terminal on the solenoid and the charge lead from the dynamo or alternator. It may be convenient to connect it in series between the control box A1 terminal and the lead removed from the terminal – as such a joint will carry the full charge and discharge current of the battery/generator system it must be made to a high standard. Soldering the joint is advised, although a good quality, heavy duty insulated barrel connector can be used. The wiring of the ammeter should be of sufficient current

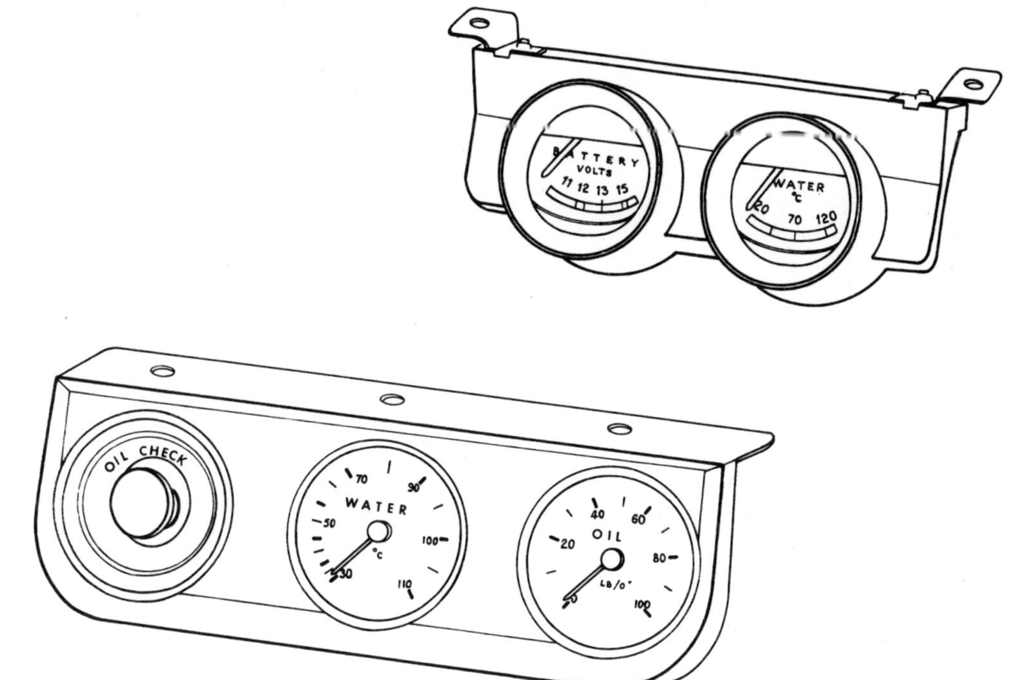

FIG 9:15 Auxiliary instrument panels

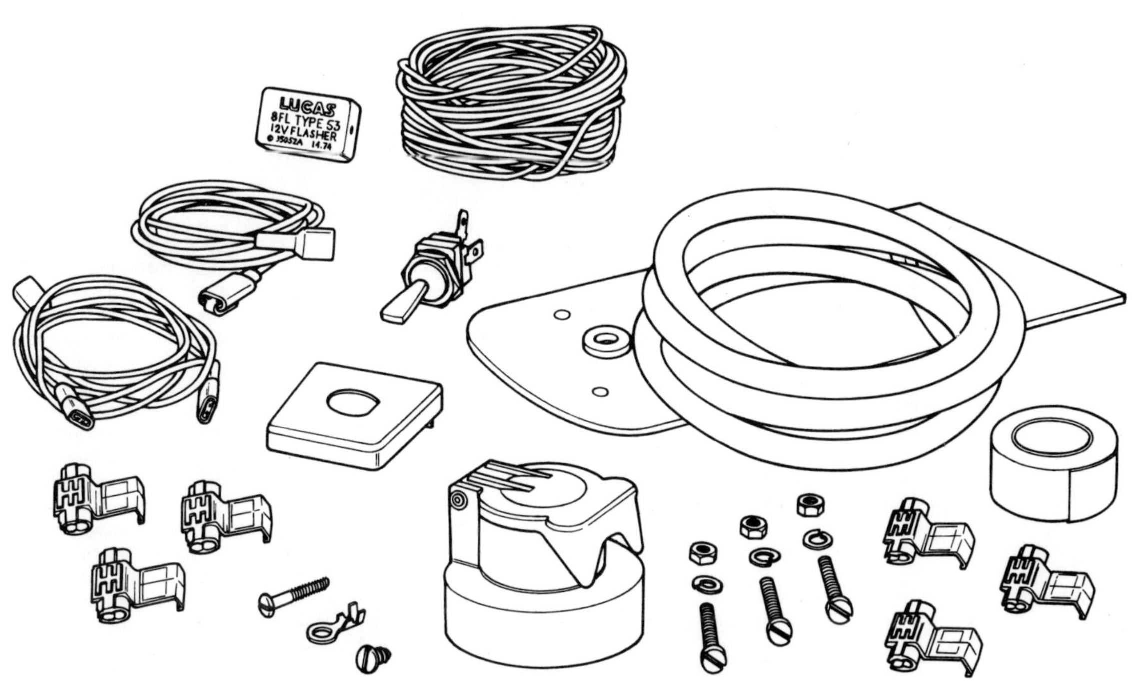

FIG 9:16 Caravan connector kit

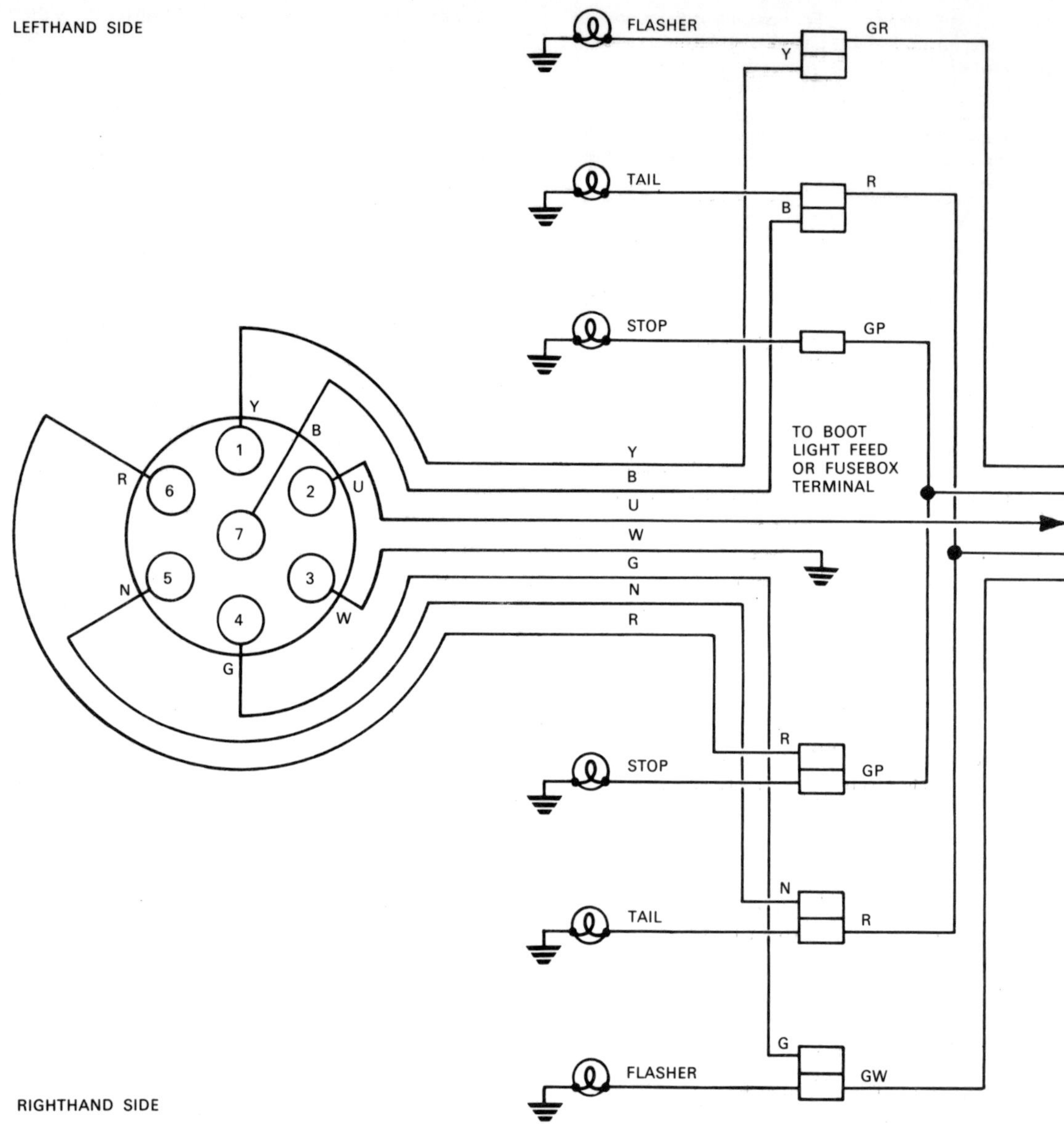

FIG 9:17 Caravan connector circuit with standard pin arrangement

carrying capacity to accept the heavy loads flowing in this circuit (see wiring grades and applications – **Chapter 2, Section 2:2**). Terminal connections at the rear of the instrument should be made with tag connectors or heavy duty Lucar types. It is wise to wrap the joints at the rear of the ammeter with insulating tape.

The voltmeter or battery condition indicator must be wired to a point in the car's main supply circuit. A convenient connection in the area of the instrument panel can be to the battery terminal of the instrument voltage stabiliser. Secure the earth lead from the voltmeter to a good earth point on the car body with a tag connector.

Dial illumination lamps inside instruments can be wired to the existing instrument panel lighting using insulation piercing connectors such as the 3M Scotchlok type. If the car has a printed circuit for instrument panel wiring take the dial illumination supply lead from a point on the main lighting circuit between the main light switch and the dipswitch.

As far as possible use existing holes in the engine compartment bulkhead to feed instrumentation leads through to the facia. If it is necessary to make additional holes drill carefully to avoid damage to existing wiring and make a hole large enough to accept a protecting grommet.

Site instruments carefully on the newly designed facia or

subsidiary instrument panel. For instance vacuum gauges and non-electric oil pressure gauges should be mounted in a position that affords easy kink-free access for the pressure tubes. These two instruments and the ammeter should always be placed near to the driver's line of sight to make checking easier without adding too much to the distraction from the road ahead. Switches for other accessories should be grouped according to their function and clearly labelled; lighting switches should all be together, heated rear window and electric washer switches should be closely grouped.

There are many types of subsidiary instrument panels available for mounting in particular places on or above the existing facia – they can be a great help in organising instrument fitting.

9:9 Heated rear windows

Heated rear window filaments or panels can be fitted to most cars and there are a number of different makes on the market. Individual fitting instructions vary but the best general advice is to ensure that the window is clean before attempting to fix the filament or heater panel in place. A proprietary glass cleaner or windscreen wash additive applied with a soft clean cloth will perform the job satisfactorily.

Heated rear window accessories have a high current demand ($7\frac{1}{2}$ to 10 amps) and wiring must be of a suitable grade to accept this loading. Most kits are supplied with a facia switch and parallel warning lamp. The supply to the switch should be connected to the ignition switched fuse or, if this would overload the main fuse, a subsidiary fuse box.

Observe the wiring instructions in **Chapter 2** – with an accessory consuming this amount of current some additional protection to the long run of wire from the rear to the front of the car is essential.

Cars with 6 volt systems (earlier models from Renault, DAF, VW) cannot be fitted with a conventional 12 volt heated rear window panel. It is best to consider fitting one half panel from the Smiths Industries kit designed for van door windows.

9:10 Connections to trailers and caravans

Special kits of parts are available to make the electrical connections between the car's brake, indicator and rear light circuits and those of a trailer or caravan. The kits consist of a seven-pin weather protected connector box for fitting to the car's rear panel or towing bracket. A heavy duty flasher to replace the normal indicator flasher unit is provided and there is also a warning light to provide a check that the unit is operating.

If the car has a hydraulic pressure brake light switch, the additional current load in the circuit can cause arcing of the switch contacts. A relay must be fitted to protect this switch.

Fitting these electrical connectors is not a complex job – the essential thing is to ensure that the correct leads are connected up to each car circuit. Connections should be firmly made with Lucar or bullet connectors. If there is any difficulty consult the main agents for caravan or car, or the technical advisers of one of the motoring and caravanning organisations.

Index